DELAWARE TRIBE IN

A CHEROKEE NATION

Delaware Tribe in a Cherokee Nation

BRICE OBERMEYER

UNIVERSITY OF NEBRASKA PRESS ❧ LINCOLN AND LONDON

Library of Congress
Cataloging-in-Publication Data
Obermeyer, Brice.
Delaware tribe in a Cherokee
nation / Brice Obermeyer.
p. cm.
Includes bibliographical references and index.
ISBN 978-0-8032-2295-3 (cloth : alk. paper)
1. Delaware Indians – Oklahoma – Politics and
government. 2. Delaware Indians – Relocation.
3. Delaware Indians – Government relations.
4. Self-determination, National – Oklahoma.
5. Cherokee Indians – Oklahoma – Politics and
government. 6. Oklahoma – Ethnic relations.
7. Ethnology – Oklahoma. I. Title.
E99.D2024 2009
305.897′3450766 – dc22
2009019436

Set in Arno by Bob Reitz.
Designed by Nathan Putens.

For Dennis and Carole

Proceeds from the sale of this book will be donated to the Delaware Tribe's Elder Nutrition Program to support their ongoing efforts to provide for the elderly members of the local community.

Contents

	List of Illustrations	ix
	Acknowledgments	xi
1	Introduction	1
2	Removal and the Cherokee-Delaware Agreement	35
3	Delaware Country	66
4	Government to Government	117
5	Self-Determination	146
6	Cherokee by Blood	179
7	Single Enrollment	219
8	Conclusion	256
	Notes	279
	References	291
	Index	307

Illustrations

PHOTO

1 Delaware Tribal Seal   112

MAPS

1 Delaware Homeland   39

2 Delaware and Cherokee Removal   46

3 Cherokee Nation, 1870   56

4 Delaware Line Communities   88

5 Delaware Allotments   91

6 Cherokee Nation and Delaware
  Tribe Service Areas   102

7 Delaware Administrative
  Centers and Cultural Sites   110

8 Dewey and Delaware Allotments   122

9 Cherokee Nation Health Services   207

FIGURE

1 Delaware Tribe Population
  Growth, 1867–2001   143

TABLES

1 Chairmen and Chiefs of the
  Delaware Tribe, 1856–present   171

2 Cherokee CDIB Labels   190

3 Tribal Enrollment in the
  Cherokee Nation   226

4 Delaware Enrollment Options   227

Acknowledgments

The first acknowledgment is rightfully given to the Delaware Tribe, as the pages that follow reflect the Delaware Tribe's long-standing assertion of self-determination that certainly deserves, at the very least, my first recognition. My formal thanks are offered to Chief Dee Ketchum, Chief Joe Brooks, and Chief Jerry Douglas, under whose administrations this research was carried out, as well as to the Delaware Tribal Council and Trust Board for allowing me the opportunity to complete my self-chosen task. Among the many who have served on the Delaware Tribe's government that helped me learn about tribal politics were Curtis Zunigha, Bucky Buck, Annette Ketchum, Wayne Stull, Rosetta Coffey, Edna Havens, Raymond Cline, Doyle Hayes, Micky Morrison, and Verna Crawford. The staff at the Delaware Tribe and Housing Authority also deserve my gratitude. Anchoring the staff of the Delaware Tribe is Enrollment Director Marilyn Cole, and her support and assistance for this project are sincerely appreciated and highly valued. My other co-workers at the tribal headquarters also found the time in their hectic schedules to help me find my way as I stumbled through the bumpy terrain of Delaware politics and tribal governance. It was indeed a pleasure to work with, among many others who shared the task of tribal operations, Dennis Artherton, Vicki Bratton, Levi Randoll, Lisa Steele, Gina Parks, Anne Swearingin, Dennis Frenchman, Ernest Tiger, Johnny Tucker, Marylin Coffey, Connie Collier, Sherry Radcliff, Faye Thomas, Walter Dye, Chad Killscrow, Carolyn Wilson, Sammy Buoy, Sandra Crawford, Kathy Davis, Travis Forth, Scott George, John Hunt, and Dalen Jackson. My research is also particularly indebted to the work of tribal lawyer Gina Carrigan and her co-author, Clayton Chambers. The analysis I present would not have been possible without their work to locate and compile an archive on Delaware social and legal history, portions of which the Delaware Tribe published in the form of a legal brief in 1994.

While many at the tribal headquarters made important contributions to this work, my presentation of the Delaware Tribe would have never been possible without the generosity, graciousness, and hospitality of the Delaware community. The best place to continue with my long list of thanks is thus with the people who were responsible for my first introduction to the Delaware community and who continue to remain good friends. Michael Pace and his wife Ella deserve my most special gratitude for opening the Delaware community to me as well as for the kindness they have extended to me, my family, and my students over the past many years. Mike's dedication to the Delaware community and his commitment to preserving, practicing, and teaching about Delaware heritage (while not forgetting to have a good time in the process) are always rewarding to witness, and I am thankful for being allowed to take part.

It was also a distinct pleasure to explore and learn about the history and significance to be found along the back roads of Delaware Country with the many folks who shared with me the locations of abandoned settlements and old churches now marked by the many rural cemeteries that are considered vitally important to Delaware heritage in Oklahoma. Perhaps one of the more significant and most widely known spaces is the Delaware Powwow Grounds in Northern Washington County. Here were shared invaluable memories and experiences that are interwoven throughout the more analytical portions of the book. It was here that the Paces first allowed me the much needed tent space to begin my introduction to the Delaware Community, and the powwow grounds remain a deeply important background for many events in the book. Equally deserving of my gratitude are other family camps who gladly shared food, space, and fellowship that is an important element of the Delaware Powwow. Forest and Judy Yearout graciously hosted and welcomed my family and students who accompanied me on a few occasions to the Delaware Powwow, as did Dee and Annette Ketchum and Paula Pechonick and her daughter Jenifer, all of whom I am honored to count as good friends. I and this book are also deeply indebted to the hospitality of many other Delaware family camps at the powwow grounds such as the Waters, Jackson, Thaxton, Falleaf, Artherton, and Brooks families, who invited me into their family circles for meals and social gatherings. Whether it was trading stories by campfire after an evening meal or passing the time under a much needed shelter during a late spring thunderstorm, my valued experiences at the Delaware Powwow grounds were, and continue to be, an important foundation upon which this work is based.

Beyond the powwow grounds, the Delaware Community Center was another equally important institution that provided a comforting space for meetings and events that also facilitated my participation and collaboration. Here this book benefited from the many experiences at Delaware events such as the General Council and Tuesday night social dances, but most influential were my deeply valued friendships with the regular attendees at the weekday lunches sponsored by the Elder Nutrition Program. Most of my fellow daily diners were elders in the Delaware community, and an immense degree of gratitude is extended to all who provided me with important insights. I can only hope to honor their trust and friendship in the pages that follow. Heartfelt thanks are gratefully extended to Bonnie Thaxton, Rosetta Coffey, Jean Kirkendall, Elgia Bryan, Evelyn Thomas, Mary Watters, Lew Ketchum, Don Wilson, Eddie Barnes, Howard Barnes, Ray Barnes, Kay and John (Sonny) Anderson, Ed Wilson, Sandy Tompkins, Verna Sue Artherton, Nancy Falleaf, Bea Freeland, Mary Lou Dershem, Jan Brown, and Jack Tatum. My gratitude is similarly extended to those who agreed to a formal but anonymous interview for use in this book as well as the many other friends and acquaintances who worked to help me learn about Delaware society and acknowledgment in less formal settings at Delaware homes, tribal buildings, social gatherings, and religious events.

Other tribal institutions exist beyond Washington County and include the spaces near the towns of Nowata, Delaware, Lenapah, Coody's Bluff, and Chelsea. My very special appreciation is extended to all who welcomed me in such communities and shared with me the histories and memories of these communities. The Delaware are structured by many different families, each associated with a region of Delaware Country, and I have attempted to honor such regional diversity with this book. My acknowledgment of Delaware diversity and important spaces throughout Delaware Country is deeply indebted to Edna Havens and the many friends and family members to whom she provided introductions. Edna's work has encouraged me to bring out this important aspect of Delaware society that is all too often not acknowledged but is important in structuring the course of modern Delaware society. I would also like to acknowledge the Dushane and Martin families for allowing me to gain an appreciation for the small but important Shawnee-Delaware Community near Chelsea-White Oak that remains active in Shawnee Ceremonialism and the Native American Church.

It would be nearly impossible for me to rightfully thank everyone who contributed to this book as the Delaware Tribe has a constituency that extends nationwide, and the voices of the local and nonlocal members are included. It would also be as impossible to remember every encounter, event, and conversation that has contributed to my understanding of Delaware society. As I began to attempt such a list of everyone whose voices are reflected in this book, it soon became apparent that my list would ultimately end in utter failure. Either I would name someone whose anonymity was promised, or I would mistakenly exclude others who had contributed substantially to this work. A very deep expression of thanks is thus extended to all who had a hand in shaping this book.

While the list of Delaware contributors is long, special thanks is rightfully due to my friend and colleague at the Lenape Language Program, Jim Rementer. Jim's tireless work documenting Delaware history and language over the past four and a half decades has resulted in a singularly important accumulation of Delaware documents, knowledge, and personal experiences from which this book has benefited immensely. I thank you, my friend, for allowing me to benefit from your work and from your friendship. Jim has truly served as a mentor for me and demonstrated in his own life the way to pursue responsible scholarship in any American Indian community.

Mentoring is indeed an important academic tradition, and for his role in serving as my other guidepost I would like to also acknowledge Jason Baird Jackson. Jackson's work with the Yuchi has served as a model for me in my ethnographic pursuits, serving as an example for how good ethnography should be performed and usefully applied. In many instances when I had certain doubts while carrying out research or while preparing this manuscript I found myself turning to Jason's example for insight. The answers that would eventually come generally worked, and many are found throughout the book, which bears both Jim's and Jason's considerable and well-respected influence. Jim and Jason have both read, and provided substantial comments on, earlier drafts of this book, and it is to their academic character that I credit the end result.

Though my work with the Delaware Tribe would not have been possible without Delaware generosity and significant academic mentoring, it would also not have been feasible without substantial financial support. My early work with the Delaware was supported by another ethnographic project with the historically black towns of eastern Oklahoma on which I was fortunate to work. I extend my appreciation to Morris Foster for the opportunity to work on his National Institute of Health (NIH)–funded project, "African American Community Review of Genetic Research," which provided me with the economic capability to make the move to Tulsa and begin this ethnography. After being hired by the Delaware Tribe to serve as their Native American Graves and Repatriation Act (NAGPRA) representative in 2003, we were successful in achieving further funding from a 2004 NAGPRA Documentation Grant and a NAGPRA Repatriation Grant. Although the projects funded by NAGPRA were not directly related to this work, the funding allowed me to continue the collaborative research that had already begun with the Delaware Tribe and community. I would also like to thank Ara Carboneau, who performed the transcriptions of the recorded interviews, and acknowledge the considerable financial support provided by Emporia State University's Research and Grants Center, which provided the funding for the transcription work. Similarly funded by Emporia State was Rebecca Dobbs's work on the maps for this book, which do an excellent job of revealing the geography of the Delaware's past and present homelands.

Also important were the editing comments from Delaware colleagues. Mike Pace and others in the Delaware community such as Don Wilson, Jerry Douglas, Jennifer Pechonick, and Nicky Michaels were willing to read earlier versions of this manuscript, and their editing comments offered helpful guidance throughout the development of this book. Collaboration with colleagues beyond the Delaware community has also influenced this book. As this work began while I was still a doctoral student in the Department of Anthropology at the University of Oklahoma, I am especially grateful to the possibilities provided by my committee members and fellow students. Morris Foster, Loretta Fowler, Steven Perkins, Michael Nunley, John Monaghan, Patricia Gilman, Bob Brooks, and Joe Whitecotton are among the many anthropologists whose instruction and research deserves my recognition. The most influential of the Oklahoma faculty was Circe Sturm, whose instruction provided the valuable theoretical tools that frame this work. Strum's (2002) work on the

Cherokee Nation significantly shaped my understanding of issues of race and nationality for the Delaware. Susan Vehik and James Treat are also acknowledged for their editorial suggestions, which have only strengthened this work. It is my hope that what I offer will show the respect I have for their willingness to take the time required to help encourage my academic development when it was clearly in its infancy.

My graduate experience was equally rewarding, and I appreciate my inclusion in the fold of an excellent cohort of ethnographers interested in work with Oklahoma's Indian communities for which the anthropology program at the University of Oklahoma has become well known. Rhonda Fair, Brian Gilley, Gus Palmer, Michelle Stokely, Pam Wallace, and Kristy Fieldhousen are among the many students-now-turned-colleagues whose influence has touched this work. My graduate training has also put me in contact with a larger group of scholars whose influence and writings are owed acknowledgment for their insight, which has informally impacted this book. Jay Miller, Terry Prewitt, Ives Goddard, Mark Miller, Pamela Bunte, and James Brown are among those whose works have substantially influenced this book. Also acknowledged is the support for this work extended by my colleagues in the Sociology/Anthropology Department at Emporia State University including Gary Wyatt, Jannette Borst, Alfredo Montalvo, Evandro Camara, Nathanial Terrell, and administrative assistant Debbie Roether. The anonymous reviewers of this book should also be commended for their careful consideration and substantial contribution to the final editing. Their many excellent suggestions included the recommendation that I explain Cherokee motivations for either challenging or supporting the federal acknowledgment of the Delaware Tribe. Realizing that such an addition was sorely needed, I carried out an interview with Cherokee Chief Chad Smith in order to better incorporate the Cherokee perspective on the issue of Delaware acknowledgment. Chief Smith graciously agreed to the interview, and his comments add greater balance to the final presentation.

To those nearest to my heart, thank you for tenderly reminding me of life's purpose. This book would not be worth completing without the love and encouragement I receive from my wife, Cheri, and my children, Cory, Kyle, and Amber. Cheri's patience and acceptance of my dream have only fortified my resolve to make her aspirations and the future goals of my children a reality. I thank my parents and grandparents for their hard work and sacrifice that have allowed me to pursue my passion and realize a life goal. Each word that follows should be read as a testament to their love for family and commitment to education, which have been instilled in their progeny.

DELAWARE TRIBE IN

A CHEROKEE NATION

① Introduction

Welcome to Delaware Country!
CHIEF DEE KETCHUM, 2003

The chief of the Delaware Tribe and the principal chief of the Cherokee Nation were both invited to speak at the annual Wild Onion Dinner hosted by the Bartlesville Indian Women's Club at the fairground building in Dewey, Oklahoma. The Cherokee leader was present because both the towns of Bartlesville and Dewey are a part of the Cherokee Nation's Tribal Jurisdiction Area, and the Delaware chief was involved because the two cities are also the heart of the area locally understood as Delaware Country and included within the Delaware Tribe's Service Area. The two tribal leaders each delivered inspiring yet diplomatic speeches to an approving intertribal crowd who were aware of the tensions that existed on the stage before them. Nothing political was ever formally aired during the speeches, and the packed house of over seven hundred Delaware, Osage, Cherokee, Shawnee, and non-Indian attendees was content with meeting new people, visiting with friends, and enjoying extra helpings of the popular wild onion peppered scrambled eggs.

The Delaware chief later confided in me that he had initially considered opening his speech with "Welcome to Delaware Country!"

He ultimately decided to refrain from what might be perceived as an inflammatory introduction in order to maintain the decorum of the event. In retrospect, however, the Delaware chief wished that he had made such an invitation in order to declare his views on the unusual situation that existed between the Cherokee Nation and the Delaware Tribe. As the speeches explained, the Delaware Tribe and the Cherokee Nation are both independent tribal governments, each with their own separate history, culture, and tribal organizations. The Delaware came to the Cherokee Nation in 1867 when the tribe was removed from their former reservation in Kansas and subsequently took up residence along the river valleys of what was then a northwestern portion of the Cherokee Nation. What was not mentioned in the speeches was that since removal the Delaware and Cherokee have had a sometimes strained relationship over the issue of Delaware rights as residents and potential citizens of the Cherokee Nation. This historically uncertain relationship began a new chapter in recent years when the Delaware Tribe achieved federal acknowledgment in 1996. In response the Cherokee Nation appealed the Delaware Tribe's acknowledgment decision and was, at the time that the speeches were being delivered at the Wild Onion Dinner, seeking the judicial termination of the Delaware Tribe in order to maintain Cherokee jurisdiction in that same northwestern region of the Cherokee Nation that has come to be known as Delaware Country. Since the 1996 acknowledgment, the Delaware Tribe was achieving significant advances in administering tribal programs and was fighting the Cherokee appeal in order to preserve their federal recognition and continue to provide programs and services for Delaware Country. While the Delaware and Cherokee chiefs chose not to discuss such actions at the Wild Onion Dinner out of respect for the event, this book describes what the tribal leaders could not. Presented here is an ethnographic study of the Delaware Tribe in the Cherokee Nation, a study that documents the cultural and political persistence of the Delaware Tribe, which continues to maintain its independence from the Cherokee Nation despite Delaware enrollment with and residence in the Cherokee Nation.

DELAWARE TRIBE AND THE CHEROKEE NATION

While the Delaware Tribe maintains its independence from the Cherokee Nation, it is clear that Delaware history has also become interwoven with that of the Cherokee Nation. The Cherokee Nation is today one of the largest federally recognized tribes in North America and is perhaps the most commonly referenced but least understood American Indian group. The Cherokee Nation is one of three federally recognized tribes that descend from the Iroquoian-speaking inhabitants of the southern Appalachian Mountains. Cherokee interaction with the nineteenth-century American government both set the judicial foundations for the status of Indian tribes today and provided the most tragic example of the removal period. In 1835 many Cherokee were forcibly removed from their eastern homelands to what is today eastern Oklahoma, where the modern Cherokee Nation of Oklahoma now exists and within whose jurisdiction the Delaware Tribe resides. Despite residence in the Cherokee Nation, the Delaware Tribe maintains its independence and is one of three American Indian tribes and three Canadian First Nations that are the descendants of the original inhabitants of the Hudson and Delaware River valleys who first met the seventeenth-century European explorers along the coasts of northeastern North America. Known as the grandfathers to other northeastern Algonquians, the Delaware are chronicled as the original owners of the regions encompassed by such American metropolises as New York City and Philadelphia and were the first American Indian tribe to sign a treaty with the then fledgling United States of America. The Delaware's centuries-long treaty alliance with the United States was eventually rewarded with removal to the Cherokee Nation following the Civil War. As a consequence of federal removal policies, the Delaware and the Cherokee were thus removed from their eastern homelands, and the Delaware were required to take up residence on lands within the relocated Cherokee Nation.

The Delaware are not the only non-Cherokee Indians that were forced to remove to and reside within the Cherokee Nation. Other non-Cherokee people in the Cherokee Nation include groups of Shawnee and Natchez and a few Muscogee or Creek, and the descendants of such groups continue to hold potential citizenship rights in the Cherokee Nation today as do the Delaware. Before Oklahoma statehood in 1907 intermarried whites and Cherokee freedmen were also citizens of the Cherokee Nation. Neither group holds full citizenship rights today, although the descendants of the Cherokee freedmen are currently active in efforts to regain Cherokee citizenship. The Cherokee freedmen are the modern descendants of the former African American slaves who were once owned by some nineteenth-century Cherokee Indians who removed to Indian Territory. Some Cherokee freedmen also have Cherokee Indian ancestry but have been unable to successfully document their lineage (Obermeyer 2005:56–60). The intermarried whites of pre-statehood days were the European-descended individuals who obtained Cherokee citizenship through intermarriage with Cherokee citizens. Intermarried whites are no longer members of the Cherokee Nation, and I am not aware of any organized effort to return citizenship to the non-Indian descendants of intermarried whites. Thus, the Cherokee Nation was once composed of multiple Indian tribes as well as non-Indian citizens but today consists of only those with documented Indian descent, with some holding Indian descent from non Cherokee ancestors.

Federal Indian policy thus brought the Delaware and others to the Cherokee Nation and continues to play a role in shaping the modern politics between the Delaware Tribe and the Cherokee Nation, who are now in opposition over the issue of Delaware acknowledgment.

Since removal to the Cherokee Nation, the Delaware have remained identifiable as both an Indian tribe and Indian community living within the Cherokee Nation as evidenced by both the extensive ethnographic literature on the Delaware as well as in the sustained federal interactions with the Delaware Tribe. Revealed in this text is the continued vitality of the distinctive Delaware community in eastern Oklahoma that has both perpetuated a unique sense of group identity while ever adapting to the constantly changing world of both federal policy and the regional political economy of the twentieth century. The Delaware Tribe's most recent struggle with the Cherokee Nation began approximately thirty years ago when federal recognition of the Delaware Tribe was administratively terminated by the Department of the Interior at the urging of the Cherokee Nation (Butler 1979). Recognition was subsequently restored to the Delaware Tribe in 1996 but was judicially terminated in 2004 as a consequence of the appeal filed by the Cherokee Nation. At the time of this writing the Delaware Tribe lacks acknowledgment and is obliged to seek acknowledgment, enrollment, and federal services through the Cherokee Nation. The Delaware's struggle to remain Delaware in an uncertain time in which they have recently been placed under Cherokee control is thus the book's focus. The Delaware's effort to remain independent from the larger and more powerful Cherokee Nation is presented because it holds implications for both the continuation of the Delaware Tribe as well as the broader issue of federal acknowledgment for tribes like the Delaware in the self-determination era.

SELF-DETERMINATION, FEDERAL ACKNOWLEDGMENT, AND CONSTITUENT TRIBES

The Delaware, like many other American Indian tribes, have faced removal, reservation, and allotment as well as New Deal-, termination-, and self-determination-era programs. In the process the Delaware have dealt with each new shift in federal policy and negotiated the imposition of new forms of federal control through the mechanisms of their own tribal governance. The present self-determination era has brought a new set of challenges for the Delaware, some of which are shared by other tribes while others are unique to tribes that are included within larger, federally acknowledged tribes. This section places in historical context the relationship between federal policy and tribal governance and concludes with a presentation of the problems that are unique to tribes like the Delaware, given the current pressures and expectations implicit in self-determination policy. A clear explanation of federal policy is thus presented here in order to provide the background for the struggles and decisions faced by the Delaware Tribe, which continue to be influenced by federal policy and which are described in the following chapters.

Bruce Granville Miller (2003) offers a very useful ethnology of both recognized and unrecognized indigenous groups throughout the world to demonstrate how nation-states use legislation, treaties, policy, and administrative practices to ultimately limit the number and power of indigenous groups by classifying and consolidating indigenous populations. Such state practices often lead to the official denial of indigenous status for many deserving groups that are either lumped with existing groups or simply ignored. When placed against the backdrop of Miller's analysis, the Delaware situation appears to be another case confirming Miller's conclusion. The Delaware Tribe is, at the time of this writing, an unacknowledged tribe that remains so as a consequence of state policies restricting and consolidating the number of recognized indigenous groups within the boundaries of the United States. Indeed, American Indian history in general has been accurately characterized as a process guided by a colonial policy in which tribal groups were artificially created and consolidated in order to expedite state administration, control, and assimilation of indigenous groups (B. Miller 2003:68–70).

The fact that modern tribal organizations in the United States are the product of federal consolidative and assimilative pressures and either hold or do not hold federal acknowledgment brings into focus the politically constructed nature of federally recognized tribal governments. Today's American Indian tribal governments and their constituent populations were constructed in response to removals and years of federal pressures and the composition of contemporary Indian tribes cannot be adequately understood unless the substantial role of federal intervention in their establishment is recognized. While the federal government has molded today's tribal governments into what some scholars characterize as functioning extensions of federal control and surveillance over Indian people, it is also important to recognize that modern tribal governments were also co-produced and crafted by local Indian leaders as well (Biolsi 1992; Esber 1992). Out of a process of negotiation and indigenization, community representatives worked with federal agents to make selective use of federal policy in ways that either solidified or modified existing political systems to allow for greater representation and authority in the federal system (Fowler 2002). Thus, today's tribal governments are best understood as the result of a series of historical negotiations between situated actors with vested interests that have attempted to balance the needs of constituent Indian populations against the imposed policies and authority of the federal government. The constructed nature of tribal governments and coalescence/dispersal of different Indian societies under federal jurisdiction, an artifact of colonialism itself, is thus a complex process of domination and resistance that continues today as tribal leaders must navigate through federal policies and practices that are still influenced by invented notions of the "tribe" in ways that are perceived as advantageous by their constituents and that are made available by the federal government. In step with such goals, modern self-determination policy, a seeming advancement and benefit for Indian people, maintains the ultimate directive of limiting and consolidating what were once artificially created units through a single enrollment requirement that pervades federal policy — particularly in the granting of contract services under Public Law 638 and in the criteria used in the Federal Acknowledgment Process. It is therefore necessary to outline the continued role of federal policy in the Delaware's struggle to remain independent from the Cherokee Nation.

The modern era of federal policy is the one in which the Delaware struggle plays out today. The self-determination era was formally established with the passage of the Indian Self-Determination and Education Assistance Act of 1975, or Public Law 93–638. The intent of the act was to provide for the "orderly transition from federal domination of programs for and services to effective and meaningful participation by the Indian people" (Esber 1992:213). The act specifically intended to carry out meaningful participation by empowering the secretaries of the Department of the Interior and the Department of Health, Education and Welfare "to enter into a contract or contracts with any tribal organization of any such Indian tribe to plan, conduct, and administer programs or portions thereof," upon the request of any Indian tribe (Fowler 2002:xiv). Thus, this federal legislation provided the opportunity for Indian tribes to take over the administration of programs and services that were initially promised by treaty and were then provided directly by the BIA.

The effects of self-determination have been double-edged, and such impacts of recent federal policy are linked with the politics surrounding the federal acknowledgment of Indian tribes. Of the more beneficial outcomes have been the relative empowerment of acknowledged Indian tribes who are able to operate under self-determination. The administration of federal Indian programs and services has given such acknowledged tribal governments access to, and control over, millions of dollars of federal resources. The increased financial budgets have given tribal governments more political influence both locally and on the national level. On reservations and in tribal communities the service centers operated by tribal governments often provide employment opportunities and needed federal aid, and thus the ability to provide for the local population increases the authority of the tribal government. The tribal government can then become both the governing body and the provider of federal services and can gain in status in the minds of tribal members. As the administrative agency, the tribal government is also consulted and included on budgetary decisions on a more equal level with the BIA and other departments headquartered in Washington DC. Some of the more powerful self-governance tribes such as the Cherokee Nation even maintain a separate tribal office in Washington DC. Thus, decision making at the national level is heavily influenced by the consultations with tribal governments, especially those with the resources to have offices in our nation's capital. Acknowledgment in the self-determination era also provides a tribe with eligibility for certain federal grants and programs as well as the possibility of developing casino gaming operations. Also of importance is the formal acknowledgment that helps to perpetuate, through federal funding and government-to-government relations, the legal existence of an Indian tribe. At stake with federal acknowledgment is thus a status that provides tribal governments with direct access to certain federal Indian services and programs, eligibility for federal grants, and legal rights reserved for recognized Indian tribes.

Critiques of self-determination, however, accurately point out the inconsistencies of the legislation and the continued expectation for conformity in the self-determination and acknowledgment policies. Rather than the law allowing for self-determination, George S. Esber Jr. (1992) argues that Public Law 93–638 actually is more correctly interpreted as an invitation for tribes to participate in the federal structure created by a non-Indian society. The programs and services for which a tribe may contract are not Indian programs designed by

Indian tribes for Indian people but programs initially designed by non-Indians. For critics, self-determination policy has not achieved the ideal of tribal sovereignty and independent decision making but has made substantial financial incentives available to those tribal governments that are willing to conform to the model outlined by the federal acknowledgment criteria. In other words self-determination and acknowledgment have in some ways used economic coercion to mold tribal governments into familiar entities and in the process have influenced the transformation of acknowledged Indian tribes into functioning extensions of the federal government. As an illustration of such a critique, there are currently 561 federally recognized Indian tribes in North America, and many acknowledged tribal governments have a single enrollment policy as well as an organization that reflects the structure and practices of the federal government.

Despite the precision of such critiques, tribes maintain and pursue acknowledgment for the advantages that come with inclusion in the federal circle. However, tribes overwhelmingly attempt to maintain the federal relationship on their own terms and in ways that protect and preserve importantly held practices, ideals, beliefs, and community structures. For the Delaware, beliefs surrounding their independence from the Cherokee Nation have been historically significant. For instance, the Delaware Tribe reorganized in 1982 in an effort to regain federal acknowledgment. The Delaware ratified a new constitution and bylaws and adopted a tribal council form of government to replace the former business committee structure that had been left off of the list of federally recognized tribes. Even after reorganization, however, the BIA refused to acknowledge the Delaware Tribe because it would not include in its new constitution language that referenced the tribe's potential for membership in the Cherokee Nation. The Delaware were willing to modify their entire governmental system in order to maintain the federal relationship but were unwilling to yield their independence from the Cherokee

Nation in the process. The Delaware remained unacknowledged from 1979 until 1996 because they would not compromise their principal conviction against formalizing their membership in the Cherokee Nation. Self-determination may thus have provided greater economic and political power to tribal governments, but the strategies selected for achieving such advantages, for the Delaware Tribe and others, remain choices guided by deeply held principles, convictions, and community structures.

At issue in the question of Delaware acknowledgment in the self-determination era is thus the contested nature of the Delaware's potential membership in the Cherokee Nation. However, the Delaware are not unique as there are several Indian communities like the Delaware who, as a consequence of federal policy, are considered constituent parts of larger, federally recognized tribes. This feature of Native North America has received very little scholarly attention to date and is the situation that this book addresses. The Delaware's experience as one particular tribe that has been faced with difficulties in maintaining federal recognition because its members are considered members of another acknowledged tribe adds an as yet unstudied case to the emergent ethnology on federal acknowledgment. A review of Delaware history, contemporary society, and difficulties with tribal enrollment offers a perspective on federal acknowledgment from the vantage held by tribes like the Delaware that illustrates the prohibitive effect that single enrollment policies have for such tribes in the modern era.

Existing ethnographic work with tribes like the Delaware often documents the history, culture, and social organization of such groups and provides clear evidence of their independence from their larger, host tribe. However, such scholarship does not focus specifically on the problems that groups like the Delaware face when attempting to gain separate federal acknowledgment. Jason Baird Jackson's

(2003a) work, for instance, provides an ethnography of the Yuchi, whose ancestors are listed on the base roll for the Creek Nation. Jackson's invitation to work with the Yuchi was extended by Yuchi leaders working toward the completion of a solid application for federal recognition. Although the Yuchi effort for federal recognition is discussed, the focus of Jackson's work is Yuchi society and ceremonialism that clearly makes the case for the Yuchi's continued vitality as a distinct Indian tribe. Similarly, Pamela Ann Bunte and Robert J. Franklin's (1987) work provides an ethnography of the San Juan Southern Paiute, who were incorporated into the Navajo Nation at the time of their work. Bunte and Franklin (1987:281–296) outline Paiute history and document San Juan Paiute persistence in the twentieth century in a manner that solidified the Paiute's eligibility for acknowledgment.[1] Following the authors' publications, the Southern Paiute received federal recognition in 1989 and negotiated a land base from the Navajo Nation in 2000. James Howard (1970, 1980) also provided ethnographic accounts of the Natchez and Loyal Shawnee who were considered members of the Cherokee Nation at the time of his work. To date, the San Juan Southern Paiute and the Shawnee Tribe are federally recognized while the Yuchi, Natchez, and Delaware remain unacknowledged tribes whose members can potentially enroll with other acknowledged but foreign tribes.

While the Delaware's relationship with the Cherokee Nation is not unique, it is a relationship that is identifiable from the situation faced by other tribes who are constituent members of larger acknowledged tribes. It is therefore important to clarify how the issues that face the Delaware and the above-named groups are different from other formerly consolidated constituent groups. The phenomenon of consolidated tribes occurs with such regularity that it is possible to identify multiple situations in which the experiences are substantially different from the Delaware. There are those tribes that share a cultural connection with the larger tribe that holds federal acknowledgment, and thus all entities maintain a cultural affinity with the larger, federally acknowledged tribe. In some cases, but not all, the culturally affiliated tribes hold federal acknowledgment as does the larger, federally acknowledged tribe. The Muscogee (Creek) Nation is one example in which there are three Creek Tribal Towns that hold federal acknowledgment, and the members of each town can also be members of the larger Muscogee (Creek) Nation within which Tribal Town members and those Creeks without town membership are included. There are also acknowledged tribes that were consolidated as confederacies between two or more tribes that may or may not have a cultural affinity, yet each group holds equal representation on the acknowledged tribal government. For instance, the Southern Cheyenne and Arapaho Tribes of Oklahoma consist of an eight member business committee staffed by four representatives from the four Cheyenne districts and four representatives elected from the two Arapaho districts.[2] The Cheyenne and Arapaho communities remain socially identifiable, with each holding formal representation on the larger confederated tribal government. Reservation-wide tribal governments that represent multiple tribal groups that may or may not be culturally or historically related have also been established, and such governments are often governed by an elected council from which representatives could be potentially drawn from all or several of the different constituent groups. In some instances each group on the same reservation has formal representation on the larger reservation-wide federally acknowledged tribe. For instance, the Ft. Belknap Indian Community of Montana is one such reservation-wide tribal government that is governed by a community council on which sit six Gros Ventre and six Assiniboine representatives. The Gros Ventre and the Assiniboine remain separate but unacknowledged constituent groups that hold formal representation on the acknowledged tribal government that represents the members of the Ft. Belknap reservation.

From the multiple ways in which constituent tribes exist, the situation faced by the Delaware, Shawnee, Yuchi, Natchez, and San Juan Southern Paiute can be separated. Unlike culturally linked and confederated or reservation-wide tribal governments, there is no cultural connection between the Delaware and the Cherokee; they do not share jurisdiction, nor are they equally represented by the Cherokee Nation's government. The smaller tribes like the Delaware are clearly placed in a subordinate position relative to another larger federally acknowledged tribe that controls the federal relationship for both constituencies. The two largest and arguably the most powerful federally recognized Indian tribes today are the Cherokee Nation and the Navajo Nation. Ironically, both the Navajo and the Cherokee have taken political and legal action to limit foreign tribes resident within their jurisdiction from seeking federal recognition and ultimately self-governance. At issue in such Navajo and Cherokee actions is the need to protect their jurisdiction over land, certain services and programs, and legal rights reserved for recognized Indian tribes. Thus, the struggle for federal recognition for tribes like the Delaware becomes more squarely a struggle with another tribe over the control of important and often contested political, economic, and jurisdictional resources.

While *subtribe* may be the closest term that approximates the Delaware situation, it is also a term that is potentially misleading and is thus not suitable to explain the Delaware's situation. Using the term *subtribe* can liken the Delaware situation to the other constituent groups described above who hold a cultural connection with the larger acknowledged tribe or who hold the potential for equal representation on an acknowledged tribal government. Glossing the Delaware situation as similar to those groups that are part of a reservation-wide or confederated tribal government runs the risk of losing the specificity of the Delaware case. Such generalizations could also make the Delaware effort for recognition appear as similar to all other internal disputes that are also a common feature of American Indian tribes. However, the Delaware Tribe is not a faction of the Cherokee Nation, nor does it hold the potential for representation as a constituent group on the Cherokee Nation's tribal government.

Furthermore, the term *subtribe* would also be viewed as offensive by the Delaware and other such groups because the very motivation for tribes like the Delaware to pursue and achieve separate acknowledgment flows from the deeply held conviction that their tribal government is not, nor should it ever be, subordinate to any other Indian tribe. The Delaware Tribe has a long history of a government-to-government relationship with the United States and is proud of its designation among other tribes as "the Grandfathers." Their subordinate relationship within the Cherokee Nation was recently imposed without Delaware consent and continues today under federal policy despite Delaware objections. One primary reason that motivates modern Delaware efforts for recognition is the desire to abolish this subordinate relationship with the Cherokee Nation and allow the Delaware Tribe to hold the federal relationship without interference.

I have referred to the Delaware Tribe in the past as a mis-acknowledged tribe in order to reference such a unique and disenfranchised status. While labeling the Delaware and other such groups as mis-acknowledged could differentiate them from the more common existence of other constituent groups, doing so also runs the risk of suggesting that the Delaware Tribe, and other similarly placed tribes, should not be acknowledged, which is not the intention nor directive of this study. While the term *mis-acknowledged* misrepresents the Delaware situation, there is no adequate term to express the uniqueness of this situation. Despite the colonial invention and implications of the term, I defer to the Delaware's own usage and understandings of themselves as simply a *tribe* without any prefixes or adjective modifications. The term *tribe* is thus used throughout this book in order to reference the Delaware's claimed sovereignty as a culturally and politically distinct group of Dawes Roll descendants who have remained constituents of their own political body throughout American history and who should be returned to the federal relationship. In identifying the Delaware as a tribe, it is important to remember the unique position within the Cherokee Nation that the Delaware hold, which is unlike many other similarly named tribes. The Delaware Tribe does lack separate acknowledgment, and Delaware people are viewed as constituent members of the Cherokee Nation even though such a status is actively resisted by the Delaware and the Delaware Tribe's situation is very different from the various other types of tribes, acknowledged or unacknowledged, that exist throughout the United States.

Tribes like the Delaware are thus placed in an unusual situation that creates unique obstacles when pursuing federal acknowledgment. An overview of federal acknowledgment will thus clarify exactly why acknowledgment remains problematic for the Delaware and other such groups. There are three routes that a tribe can follow in order to hold status as a federally recognized tribe, and the BIA maintains and periodically updates a list of those tribes recognized by congressional, judicial, and executive action. One route to acknowledgment is the legislative path in which a tribe can be acknowledged through the passage of a congressional bill as holding a government-to-government relationship with the United States. It was through legislation that the Menominee Tribe was restored in 1973 and the Shawnee Tribe was given federal acknowledgment in 2000 (Peroff 1982:252–257; Shawnee Tribe Status Act 2000). The second avenue is to pursue recognition through the federal courts as a judicial ruling can confer or uphold federal recognition for tribal governments. The Delaware Tribe's federal recognition was initially upheld in federal court in 2002 but later terminated under appeal in 2004. The final possibility is to achieve recognition through the executive branch either by executive order or by being included on the BIA's list of federally recognized tribes. The Delaware Tribe was restored recognition in 1996 when Assistant Secretary of Indian Affairs Ada Deer added the Delaware Tribe to the list of federally recognized tribes. There is also a process carried out by the executive branch for conferring recognition to those tribes that were left off of the BIA's original list. The Federal Acknowledgment Process (FAP) was established in 1978 within the BIA to investigate the validity of tribal petitions for acknowledgment. The FAP was first carried out by the Federal Acknowledgment Project office in 1978, but this was later renamed the Branch of Acknowledgment and Research (BAR) (M. Miller 2004:44). The BAR was again reorganized as the Office of Federal Acknowledgment (OFA) and was moved to the Office of the Assistant Secretary for Indian Affairs of the Department of the Interior in recent years. Although congressional and judicial routes are still available to tribes, the federal acknowledgment process has largely secured a primary place as the model for tribal recognition.

Historian Mark Edwin Miller (2004) provides the most recent and comprehensive book-length examination of the federal acknowledgment process.[3] Miller (2004:40–45) describes how the FAP was initially developed in consultation with existing tribal governments, and the process remains in place precisely because it continues to receive the support of federally recognized tribes. Miller (2004:71–72) examines the important role played by federally recognized tribes, including the Cherokee Nation, in the politics of federal acknowledgment. Miller (2004:257–258) concludes that acknowledged tribes hold an understandable interest in the acknowledgment process and have remained vocal in many of the acknowledgment decisions handed down through the FAP. Such participation by acknowledged tribes is not always antagonistic to petitioning groups as it is clear that acknowledged tribes have been relatively open to those new groups who can demonstrate a legitimate claim for acknowledgment and meet the established criteria. Federal acknowledgment, however, whether it is through congressional, judicial, or executive action, has become a process in which federally recognized tribes often voice their support for, or opposition to, the acknowledgment decisions for petitioning tribes, and most dissenting voices from acknowledged tribes reflect the criteria used in the FAP.

There are seven criteria that petitioning tribes must meet in order to be acknowledged through the FAP, and the failure to meet only one criterion would result in a negative finding for the potential tribe. The seven criteria for tribal acknowledgment used by OFA can essentially be narrowed to three general conditions. The first two criteria ask that the petitioner demonstrate that it has existed as an Indian community from historic times to the present (now revised to have existed from 1900 to the present) and its existence is identified by outsiders and insiders alike as being distinct from other non-Indian and Indian communities. The final criteria, or termination criteria, requires that neither the petitioner nor its membership are the subject of any legislation that terminated federal recognition. The middle four criteria deal with the characteristics of the tribal government. The governmental criteria require that the petitioning tribe shows evidence of a governing body that has maintained authority over its membership, possesses a governing document or rules for political organization, and its membership consists of individuals who descend from an Indian tribe that functioned as an autonomous entity and is composed principally of persons not already enrolled in an acknowledged tribe. The requirement that a substantial portion of the petitioning group not be enrolled in another federally recognized tribe was included to ensure that the FAP would not provide for the breakup and dissolution of acknowledged tribes, many of which are tribal governments representing consolidated groups. As will be shown, this single enrollment criteria for petitioning tribes is precisely the criteria that makes acknowledgment for tribes like the Delaware uniquely problematic.

While the limiting effect of the enrollment requirement for some tribes has not been presented, the existing literature on the federal acknowledgment of Indian tribes does present the many struggles faced by unacknowledged tribes. Most often the literature on the unacknowledged is critical of the expectations in the FAP criteria and points out the challenges that individual groups have faced when pursuing federal acknowledgment.[4] Sara-Larus Tolley's (2006) ethnography of the Honey Lake Maidu acknowledgment effort takes such a critical position and points out the unreasonable expectations in the FAP given the history of federal policy that was designed to erase exactly that which is now required as proof of tribal existence. Similarly the challenges that face most unacknowledged tribes generally rest in their ability to demonstrate with documented evidence a continuous political organization or defend their status as Indian people. Such petitioning efforts never occur in a vacuum and often take place in politically charged contexts galvanized over the issues of casino gaming, access to federal programs, and the ability to hold federal trust land that comes with acknowledgment. Renee Ann Cramer's (2005) book, for instance, reviews the acknowledgment efforts of several eastern tribes and highlights the pervasiveness of discourses about gaming and racial authenticity that surrounded such acknowledgment bids. The literature on the unacknowledged has thus identified the very real difficulties that the unacknowledged face, yet such difficulties are not shared by tribes like the Delaware, who can easily demonstrate political continuity and racial authenticity according to the federal standard.

For unacknowledged tribes, the FAP requirement that is most easily met is that the petitioning group be composed principally of individuals who are not also members of an acknowledged Indian tribe. This enrollment requirement is an afterthought for most unacknowledged tribes because most of their membership is not recognized as holding a federal Indian status (M. Miller 2004:149).

However, the sixth or single enrollment criteria that is unimportant to unacknowledged groups significantly limits the eligibility of other tribes whose memberships are often included as members of an acknowledged Indian tribe. Every Delaware tribal member can hold individual federal acknowledgment as "Indian," but only if they choose to enroll as such through the Cherokee Nation. This potential for enrollment thus presents unique challenges for the Delaware Tribe that are not faced by the unacknowledged when federal acknowledgment is pursued. Any prospective group may pursue legislative, judicial, or executive recognition, but the hurdles faced by tribes like the Delaware are very different from those already described in the literature for unacknowledged tribes.

The single enrollment criterion even remained problematic for the Delaware Tribe after acknowledgment was restored in 1996 because the BIA uses the single enrollment requirement when determining a tribe's eligibility for administering federal services provided by 638 contracts and compacts as stipulated under the Self-Determination Act. A condition of most self-determination or 638 contracts is that the tribe seeking a potential contract does not have an overlapping membership with a tribe already holding a BIA contract. With this requirement, the self-determination policy (perhaps unintentionally) conflates tribal membership with service population. Because the Delaware Tribe remained unacknowledged from 1979 to 1996, most Delaware were only eligible for such federal services if they enrolled with another acknowledged Indian Tribe. Enrolling with another tribe for access to services also meant that the Delaware enrollees were considered members of the other tribe. As a consequence, even if a tribe like the Delaware where to successfully achieve federal recognition either through legislative, judicial, or executive action, it would still be limited under self-determination policy from taking over those contract services already administered by other acknowledged tribes unless the Delaware could separate their tribal membership and create a new service population. With no recourse, such uniquely situated tribes that gain acknowledgment must then convince their tribal membership to adopt a single enrollment clause in order to establish a separate service population and thus be eligible for taking over the administration of contract services. Requiring single enrollment would mean that the Delaware would be obliged to renounce their membership in the Cherokee Nation (and any other tribes as well) and forgo their inclusion in the Cherokee Nation's service population.

Although instituting such a single enrollment policy appears logical, this book demonstrates that such a move would be one that is perceived by some tribal constituents as a decision that could potentially threaten their access to important and often vital federal services. Because tribes like the Delaware have been limited from developing their own infrastructure of established programs and services as a consequence of their nonrecognition, Delaware people have been obliged to utilize the programs and services provided by the Cherokee Nation that are by now well established. Giving up membership in the Cherokee Nation's service population is thus very different in Delaware minds from revoking tribal membership in the Cherokee Nation. Turning away from Cherokee tribal membership is a choice guided by one's political allegiance while dropping out of the Cherokee service population is an economic decision that some do not have the luxury to make. It would take a considerable amount of time for the Delaware Tribe to develop an infrastructure comparable to that of the Cherokee Nation, and some Delaware simply cannot do without Cherokee-administered programs and services despite their unquestionable support for Delaware independence. By enrolling as members of the Cherokee Nation's service population for access to what are often vital or otherwise expensive social services, such individual, often necessary actions thus complicate the Delaware Tribe's efforts for acknowledgment that could be more easily secured if a separate tribal membership could be demonstrated. Thus, existent acknowledged tribes like the Cherokee Nation often hold considerable influence over their constituent tribes through the control over the federal enrollment process and the access to federal contract services that such enrollment provides. Since tribes like the Delaware generally have no other option but to enroll with their host acknowledged tribe in order to be included in a service population, a single enrollment requirement in the Federal Acknowledgment Process and self-determination contracts gives the acknowledged tribe tremendous economic and political influence over their constituent tribes through the auspices of federal contract services as well as making it more difficult for tribes like the Delaware to achieve separate recognition under the FAP.

It is crucial then that the issues faced by the Delaware Tribe and others are included in the ethnography of federal recognition as their endeavors present dilemmas that have not been significantly explored. Not only must the Delaware Tribe challenge a more powerfully situated host tribe, but they must also navigate the complex meanings of tribal enrollment in current federal policy. The primary dilemma confronting the Delaware and other similarly placed groups is therefore achieving a separate tribal membership and the direct access to, and control over, the administration of federal services that such separateness provides. In this book I explore this issue of how tribal enrollment in the modern era is not simply a political choice guided by a long-standing debate within the Delaware Tribe but is also an economic choice that is influenced by the access to federal programs and services that enrollment provides. The problem then is not that the Delaware want to be members of the Cherokee Nation but that the boundary between tribal membership (as required by the Federal Acknowledgment Process) and service population (as required by the self-determination) is not clearly defined, and the conflation of the two in federal and tribal practices complicates the Delaware's bid for regaining federal acknowledgment in the modern era. Indeed, such conflation of tribal enrollment and service population is a primary factor that significantly limits the federal recognition efforts of a small but important group of Indian tribes like the Delaware while further empowering the legitimacy of established federally recognized tribes such as the Cherokee Nation.

The ethnography of the Delaware Tribe's struggle to preserve its federal acknowledgment while resident in the Cherokee Nation is thus set in relation to the federal policy that is outlined above. Federal policy has provided the background for the Delaware struggle and continues to do so. This book reveals that the root of the problem surrounding Delaware acknowledgment does not rest with the Delaware Tribe nor the Cherokee Nation, but in the consolidative pressures inherent in a modern federal policy that conflates tribal membership with service population. The book makes clear that the Delaware have not assimilated into the Cherokee Nation and survive today as an independent Indian Tribe despite its forced inclusion in the Cherokee Nation. Suggested here is that the recourse for solving this longstanding issue may best be sought by revising federal policy toward the Delaware Tribe's position within the Cherokee Nation rather than ignoring the consolidative pressures in such federal policy while forcing the hand of Delaware and Cherokee leaders to resolve the issue in federal courts and congressional legislation.

CONTEXT AND STRUCTURE OF THE BOOK

There were two foundational contexts from which this study was conducted. The first was the Delaware Community of eastern Oklahoma, and the second was the Delaware tribal government that included elected officials and employees of the Delaware Tribe of Indians. The Delaware community consists of a social network of Delaware-descended families that live and work in the region north and northeast of Tulsa, Oklahoma. Washington and Nowata counties provide the nucleus for the small but active Delaware Community that generally numbers between one hundred and four hundred individuals. Membership is fluid with people moving in and out of the group based on varying levels of participation. It is during community-sponsored events such as the Delaware Powwow, Delaware Days, the Delaware General Council, or the wild onion dinner discussed at the beginning that the boundaries of the Delaware community are most visible. Familiar relatives and friends reunite at such events, and group identity is affirmed. Most ethnography is written through the lens provided by such community-based positioning, and it is from here that I began to develop an appreciation for the distinct and diverse Delaware society of eastern Oklahoma.

My involvement with the Delaware began in 2000 when I made the decision to take on the study of Delaware federal recognition. My participation began as an awkward and naive outsider trying to learn about an issue that appeared so straightforward to everyone else. Infrequent visits were made to important community events as well as to governmental meetings at the tribal headquarters. When it became evident that I would need to make a more serious commitment to my research, my wife and son moved with me to Tulsa in 2001 so that my commute from Delaware Country would be more tolerable and thus I would spend less time away from home. From 2001 to 2004 I was a daily participant in Delaware community life. I attended most of the Tribal Council and Trust Board meetings, every Delaware General Council meeting, Delaware Powwow, and Delaware Days held during that four-year span as well as several events hosted by community members. The Delaware Community Center in Bartlesville that held the annual General Council meeting acted as my second home where I consistently attended the once monthly but now weekly potluck suppers and social dances and was a regular at the weekday lunches provided there by the Delaware Elder Nutrition Program. I am indebted to the hospitality of the Delaware elders and community members who welcomed me at their tables and in their homes and shared with me in a way that made me feel as if I were an old friend.

The second context was the Delaware Tribe of Indians for whom I continue to serve as a tribal employee. A study that explores the impact of self-determination policy on tribal governance required that I ask questions and make observations from the perspective of a participant observer at the level of the Delaware tribal government. As a participant, I took on the responsibility of continuing the operation of the Delaware NAGPRA (Native American Graves Protection and Repatriation Act) Program in 2003. Our NAGPRA work was entirely funded by externally awarded federal grants that included a project to document and inventory Delaware human remains and funerary objects held in museums and public agencies as well as to repatriate and rebury certain human remains and funerary objects already located. Such work resulted in an inventory of over seven thousand items as well as the reburial of human remains on Ellis Island and the restoration of two eroding Delaware cemeteries in Oklahoma.

As any tribal employee who works for a perpetually underfunded but overworked tribal government is aware, we have to be able to wear many hats. My other roles included work on a tribal library and the Delaware Tribe's Indian Reservation Road (IRR) program. We were fortunate to get funding from the Institute of Museum and Library Services (IMLS) for the startup of a tribal library in 2004, and the Bureau of Indian Affairs (BIA) had previously awarded a self-determination contract to the Delaware Tribe in 1999 for the tribe to develop its own IRR program. My experience while working on the IRR program that was made available through the self-determination/self-governance legislation allowed me to see firsthand the very real opportunities for empowerment provided to tribes in the self-determination era. My involvement with the IRR program also allowed me to experience as a program director the challenges that came from the Cherokee Nation when the Delaware attempted to make use of such opportunities. Ultimately, all of my work was funded by the tribe's eligibility for federal grants and tribal programs as a federally recognized tribe. Not surprisingly, all of the programs under my direction including the NAGPRA documentation and repatriation efforts, funding for the tribal library, and the IRR program were all halted by the Delaware Tribe's loss of federal recognition in 2004.

During my employment with the Delaware Tribe, I was present at the tribal headquarters on a daily basis during the years before the loss of federal recognition. The administrative offices were then housed in the same tribal headquarters as the office for the chief of the Delaware Tribe and the meeting room that held important tribal meetings. Another social world at the headquarters revolved around the elected representatives of the Delaware community and the tribal employees, who were Delaware, non-Delaware, or non-Indian. Here the social network of the Delaware community was linked to the federal circle that included other tribal governments as well as the federal government. Rules and norms were altered here as a proficiency in what were often complex and changing rules for federal compliance had to be mastered and continuously updated. Forms, applications, reports, and formal correspondence were expected in order to facilitate record keeping, documentation, and communication. Confined to our offices and focusing on our phones and computers, the employees at the tribal headquarters would somehow find the time to visit during the day about the latest news and interact as people rather than cogs in a machine. Like most places of business, the Delaware tribal headquarters constituted its own level of community, and it is from the vista of my office desk and those of fellow workers that I observed the Delaware struggle on a level separate from that provided by my involvement with the Delaware community.

Beyond participant observation, the data for this study included formal and informal interviews, written notes from my own experiences, archival sources, published and self-published works, as well as a vitally important legal brief prepared by the Delaware Tribe. The interviews utilized for this book were collected during my field research with the Delaware from 2001 to 2004. At the Delaware Community Center, in Delaware homes, and at the local powwow grounds, I conducted over forty formal interviews that were digitally recorded with the technical support from an NIH-funded project under the direction of Dr. Morris Foster and the University of Oklahoma. There were two sets of interviews that I conducted with one question format that was focused on Delaware oral history while the other solicited responses on the current struggle between the Delaware Tribe and the Cherokee Nation. All recorded interviews were transcribed and digitally archived with support from the Faculty Research and Creativity Grant program at Emporia State University and remain in the author's possession. Notes were also compiled from informal conversations, regular participation in community events, and my employment with the Delaware Tribe and remain in the author's possession as well.

To my own experiences were added Delaware histories that were available in published, unpublished, and archival sources and that situate my contemporary observations and presentation of modern Delaware society. As this book is not a history of the Delaware Tribe, I have relied on the extensive and well-researched literature as well as oral history collections already dedicated to the subject. Most notable is my constant reference to Clinton A. Weslager's (1972, 1978) historical research that reconstructs the path and politics of Delaware removal. Weslager (1972) also includes a review of modern Delaware history in twentieth-century Oklahoma with a special focus on the Delaware land claims awards that were ongoing during the time. Anthropologist Ives Goddard's (1978) chapter on the Delaware in the *Handbook of North American Indians* was also a vital source that provided my baseline understanding for aboriginal Delaware religion, culture, and social structure as well as a supplement to Weslager's historical perspective on removal. A number of other less-known works by local authors helped bring a different perspective to the literature on Delaware history. One important source was a collection of Delaware genealogy and oral history compiled by the former curator of the Bartlesville History Room, Ruby Cranor (1985, 1991). Although some Delaware have doubts about portions of the genealogical information, her self-collected compilation of transcribed Delaware oral history compliments the other more popular oral history sources used in this book, such as the Doris Duke Collection housed in the Western History Library in Norman, Oklahoma, and the archives at the Oklahoma Historical Society.[5] During the course of this research, several other archival sources were made available to me through my work at the tribal headquarters, such as tribal documents, policies, and minutes of past meetings. Also, one collection, the Freddie Washington collection, was provided to me and helped to shed light on a crucial time in mid-twentieth-century Delaware history and is included in the book as well.

Finally, the Delaware Tribe prepared a legal brief under the direction of tribal lawyer Gina Carrigan in 1994 to support the later successful Delaware effort for federal recognition (Carrigan and Chambers 1994). Carrigan's collaboration with tribal member Clayton Chambers resulted in a compilation of important government documents and archival material that reveal Delaware governmental history in the twentieth century. The authors also prepared an eighty-page narrative based on their archival research that explains the course of recent Delaware history. Carrigan and Chambers's work was crucial to my understanding of Delaware history and often provides the foundation from which I describe twentieth-century Delaware governance.

Utilizing the above sources, this book seeks to contribute to the substantial ethnography on the Delaware, which has not been updated for a generation. My work on contemporary Delaware society should be viewed only as an addition to a long tradition of rigorous ethnographic work developed by some of the best ethnographers in the field. Initial ethnographic works were salvage efforts that thankfully recorded Delaware customs and religious practices that have since been abandoned but are not forgotten (Morgan 1959; Michelson 1912; Harrington 1913; Voegelin 1946). Such work was followed by research that emphasized the acculturation of Delaware society that was then believed to be ongoing. The ethnography done at midcentury documented the memories of the once practiced Delaware customs such as the Delaware Big House and described the new events and practices taken on by Delaware people such as the Native American church (Speck 1931, 1937; Newcomb 1955, 1956a, 1956b; Petrullo 1934; Goddard 1974; Miller 1980b; Prewitt 1981). Some scholars of midcentury Delaware society proposed the idea that Delaware identity was slowly being lost and would soon be replaced by a Pan-Indian identity (Newcomb 1955; Howard 1955).[6] Research continued, however, and reported on the continuity of a distinct and revitalized sense of Delaware tribal identity as well as an appreciation for those ways long put away by previous generations (Roark-Calnek 1977, 1980; J. Miller 1975, 1977, 1980a). My ethnographic work illustrates this continued vitality of Delaware tribal identity by emphasizing the Delaware's use of social events, customs, and even federal Indian policy as a source for tribal empowerment and persistence.

The book utilizes such sources to provide a descriptive account of Delaware society that makes regular use of Delaware narratives and personal experiences. Some chapters are opened with vignettes collected during my research in order to introduce the reader to the chapter's main objective. Delaware stories, oral histories, archived information, and excerpts from recorded interviews along with my own firsthand accounts are then selectively interspersed throughout each chapter to incorporate Delaware voices with my own understandings of, and conclusions about, the Delaware pursuit for federal recognition. My intent is to achieve some balance between my voice and the voices of the Delaware community from whom I have gained such insight. Although balance is the goal, it is the voices of the Delaware community that I have strived to amplify in my writings. However, the observations, interpretations, and conclusions presented remain my own, and any inaccuracies are my sole responsibility.

The book is structured with seven subsequent chapters that describe Delaware history and contemporary society in ways that bear on the FAP criteria. Chapters 2 and 3 demonstrate that the Delaware have existed as a distinct and identifiable American Indian community from historic times to the present. Chapter 2 begins with a historical overview of the Delaware and Cherokee separate removal experiences that ultimately brought the two tribes together in the Cherokee Nation. Once removed, the Cherokee Nation and the Delaware Tribe have been at odds over the various issues concerning Delaware rights in the Cherokee Nation as witnessed from a review of the federal court battles fought between the two tribes since the late nineteenth century. Chapter 3 then lays out the existence of a distinct Delaware community that has dwelled in the northwest portion of the Cherokee Nation since removal, where the contemporary members and Delaware tribal government reside today. In the regions north and northeast of Tulsa, the Delaware have their own unique cultural landscape that is recognized by both insiders and outsiders as Delaware Country. The persistence of the Delaware's unique space in northeastern Oklahoma is illustrated with a review of Delaware settlement history and the contemporary Delaware built environment.

Chapters 4 and 5 then address the history of Delaware tribal governance and a review of the Delaware Tribe's government-to-government relationship with the United States. Chapter 4 begins with the transition to Oklahoma statehood during which time the Delaware received land allotments in the Cherokee Nation, most of which where situated in the region locally known as Delaware Country. There the Delaware were organized by two complimentary and overlapping political bodies with the formally organized Delaware Business Committee assigned the task of dealing with the federal government and the Cherokee Nation. The other less formally organized Big House leadership focused on the internal needs of the community. The Delaware Business Committee navigated the shifts in twentieth-century federal policy and was sometimes faced with dissent from the Big House community leadership. Against the wishes of the Big House leaders, the Business Committee elected not to organize under the Oklahoma Indian Welfare Act but did pursue and was awarded significant land claims that brought a new dimension to the constituency of the Delaware Tribe. Chapter 5 then explains the continuation of the Delaware tribal government in the self-determination era despite periods of first executive followed by judicial termination. Provided is an explanation of the Delaware Tribe's bicameral system of governance created in the modern era in order to meet the needs of the Delaware community as well as the federal requirements for recognition. Also articulated is an ethnographic portrait of Delaware leadership and an analysis of the unique way in which Delaware elected representatives gain the needed votes to serve on the contemporary tribal government. It is argued here that modern Delaware government still conforms to the unique Delaware sociopolitical organization and cultural ideals forged with removal. As chapters 2–5 reveal, there is no question to all parties involved including the Cherokee Nation and the United States that the Delaware Tribe has been identified as a distinct Indian community with a governing body that has existed since historic times to the present and that the federal government has never terminated the Delaware Tribe through congressional action.

The final two chapters turn the focus to address precisely why Delaware recognition remains elusive by unpacking the issues that surround the potential for Delaware enrollment in the Cherokee Nation. Chapter 6 first describes the Cherokee-controlled Certificate Degree of Indian Blood (CDIB) enrollment process that provides the only acknowledged federal Indian identity for Delaware people. Through the perspective provided by the Delaware's own words, the reasons why the Delaware enroll as Cherokee by Blood are revealed even though the Delaware do not consider themselves to be Cherokee people or citizens and do not wish to merge with the Cherokee Nation. Chapter 7 then focuses on the tribal enrollment options beyond the CDIB card that are available to the Delaware. There are both a Cherokee tribal membership card and a Delaware tribal membership card that exist separately from the Cherokee CDIB card, and explained in chapter 7 are the options available for Delaware enrollment when such tribal cards are considered. Explained here is why most Delaware own a Cherokee CDIB and hold dual Delaware and Cherokee tribal memberships or hold a Cherokee CDIB and only a Delaware tribal membership. The possibility of Delaware tribal enrollment without the Cherokee CDIB, or single enrollment, is then explored through the frame of a recent but failed Delaware referendum to institute single enrollment. The chapter thus concludes with an explanation for why a small majority of Delaware voted against single enrollment when everyone involved in the vote were strident supporters of separate federal recognition for the Delaware Tribe. Here it is clarified why it is important to clearly separate tribal membership from service population in our modern understandings of the potential for Delaware membership in the Cherokee Nation.

A concluding chapter then follows with an overview of the most recent Cherokee-Delaware Agreement that is now being put forward as a solution. This 2007 Cherokee-Delaware Agreement comes 140 years after Delaware removal to the Cherokee Nation and will help to solidify my concluding remarks on why the issue of federal recognition for the Delaware is so complex and why the politics of tribal enrollment are so crucial to the Delaware struggle. As seen in a review of the 2007 Cherokee-Delaware Agreement, what limits the Delaware Tribe today from preserving federal recognition are the influences held by the Cherokee Nation and the single enrollment criteria in the FAP and self-determination contracts that do not clearly distinguish between tribal membership and service population.

Although not a critique of the sovereignty of acknowledged tribes, this book reports on research that suggests needed revision in federal policy toward tribal enrollment. The book invites the reader to explore whether the single enrollment criterion holds the potential to serve the best interests of all tribes and whether or not it is a provision that meets with the ideal of tribal sovereignty in the self-determination era. Is single enrollment a necessary condition of tribal government or merely a provision instituted to sustain the authority of acknowledged tribes and the bureaucratic needs of the federal government? Is the expectation of single enrollment important enough to deny the undeniable existence of the distinct Delaware community and the long history of the government-to-government relationship that has existed between the Delaware Tribe and the United States? Can we expect that the members of the Delaware Tribe will risk the prospect of single enrollment simply to meet the federal standard? Or is the single enrollment criterion flexible enough to allow for the Delaware Tribe to have a real opportunity to achieve the much needed federal recognition without risking the vital needs of the membership that they hope to serve? While answers to such questions are implicitly suggested in this book, my work is not intended to challenge the sovereignty of acknowledged tribal governments but to provide evidence for the need to find a solution that considers the unique case that is presented with tribes like the Delaware.

Removal and the Cherokee-Delaware Agreement

The children hereafter born of such Delawares so
incorporated into the Cherokee Nation shall in
all respects be regarded as native Cherokees.

1867 CHEROKEE-DELAWARE AGREEMENT

Highway 75 between Tulsa and Bartlesville was my daily
commute, and my attention during the hour-long drive often turned
to the scenery located just a few miles to the west. The escarpment
of the post oak-covered Osage Hills provided the western horizon,
and the Caney River flowed southward along the hills' eastern edge.
It was along that eastern ridge of the Osage Hills where the ninety-
sixth degree of longitude ran, and the former western boundary of
the Cherokee Nation lay. Up against this line of longitude is where
most Delaware families settled following removal in small agrarian
communities along the fertile floodplains of the Caney River and
its tributaries. Because the Delaware chose to preserve their tribal
organization while settling east of the ninety-sixth degree in 1867,
the Delaware Tribe was required to pay the Cherokee Nation for
the rights to land and Cherokee citizenship as stipulated in the 1867
Cherokee-Delaware Agreement. Ever since that time, the Delaware
Tribe has had to remain diligent with the Cherokee Nation in order
to ensure that all three rights (preservation of tribal organization,
land rights, and Cherokee citizenship) were maintained.

This chapter presents the historical background of how the Delaware have come to be in such a difficult situation with the Cherokee Nation while both tribes have very little in common. Described here are the separate cultures and removal histories of both tribes as well as the somewhat antagonistic relationship that has existed between them since the signing of the 1867 Cherokee-Delaware Agreement. The discussion shows that the Delaware and the Cherokee are not historically related nor are they even culturally similar. The only similarity is that both the Delaware and the Cherokee are Indian tribes that do not presently reside in their ancestral homelands. Both the Delaware and Cherokee were forcibly removed through different means to Indian Territory during the nineteenth century and have lived within a shared territory only since 1867.

The Delaware Tribe and Cherokee Nation did, however, enter into a formal contract in *The Articles of Agreement between the Cherokee Nation and the Delawares, April 8, 1867*, or the 1867 Cherokee-Delaware Agreement, in order to provide for the Delaware's removal to the Cherokee Nation. Although certain stipulations in the agreement have been cited as the reason for the Delaware's inclusion in the Cherokee Nation, the discussion here shows that such cited conditions were actually intended to provide for the preservation of the Delaware Tribe's political organization. An overview of the important treaties and agreements signed between the Delaware Tribe, the Cherokee Nation, and the federal government during the crucial years of 1866 and 1867 makes evident the true factor that motivated the Delaware Tribe to sign the 1867 agreement and relocate to the Cherokee Nation. Perhaps more relevant to understanding the Delaware Tribe's intention while agreeing to removal was the fact that the Delaware Tribe and the Cherokee Nation did not merge into one centralized government even after shared occupation. Rather, the Delaware Tribe and the Cherokee Nation have been at odds with one another over the terms of the 1867 Cherokee-Delaware Agreement as can be inferred from the long legacy of court cases between the two tribes. A review of the Delaware and Cherokee litigation since removal is presented in the final section of the chapter to reveal the long-standing tensions that have stemmed from what appear to be the unreasonable conditions stipulated in the 1867 Cherokee-Delaware Agreement.

DELAWARE AND CHEROKEE REMOVAL

The Delaware and Cherokee removal experiences were unique and brought significant alterations to both the Delaware and Cherokee societies. Delaware removal involved a century-long series of relocations with periodic stops at different locations throughout the midwestern United States. During the intermittent Delaware relocations the core, or main body, of Delaware sustained an independent political organization characterized by a body of male lineage and later clan representatives selected to leadership by their respective extended families. Cherokee removal, on the other hand, began with increasing non-Indian encroachment following the American Revolution and ended with the historic Trail of Tears through which the majority of Cherokee people were finally removed from their homeland to Indian Territory. Cherokee attempts to fend off removal involved the adoption of Anglo-American cultural and political practices including the reorganization of the Cherokee government into a three-branch system that mimicked the political structure of the United States. Thus, by the time that the Delaware Tribe removed to the Cherokee Nation, the Delaware Tribe had essentially sustained a kin-based representative democracy while the Cherokee Nation resisted removal through accommodation. Delaware and Cherokee removals were thus separate relocations and removal did not result in the merger of the two tribes as has been asserted by some authorities.[1]

The Delaware Tribe is one of many contemporary tribes that descend from the Unami-and Munsee-speaking peoples of the Delaware and Hudson River valleys. Munsee and Unami are two closely related Algonquian dialects that were easily distinguishable from the languages of the other coastal Algonquian groups (Goddard 1978:213). The Unami and Munsee aboriginal homeland is situated within what are today the states of New Jersey, Pennsylvania, New York, and Delaware. Munsee was the Algonquian dialect spoken in the villages along the upper Delaware and lower Hudson rivers while the Unami dialect that contained southern and northern variants existed along the lower Delaware River. The material culture differences between the Proto-Munsee and Proto-Unami villagers of the Hudson and Delaware valleys can be recognized as early AD 10,000, suggesting an antiquity in the cultural barriers between the Unami and Munsee speakers (Kraft 1984:7–8).[2]

The name collectively attributed to the descendants of such Unami and Munsee people is Delaware, yet the word *Delaware* is not of indigenous origin, nor did the Munsee and Unami speakers conceive of themselves as a united political organization until the eighteenth century. The term *Delaware* actually derives from the title given to Sir Thomas West or Lord de la Warr III, who was appointed the English governor of Virginia in 1610. When Captain Samuel Argall first explored what would later be named the Delaware Bay and River, he chose the name *Delaware* to honor the newly appointed Virginia governor (Kraft 1984:1). European colonists later applied the term in varied dialectical forms to reference the Unami-speaking groups of the middle Delaware River valley, and by the late eighteenth century the term had been extended to include all of the Unami-and Munsee-speaking peoples living in or removed from the Delaware and Hudson River valleys (Goddard 1978:213, 235; Weslager 1972:31). The southern Unami self-designation is *Lenape*, which roughly translates as "People" and was the term used by the inhabitants of the lower Delaware River. Most Delaware in eastern Oklahoma descend from such Unami speakers, with only a minority who count Munsee descent as well. Today, the southern Unami dialect is the language

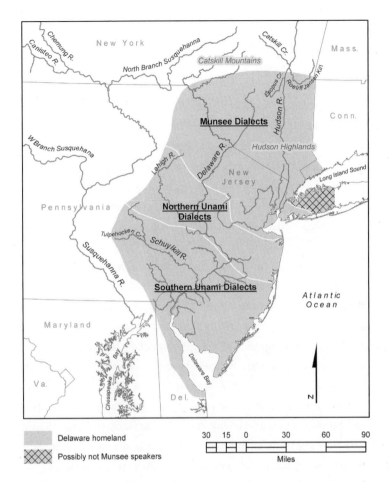

Delaware homeland

Possibly not Munsee speakers

| 30 | 15 | 0 | 30 | 60 | 90 |

Miles

1. DELAWARE HOMELAND: The seventeenth-century Delaware territory
and distribution of Munsee and Unami dialects. Adapted from Ives Goddard,
"Delaware," in Handbook of North American Indians, vol. 15: Northeast,
ed. Bruce Trigger and William Sturtevant (Washington DC: Smithsonian
Institution, 1978), p. 214, figure 1. Map by Rebecca Dobbs.

learned and used by the Delaware in eastern Oklahoma, and *Delaware* is the tribal name used by most tribal members, with *Lenape* as an often used synonym.

In the seventeenth century, Munsee-and Unami-speaking groups lived in approximately forty politically autonomous bands of a few hundred members each that were linked through cultural similarities, periodic alliances, and marriage (Goddard 1978:213–216). The Munsee and Unami bands were horticulturalists who cultivated gardens of corn and other cultigens in dispersed villages located along the floodplains of the Delaware and Hudson River valleys. Each village housed several matrilineages, each with their own understood hunting territory. Each lineage belonged to one of at least three clans, and both the clans and lineages were exogamous. During the winter months the villagers would disperse as each lineage would break up into smaller family foraging groups and make greater use of their lineage's hunting territory that surrounded the centrally located village. The villages were likely settled in the same location for long periods of time, and each was governed by a group of male sachems or lineage representatives. Although the sachems were male, the matron of each matrilineage was the chief-maker, as it was she who named and could replace lineage sachems. The villages were thus relatively egalitarian with political decisions ultimately being made by consensus within each lineage and the sachems acting as the political voice for the lineages of each autonomous village (A. Wallace 1947:11–20).

Though once politically, regionally, and dialectally separable, the villagers of the Delaware and Hudson rivers followed a religion anchored by a vision experience carried out just before puberty and expressed through an annual harvest ceremony, war dances, curing rituals, and family-sponsored ceremonies (Goddard 1978:220, 231–234). A vision gave to an individual a supernatural mentor, and such experience was enacted in song and dance by each visionary as the central event in the fall harvest ceremony, which later became known as the Gamwing or Big House Ceremony (J. Miller 1997). The Big House Ceremony was an annually held twelve-day thanksgiving and world renewal ceremony during which the Delaware gave thanks to Kishelemukong, or the creator, and vision songs and dances were performed. The ceremony was performed in the Xingwikaon, or Big House Church, which was a rectangular log building with a pitched shingle roof supported by one central ridge pole running the length of the structure. Although the Xingwikaon is similar to the longhouses common to other northeastern Indians, the Big House structure and ceremony were unique to the Delaware (Grumet 2001:xi–xv).

The Unami and Munsee bands felt the pressure of European encroachment since the early seventeenth century beginning with Swedish and later Dutch colonization. Initial relations with the Dutch generally revolved around the fur trade and land cessions. The Unami and Munsee had access to European trade goods such as guns and steel through the Dutch but in turn had to deal with the population loss that resulted from the early introduction of European diseases and warfare.[3] By the time that the English wrested possession of the region from the Dutch in 1664, the Unami and Munsee had already been pressured to leave portions of their original homelands (Weslager 1972:98–136; Goddard 1978:220). The British subsequently established new settlements or renamed existing Dutch villages, and the growing number of English immigrants arriving in the late seventeenth century put further pressure on the Unami and Munsee to cede more land (Weslager 1972:137–152).

Two centuries of European encroachment ultimately led to the removal of the Unami and Munsee speakers from the Delaware and Hudson River valleys to the frontier of English occupation. The allied Six Nations and the English combined forces in the eighteenth century and relied upon misleading treaty agreements and the threat of military force to ultimately push the Unami and Munsee people to abandon their remaining homelands and move west. By the mid-eighteenth century, the majority of Munsee and Unami speakers had joined several villages along the Susquehanna, Allegheny, and Ohio rivers and were by then referred to collectively as the Delaware (Goddard 1978:213–216). Other displaced coastal and interior Algon-quians such as the Shawnee, Conoy, and Nanticoke often joined the Delaware villages on the frontier (Weslager 1972:173–193; Goddard 1978:221–222). The refugees were then settled within territory claimed by the Iroquois, and the newly arrived residents were obliged to live as protectorates of the Six Nations (Weslager 1972:180, 196–208).[4] Since authority among the Delaware villagers rested in a group of sachems, British officials and Iroquois diplomats were often frustrated in their attempts to deal with the displaced peoples and broker land deals with the refugee villagers. The Iroquois and the English subsequently pressured the Delaware groups to name a king who could represent the different villages and with whom the colonial government could engage treaty negotiations (Weslager 1978:14–15). Though paramount leaders were named for the displaced villagers, it is clear that such designated Delaware chiefs of the eighteenth century held a somewhat tenuous authority over the entirety of their people (A. Wallace 1970; Weslager 1972:209; Goddard 1978:223).

As the independent Munsee and Unami bands coalesced in frontier villages, the political life of such groups followed a pattern by which the independent village sachems centralized under a clan-based governing body. The Delaware political system that emerged in the mid-eighteenth century consisted of three clan chiefs who represented three matrilineal clans, the Wolf, Turkey, and Turtle clans. One clan chief acted as the first among equals and served as the Delaware spokesman (Goddard 1978:222; Weslager 1972:250). Each clan chief was also attended by councilors and war captains of the same clan. War captains were responsible for declaring war and protecting the people, while only the clan chiefs could declare peace. The councilors served as personal advisers for each clan chief (Zeisberger 1910:98).[5]

The tumultuous years surrounding the American Revolution led to a Delaware diaspora that would further define the nucleus of the Delaware Tribe and create the boundaries between the many Delaware-descended groups that exist today. By the eve of the American Revolution, most Delaware groups were living along the Ohio and Allegheny rivers. The pro-British Delaware groups were living in what is today the northwestern portion of Ohio, and pro-American Delaware groups were settled near the frontier city of Pittsburgh (Goddard 1978:222–223). Despite the mixed alliance, the Delaware were largely treated as defeated British allies at the close of the war. Following the American Revolution, different Delaware groups migrated north and west to Canada and Spanish Territory in order to escape American retaliation while others stayed within the Ohio Territory.[6]

Three groups relocated to Canada following the American Revolution. The first group consisted of a few Northern Unami bands who had not followed the main body to the frontier and who joined the Iroquois on the Six Nations Reserve along the Grand River in what is today Ontario (Goddard 1978:222). The Delaware living on the Six Nations Reserve have maintained an identity separate from the Iroquois but are today considered members of the Six Nations of the Grand River Territory, a recognized First Nation of Canada. A second group of Canadian Delaware were originally Christian converts who followed the Moravian missionary David Zeisberger north to Canada after the American Revolution and, in 1792, established what would later become known as Moraviantown along the Thames River in Kent County, Ontario. The Moravian migration followed the Gnadenhutten Massacre of 1782 when the American militia slaughtered ninety peaceful Moravian Delaware living in the mission village of Gnadenhutten, Ohio (Goddard 1978:223). The third group relocating to Canada was a collection of pro-British Munsee bands who lived in northwestern

Ohio during the American Revolution and who elected to settle at Munceytown along the Thames River in Canada prior to the arrival of the Moravian Delaware. Both the Moravian Delaware (Delaware of the Thames) and the Munceytown Delaware (Muncee-Delaware) are recognized today as First Nations in Canada.

Other Delaware groups decided to move further west to Spanish territory or remain within the boundaries of the new American state. The earliest movement consisted of both Unami and Munsee speakers who elected to move further west in 1789 to a settlement near what is today Cape Girardeau, Missouri, at the invitation of the Spanish after the American Revolution. Following a series of subsequent removals, the Cape Girardeau Delaware would later settle in Texas and eventually end up on a reservation with the Caddo and Wichita in what is today western Oklahoma. The western Oklahoma Delaware are federally recognized today as the Delaware Nation and are headquartered in Anadarko, Oklahoma (Goddard 1978:223; Hale 1987). A second migration consisted of a few small groups of Christian Munsee and Unami converts who managed to remain behind along the Hudson and Delaware River valleys following the American Revolution. The converts were eventually relocated with other Munsee and Mahicans living at Stockbridge, Massachusetts, to a reservation in Wisconsin. The descendants of such Munsee, Unami, and Mahicans are a federally recognized tribe today known as the Stockbridge-Munsee Band of Mahican Indians (Goddard 1978:222). A third group of predominately Munsee speakers settled with the Senecas along the Allegheny River in 1791, where they eventually merged with the Seneca by the twentieth century (Goddard 1978:223). Today, the descendants of such assimilated Munsee are members of the Seneca Nation of Indians who are located on the Allegany Indian Reservation in southwestern New York and are also a federally recognized tribe. Munsee and Unami descendant groups are thus scattered widely throughout North America, and most are recognized as members of acknowledged Indian Tribes in the United States or as First Nations in Canada.[7]

The Delaware Tribe of today is composed of the descendants of the so-called main body of Delaware who elected not to relocate north or west but remained in Ohio following the American Revolution. There the Delaware Tribe became a powerful frontier force that participated in the intertribal resistance to the new American government during the late eighteenth century (Weslager 1972:317–322; Goddard 1978:223). Delaware military action against the United States ultimately ended when the Americans defeated the intertribal confederacy that included Delaware, Shawnee, and other woodland Indian forces at the Battle of Fallen Timbers in 1795. Following the defeat, the Delaware and others surrendered to the United States and signed the Treaty of Greenville after which they would never again take up arms against the Americans (Weslager 1972:322). The main body then joined other Delaware who had earlier settled, at the invitation of the Miami, along the White River in what is now Indiana (Weslager 1972:333; Goddard 1978:224).

It was along the White River that leadership became further centralized and a new, religiously conservative Delaware government emerged. A revitalization movement took place among the Delaware settled along the White River that institutionalized a renewed sense of Delaware identity in opposition to Christianity. The new leadership blamed the Christian influence for the Delaware's inability to defeat the Americans. Missionaries were banned from Delaware lands, and the clan chiefs selected to govern were those men who were also ceremonial leaders and visionaries within the revitalized Big House Ceremony. Clan membership still determined the appropriate leaders, but now participation in the Big House Ceremony further strengthened one's ability to gain support within the clan (A. Wallace 1956:16; J. Miller 1994:246–247). During the settlement along the White River the Delaware began to recognize the ascendancy of a principal chief among the clan chiefs as

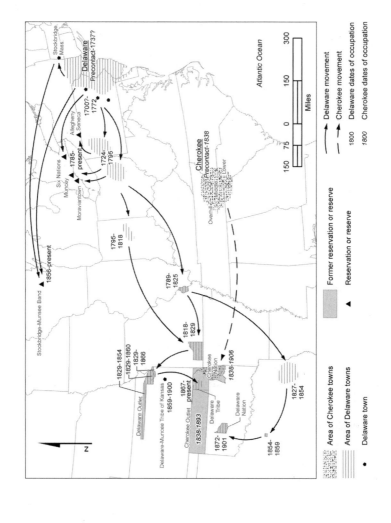

N

Stockbridge, Mass.

Delaware
Precontact–1737?

1700?–1772

Allegheny
Seneca

Six Nations

1785–present

Muncey

1724–1795

Moraviantown

Stockbridge-Munsee Band

1856–present

1795–1818

1789–1825

1818–1829

Cherokee
Precontact–1838

Overhill
Middle
Lower

1829–1854
1829–1860
1829–1866

Delaware Outlet

Delaware-Munsee Tribe of Kansas
1859–1900

Cherokee Outlet

Cherokee
Nation

Delaware
Tribe

1867–present

1838–1883

1872–1901

Delaware
Nation

1838–1906

1827–1854

1854–1859

Atlantic Ocean

Miles

150   75   0   150   300

Former reservation or reserve

Reservation or reserve

Area of Cherokee towns

Area of Delaware towns

Delaware town

Delaware movement

Cherokee movement

1800   Delaware dates of occupation

1800   Cherokee dates of occupation

2. DELAWARE AND CHEROKEE REMOVAL: The chronology and routes of the separate Delaware and Cherokee removals to Indian Territory. Official dates are given, but occupation may have preceded and followed these dates. Many additional Delaware settlements and movements existed, and the divisions between the seven identified Delaware groups cannot be traced to the eighteenth century, as smaller groups consistently moved back and forth between what appear as bounded groups into the twentieth century. Adapted from Ives Goddard, "Delaware," in Handbook of North American Indians, vol. 15: Northeast, ed. Bruce Trigger and William Sturtevant (Washington DC: Smithsonian Institution, 1978), p. 214, figure 1, and p. 222, figure 5, and from Raymond D. Fogelson, "Cherokee in the East," in Handbook of North American Indians, vol. 14: Southeast, ed. Raymond D. Fogelson and William Sturtevant (Washington DC: Smithsonian Institution, 2004), p. 338, figure 1. Map by Rebecca Dobbs.

the Delaware elevated Chief Anderson's position from a first among equals to the position of principal or head chief (Cranor 1991:5).

By 1821 the Delaware on the White River in Indiana were again forced westward by the U.S. government to what is today a southwestern portion of Missouri. Given land along the James Fork of the White River in the hilly regions of the Ozark Plateau, the Delaware found it difficult to farm and grew increasingly unhappy (Eaton n.d.; Powell and Lopinot 2003).[8] Beginning in 1829 and ending by 1831, the Delaware Tribe moved again, this time to the junction of the Kansas and Missouri rivers in present-day northeastern Kansas (Weslager 1972:357–372; Goddard 1978:224). The Delaware reestablished towns along the Kansas River and soon prospered from the emerging industry surrounding the migration of American settlers to the West for which the Delaware served as traders, ferry operators, military scouts, and guides (Farley 1955).

The anti-Christian sentiment of the early nineteenth century lapsed on the Kansas reservation, and Christian missionaries were allowed to return.[9] The missionaries soon set up schools and churches on the Delaware reservation, and many influential Delaware were either educated or converted by the Baptist, Methodist, or Moravian missions (Farley 1955; Weslager 1972:373–387). By the 1860s

Removal and the Cherokee-Delaware Agreement ◄ 47

some of the clan leaders constituting the Delaware Council were also Christian converts (Weslager 1972:384–388). While the influence of Christianity on the Delaware Tribal Council was apparent, leadership positions continued to be achieved through matrilineal clan ascendancy until the mid-1860s (Weslager 1972:388).[10] Thus, by the time of the Delaware's last removal to the Cherokee Nation, Delaware society was a religiously diverse population living in agrarian frontier villages with a clan-based political organization that maintained a strong alliance with the United States.[11]

The Cherokee, on the other hand, not only have a separate removal experience but are unlike the Delaware culturally and historically. The Cherokee are an Iroquoian-speaking people originally from the Southern Appalachian Mountain region of the southeastern United States that is today encompassed by the states of Alabama, Georgia, South Carolina, North Carolina, Virginia, Kentucky, and Tennessee (King 1979:ix). Five regional Cherokee settlements existed in the Appalachians among which were shared three Iroquoian dialects. The Elati dialect was spoken among the Lower towns that were situated along the Savannah River; Kituhwa or Keetoowah was the dialect of the Middle and Out towns located along the upper portions of the Little Tennessee River and east into what is today western North Carolina. Along the lower portion of the Little Tennessee River and the Hiwassee River were the Overhill and Valley towns that shared the Alati dialect (King 1979:ix). As Iroquoian speakers, the seventeenth-century Cherokee were distinctly different from their surrounding Muskogean-and-Siouan-speaking neighbors in the southeast. Some have suggested that the name *Cherokee* is derived from the languages of the Muskogean southeasterners, but the term could just as easily be the English version of the Lower Cherokee self-designation, *Tsaragi* (Fogelson 2004:349–350). Today, *Cherokee* is the tribal identifier most commonly used by Cherokee people.

While the Iroquoian dialects of the Cherokee villages contrasted sharply with the surrounding languages, the Cherokee shared similar cultural and religious traditions associated with southeastern peoples while retaining specifically Cherokee beliefs and rituals. The Creek, Chickasaw, Choctaw, Natchez, Seminole, and Yuchi are among the contemporary southeasterners with which the Cherokee share the most cultural affinity. A general cultural complex was and continues to be shared by such peoples that involves annually held religious ceremonies, periodic observances to achieve individual or group goals, and rites of passage that mark the life cycle (Hudson 1976:317). Most important in the southeastern religious calendar is the Green Corn Ceremony, which continues to be performed in late summer by a small number of Cherokee people in both Oklahoma and North Carolina (Hudson 1976:371–375). While the Green Corn Ceremony is the central expression of religious life among southeastern peoples, the observance is also practiced by other woodland peoples from the interior and northeast, such as the Shawnee and Oklahoma Seneca. The basic structure for the Green Corn Ceremony is a multiday first fruits ceremony, and each group adds individual qualities to the performance to create tribally specific observances (Witthoft 1949; Hudson 1976:366–367).[12]

Protohistoric Cherokee settlements consisted of sedentary horticultural villages and homesteads nestled along the thin but fertile floodplain environments of the southern Appalachians. Cherokee towns were permanent municipalities that were occupied year-round and possessed their own territory and membership. Political authority rested at the level of each Cherokee town with membership in each town defined through the mother, and seven matrilineal clans connected residents of the politically autonomous Cherokee towns. Though no town could exert control over the other, towns did share the same political structure (Gearing 1962:21; Sturm 2002:37–39). Such protohistoric Cherokee towns were first visited by Spanish explorers in the sixteenth century. Infrequent contact with non-

Indians ensued and was slowly replaced with increased interaction and trade following the arrival of the English, whose encroachment on Cherokee lands intensified in the early eighteenth century (Fogelson 2004:338–339). The Cherokee responded to British pressure by adopting a more centralized political system modeled after the structure of governance at the town level. Previously autonomous Cherokee towns began organizing into a larger confederacy, or tribal council, with each sending delegates to represent the interests of each Cherokee town and clan (Gearing 1962:85–105; Sturm 2002:40–42). Following their defeat by the British in the French and Indian War, the Cherokee Council established an alliance with the British that would last through the American Revolution. Through such a British alliance, the Cherokee agreed to substantial land cessions in exchange for the promise of protection and peace, yet encroachment from colonial settlers continued (Fogelson 2004:339–341).

The Cherokee were thus treated with hostility by the new American government after the close of the Revolution as a consequence of their British alliance. The Cherokee were eventually removed from their Appalachian homelands and relocated to what is today northeastern Oklahoma following a series of voluntary and involuntary removals that spanned from the end of the American Revolution to the early nineteenth century. American harassment continued after the Revolution, and several different Cherokee groups relocated to regions west of the Mississippi River beginning in the late eighteenth century. The first groups of Cherokee migrants were known as the Old Settlers who moved to the Ozark Plateau region of what is now northeastern Oklahoma, northwestern Arkansas, southwestern Missouri, and southeastern Kansas by the early nineteenth century. Their early migration was motivated by the desire to escape American encroachment and a generally shared disillusionment with the more accommodative posture of the Cherokee government in the early nineteenth century (King 2004:354–357).

Following the American Revolution, the Cherokee political leaders who remained in the Appalachian region had adopted a more diplomatic strategy with the U.S. government and sought accommodation in order to counter the threat of removal. By the early nineteenth century the Cherokee welcomed Christian missionaries and incorporated many of American cultural, political, and economic practices. The wealthier Cherokee families adopted plantation agriculture, owned slaves, and sent their children to be educated in mission schools. As the threat of removal loomed, the Cherokee restructured their tribal government into a constitutional republic complete with a written constitution, judiciary, principal chief, and a two-house legislature. A Cherokee leader named Sequoyah established the Cherokee syllabary, and in 1828 the Cherokee Nation began publishing the *Cherokee Phoenix*, a newspaper printed entirely in the Cherokee language (King 2004:357–358).

Not long after gold was discovered on Cherokee lands, the Indian Removal Act was passed in 1830. As land speculation and harassment mounted, the Cherokee Nation brought suit against the state of Georgia in the U.S. Supreme Court to force an end to the threat of removal. In two landmark cases (*Cherokee Nation v. Georgia*, 1831, and *Worchester v. Georgia*, 1832), the U.S. Supreme Court ruled that the Cherokee Nation was not a foreign nation but a domestic dependent nation that occupied its own territory in which the laws of Georgia had no force (Prucha 1975:58–62). The state of Georgia and President Andrew Jackson ignored the ruling, and President Jackson began the process of removing the Cherokee Nation by treaty under the Indian Removal Act.

The second Cherokee removal began when a small number of Cherokee leaders, known collectively as the Treaty Party, felt that further resistance to removal following the Supreme Court cases was futile. In 1835 prominent members of the Treaty Party signed the Treaty of New Echota and agreed to move west to land set aside for Cherokee settlement in Indian Territory. Once relocated in the West, the Treaty Party and their followers largely merged with the towns already established by the first Settlers in Indian Territory. The third removal occurred a few years later and is the event that has been memorialized as the Trail of Tears. Most of the Cherokee who resided in the Appalachians refused to move voluntarily following the 1835 Treaty of Echota and had to be removed by force beginning in 1838. Many did not survive the forced removal. Historians estimate that approximately four thousand Cherokee died along the arduous trip to Indian Territory (King 2004:358–359). Some Cherokee did manage to evade the removal from the Appalachians and remained in their homelands. The descendants of those who escaped removal survive today as the Eastern Band of Cherokee, a federally recognized tribe headquartered in the Appalachian Mountains of far western North Carolina.

Upon reaching Indian Territory, the three removed Cherokee groups eventually worked out their internal differences and reestablished their government, towns, newspapers, and industry. The Cherokee rebuilt their tribal government at the town of Tahlequah in Indian Territory with a three-branch structure similar to that of the pre-removal government, and the *Cherokee Phoenix* continued publication. Many of the Cherokee towns from the Appalachian Mountains were re-established with the same names and were located in the Ozark Plateau region along what is today the Oklahoma-Arkansas border (Warhaftig 1968). Remarkably, the Ozark topography was similar to the familiar mountains and valleys of the Appalachians. Cherokee families thus resettled in small frontier farms along the Ozark hollows while the wealthiest re-established plantation agriculture staffed with African slaves brought along during removal (King 2004:363). Thus, the Cherokee society that existed prior to the Civil War was highly stratified with an elite class in control of the Cherokee government who had largely embraced the culture, religion, and economic strategies of the Anglo-American South (Sturm 2002:68).

Following the Civil War, white encroachment and railroad speculation increased, and the Delaware were pressured to cede their lands
in Kansas and relocate to Indian Territory (Weslager 1972:399–429;
Goddard 1978:224). In 1866 the U.S. government signed its final
treaty with the Delaware Tribe, ending one of the longest ongoing
treaty relationships between the federal government and an Indian
tribe.[13] Under the Treaty with the Delaware, 1866, or 1866 Delaware
Treaty, the Delaware Council agreed to give up their reservation in
Kansas and move to a region of their choosing on lands ceded to the
federal government by the Choctaw, Chickasaw, Creek, or Seminole,
"or which may be ceded by the Cherokees in the Indian Country"
(Carrigan and Chambers 1994:A4). The lands to be chosen by the
Delaware were to be selected in as compact a form as possible and
include an area equal to 160 acres for each man, woman, and child
who chose to relocate. Given that a total of 985 Delaware eventually removed to the Cherokee Nation, the land selected for removal
would have had to be equivalent to 157,600 acres or roughly 250
square miles. A handful of Delaware elected to remain in Kansas,
and according to the treaty such individuals could do so only if they
dissolved their membership in the Delaware Tribe. The Delaware
who stayed in Kansas subsequently became American citizens,
and their land was held in severalty by the secretary of the interior
(Weslager 1972:423). Clinton A. Weslager (1972:516–517) lists the
nineteen Delaware families who chose to stay in Kansas, but the
Delaware Tribe did reinstate a few families who later decided to
join their relatives in Indian Territory following removal.[14] Today,
the Delaware-Munçee Tribe is headquartered in Ottawa, Kansas,
and is recognized by the state as the descendants of those Delaware
who elected not to remove to the Cherokee Nation.

It was thus made clear to the Delaware by the 1866 Delaware Treaty that removal was the only route available to ensure the continuation of the Delaware Tribe. Cognizant of the mounting pressure for removal and the desire to preserve the Delaware Tribe, Delaware clan leaders began exploring and scouting different locations for a new reservation in Indian Territory as stipulated by the 1866 treaty. It was determined that the Delaware desired the unoccupied lands in what is now northeastern Oklahoma immediately east of the ninety-sixth degree of longitude (Weslager 1972:423–424). Since the land belonged to the Cherokee Nation at the time, the Delaware decided to purchase a 10-by-30-mile tract of land from the Cherokee Nation that was situated along the upper Caney River valley. In an 1866 letter from principal Delaware chief John Conner (maternal grandson of Delaware chief William Anderson) to Cherokee chief William P. Ross, Conner explained that the Delaware had selected a tract east of the ninety-sixth parallel because of the perceived productivity of the land and in order to preserve the Delaware tribal organization (Conner 1866). Consistent with the 1866 treaty, the Delaware had selected a compact area of land that contained 300 square miles or 192,000 acres, only slightly larger than the required 250 square miles or 157,600 acres.

Chief Conner's request for the right to purchase a 10-by-30-mile tract of land from the Cherokee Nation was also consistent with the Treaty with the Cherokee, 1866, a treaty being signed at the same time between the Cherokee Nation and the federal government. In this treaty the Cherokee Nation agreed to sell their lands west of the ninety-sixth degree of longitude for the resettlement of friendly Indians. The relocated friendly Indians were to pay the Cherokee Nation for the land and afterward would hold the land as their own separate reservation. From the land cession, the federal government then had the space to remove what were primarily tribes from the newly organized states of Kansas and Nebraska to reservations in

Indian Territory.[15] Land east of the ninety-sixth degree of longitude, however, remained in the possession of the Cherokee Nation but was made available for the resettlement of what the federal government referred to as "civilized Indians."

The 1866 Cherokee Treaty spelled out two options that were available for civilized Indians wishing to settle within the boundaries of the Cherokee Nation. The first option, also known as the incorporation option, was for the Indian tribe being removed to abandon their tribal organization and become Cherokee citizens. Tribes who wished to adopt Cherokee citizenship had only to pay the Cherokee Nation a sum of money for the right to citizenship, and they would ever after be treated as native citizens. On the other hand the second option, also known as the preservation option, allowed for the Indians being removed to preserve their tribal organization in ways that were not inconsistent with the constitution and laws of the Cherokee Nation. Tribes who selected the preservation option in order to continue their tribal structure were required to pay two separate payments to the Cherokee Nation. The first payment was for citizenship that granted the relocated tribe the right to hold all rights as native Cherokee citizens. The second payment was for a parcel of land equal to 160 acres per man, woman, and child that would be set aside for the occupancy of the relocating tribe. It would appear then that the letter from Chief John Conner was informing the Cherokee Nation of the Delaware Tribe's intent to pursue the preservation option as stipulated by both the 1866 Delaware Treaty and the 1866 Cherokee Treaty with the United States. The Delaware thus agreed to removal so they would not become American citizens and chose the preservation option in the 1866 Cherokee Treaty in order to preserve their tribal government and not merge with the Cherokee Nation upon removal. The purchase of land equivalent to 160 acres per removed Delaware was pursued in order to sustain an independent Delaware Tribe that was now going to occupy lands in the Cherokee Nation.

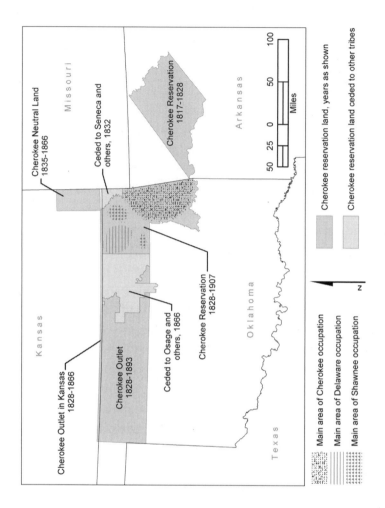

Map labels:
- Kansas
- Missouri
- Cherokee Neutral Land 1835–1866
- Ceded to Seneca and others, 1832
- Cherokee Reservation 1817–1828
- Arkansas
- Cherokee Outlet in Kansas 1828–1866
- Cherokee Outlet 1828–1893
- Ceded to Osage and others, 1866
- Cherokee Reservation 1828–1907
- Oklahoma
- Texas
- 50 25 0 50 100 Miles
- N
- Cherokee reservation land, years as shown
- Cherokee reservation land ceded to other tribes
- Main area of Cherokee occupation
- Main area of Delaware occupation
- Main area of Shawnee occupation

3. CHEROKEE NATION, 1870: The Cherokee Treaty lands in the West and
the dates that such lands were transferred to other Indian tribes or the U.S.
government, or lands on which the Delaware and Shawnee had settled by
1870. Adapted from Duane King, "Cherokee in the West: History since 1776,"
in Handbook of North American Indians, vol. 14: Southeast, ed. Raymond D.
Fogelson and William Sturtevant (Washington DC: Smithsonian Institution,
2004), p. 355, figure 1. Map by Rebecca Dobbs.

The civilized Indians allowed for in the 1866 Cherokee Treaty would indeed become the Delaware Tribe and Shawnee Tribe who then occupied diminished reservations in northeast Kansas. Following the stipulations of the 1866 Cherokee Treaty, the Cherokee Nation entered into separate agreements with the Delaware Tribe and the Shawnee Tribe to provide for each tribe's removal to lands east of the ninety-sixth degree of longitude. In the Articles of Agreement between the Shawnees and the Cherokee, dated June 7, 1869, the Shawnee elected to abandon their tribal organization and thus paid for the right to Cherokee citizenship but not for a separate land base as consistent with the incorporation option. In the Articles of Agreement between the Cherokee Nation and the Delawares, April 8, 1867, the Delaware Tribe selected the preservation option as it was clearly the Delaware's intent to sustain their tribal organization. The 1867 Cherokee-Delaware Agreement stipulated that the Delaware would pay for both Cherokee citizenship and their own land base as was provided for by the 1866 Cherokee Treaty for those civilized Indians wishing to preserve their tribal organization. As the 1867 Cherokee-Delaware Agreement stipulated, "The Cherokees . . . agree to sell to the Delawares for their occupancy, a quantity of land east of the line of the ninety sixth degree of west longitude" (Carrigan and Chambers 1994:A24). The Delaware did purchase a quantity of land east of this line of longitude in the aggregate total equal to 160 acres for each removed Delaware tribal member; a total of 157,600 acres for which they paid $1 per acre. The Delaware also paid $121,824 into the Cherokee National Fund for the right to Cherokee citizenship. The 1867 Cherokee-Delaware Agreement stipulated that the Delaware "shall become members of the Cherokee Nation with the same rights and immunities, and the same participation (and no other) in the national funds, as native Cherokees . . . and the children hereafter born of such Delawares so incorporated into the Cherokee Nation shall in all respects be regarded as native Cherokees" (Carrigan and

Chambers 1994:A24). Thus, while the Shawnee Tribe elected the incorporation option, the Delaware Tribe clearly chose the preservation option as is evident in the Delaware Tribe's dual payments for land and citizenship as stipulated in the 1866 Cherokee Treaty.

Under the 1866 Delaware Treaty, the Delaware were given the option to stay in Kansas and become U.S. citizens or to move to the Cherokee Nation and remain a member of the Delaware Tribe. The decision to move from Kansas plus the dual purchase of land and citizenship in the Cherokee Nation reflects the Delaware Tribe's desire to sustain their own tribal government in the Cherokee Nation as stipulated under the 1866 Delaware Treaty and the 1866 Cherokee Treaty. The 1867 Cherokee-Delaware Agreement is shown here to simply be a formalized agreement that allowed for Delaware removal to the Cherokee Nation under the preservation option that was provided for by the 1866 Cherokee Treaty.

THE DELAWARE TRIBE AND THE CHEROKEE NATION: A LEGAL REVIEW

Despite the fact that the Delaware Tribe did make dual payments for the rights to land and citizenship in the Cherokee Nation, the question of the Delaware's status as a result of the 1867 Cherokee-Delaware Agreement has been tried multiple times in the federal courts. In no less than three Supreme Court cases and several appeals in the federal circuit and district courts, the issue of Delaware rights and recognition has been put forward. A review of such cases demonstrates the lack of consistency in the judicial record and shows that no decision is immune to reinterpretation. In two early cases the Supreme Court upheld the Delaware's rights to Cherokee citizenship and land occupancy in the Cherokee Nation. In the third the Supreme Court found that the Delaware Tribe was a federally recognized tribe. Thus, the Supreme Court has affirmed that the Delaware Tribe is a federally recognized tribe whose membership held full citizenship and land rights in the Cherokee Nation. More recent appeals from the Cherokee Nation have led to a series of decisions by federal court judges that have both confirmed and denied Delaware federal recognition although such contradictory decisions have been based on the same conditions as stipulated in the 1867 Cherokee-Delaware Agreement and the Supreme Court rulings.

A brief review of the federal court cases between the Delaware and the Cherokee indicates that the stipulations of the 1867 Cherokee-Delaware Agreement were not only unreasonable but could never be adequately kept by two tribal governments wishing to preserve their own sovereignty. The Delaware were not willing to become members of the Cherokee Nation at the expense of loosing an affiliation with the Delaware Tribe, and legal action was later needed in order to protect Delaware interests as landowners in the Cherokee Nation. The Cherokee Nation, on the other hand, never intended to truly allow the Delaware to share full rights as citizens unless the Delaware gave up their tribal affiliation as Delaware despite the fact that the Delaware had selected the preservation option. The Delaware were thus placed in an unusual situation as a tribal government that wished to preserve its sovereignty while representing the interests of the Delaware people who owned land and citizenship in a foreign Indian Nation.

The Delaware's early experience in the Cherokee Nation was thus marked by two Supreme Court cases in which the Delaware sought to sustain their land and citizenship rights in the Cherokee Nation at a time when the Cherokee Nation hoped for precisely the opposite. Of immediate concern following removal was that the Delaware were not enjoying the rights to Cherokee citizenship for which they had paid under the 1867 Cherokee-Delaware Agreement. The most obvious breach of the agreement was that the Cherokee Nation consistently refused to share with the Delaware the income from the per capita payments that came with periodic land sales. The Delaware Business

Committee eventually took the Cherokee Nation to the U.S. Court of Claims, which ruled that the Cherokee were obligated to share the per capita payments. The Cherokee Nation appealed the decision, but the Court of Claims verdict was upheld by the Supreme Court in *Cherokee Nation v. Journeycake* (1894). The high court ruled that the Delaware were entitled to any and all rights enjoyed by Cherokee citizens by virtue of the 1867 Cherokee-Delaware Agreement (Haake 2002a:27; Carrigan and Chambers 1994:26–27).

With the threat of Oklahoma statehood on the horizon in the late nineteenth century, the Delaware were also concerned about their purchased land rights. The Delaware believed that they owned the 157,600 acres that they had purchased from the Cherokee Nation under the 1867 Cherokee-Delaware Agreement. The Cherokee, on the other hand, took the position that the payment only entitled the Delaware to the right of occupancy. The issue of Delaware land tenure was later tried in the U.S. Supreme Court, which ruled in favor of the Cherokee's position. In *Delaware Indians v. Cherokee* (1904), the high court ruled that the Cherokee Nation did not possess the right to sell the land in fee simple, and thus the Delaware had only purchased right of occupancy. Though the Cherokee's position and the Supreme Court's decision were inconsistent with the Delaware's 1866 treaty with the United States, the Supreme Court did grant that the Delaware who were born in Kansas prior to 1867 had retained the right to 160 acres in the event of allotment (Weslager 1972:453–454; Carrigan and Chambers 1994:26–27). When allotment did take place at the beginning of the twentieth century, those Delaware born in Kansas did receive 160-acre land allotments as opposed to the smaller allotments received by all other Cherokee citizens.

Judicial tension between the Delaware and the Cherokee quieted following Oklahoma statehood, and the legal battles fought by the Delaware Tribe turned to the issue of land claims with the United States. One important case was *Delaware Tribal Business Committee v. Weeks* (1977), which initially began when the Delaware-Muncee of Kansas appealed the federal government's decision to distribute the claim money from the sale of lands in Kansas to only the descendants of the Delaware Tribe and the Delaware Nation in Oklahoma. The Delaware-Muncee sued to be included in the award on the grounds that they were also the descendants of the Delaware living on the former Kansas reservation. The Supreme Court ruled that the Delaware Tribe and the Delaware Nation were federally recognized tribes and as a result were exclusively entitled to the award because of their special status as an Indian tribe. Although the Delaware-Muncee were later included in the award as lineal descendants, the Supreme Court had specifically identified the Delaware Tribe as a federally recognized tribe in the 1977 ruling (Carrigan and Chambers 1994:46–50).

Despite the Supreme Court ruling, however, the BIA administratively terminated the Delaware Tribe two years later in 1979. At the urging of the Cherokee Nation, the Delaware Tribe was left off of the first list of recognized tribal governments issued by the Department of Interior (Carrigan and Chambers 1994:A73–A80). After much work on the part of elected and non-elected Delaware leaders as well as tribal attorneys, the Delaware Tribe was finally restored federal recognition by the Department of the Interior (DOI) in 1996. However, the restored Delaware Tribe and the DOI soon faced opposition once again from the Cherokee Nation. That same year, Cherokee chief Joe Byrd filed a lawsuit against the Department of the Interior, which began as the *Cherokee Nation of Oklahoma vs. Babbitt* (1996). In the suit the Cherokee Nation alleged that the department violated the Administrative Procedures Act (APA) by extending recognition to the Delaware Tribe. The district court initially dismissed the suit on the grounds that the Delaware Tribe was an "indispensable party that could not be joined because of sovereign immunity" (*Cherokee Nation v. Norton*, 241F Supp. 2d 1368 [2004]:4). The Washington DC Circuit Court later reversed the decision in *Cherokee Nation of Oklahoma v.*

Babbitt (1997) but transferred the case to the Northern District Court in Tulsa, Oklahoma, because the DC court lacked jurisdiction over the Delaware. The decision before the Northern District in Tulsa was whether the Delaware gave up their tribal organization in the 1867 Cherokee-Delaware Agreement (*Cherokee Nation v. Norton,* 241F Supp. 2d 1368 [2004]:4).

In *Cherokee Nation of Oklahoma v. Norton* (2002) the Northern District Court of Oklahoma found that the Department of the Interior did not violate the APA and reasoned that the Delaware were a federally recognized tribe based on the Supreme Court's finding in *Delaware Tribal Business Committee v. Weeks* (1977) and in previous executive dealings with the Delaware Tribe. The Cherokee Nation appealed the Northern District Court's decision to the U.S. Court of Appeals for the Tenth Circuit in Denver. The Denver court reversed the Tulsa court's decision in *Cherokee Nation of Oklahoma v. Norton* (2004). The appeals court ruled that the Department of the Interior had violated the APA and had not followed the appropriate administrative procedures for establishing Delaware federal recognition. The court further reasoned that the Supreme Court's ruling in *Delaware Tribal Business Committee v. Weeks* (1977) only established the Delaware Tribe as a federally recognized tribe for the purpose of land claims. The Denver court also declared that all executive actions based on the 1996 federal recognition were to be considered void, and the Delaware Tribe was then judicially terminated with the 2004 ruling. The court did, however, concede that its opinion was based solely on the language in the 1867 Cherokee-Delaware Agreement and the BIA's accused procedural violations under the APA, and it would therefore "leave for another day what effect, if any, the post 1867 legislative and executive dealings with the Delawares had on their alleged status as a tribe" (*Cherokee Nation v. Norton,* 241F Supp. 2d 1368 [2004]:7n2). The Delaware Tribe thus lost federal recognition as an ultimate result of the Cherokee Nation's 1996 appeal.

The Delaware case is unique among tribal governments today. Rare is the situation when a tribe's federal recognition is appealed by another federally recognized tribe. However, what can be seen in a review of federal court cases is that the tensions between the Delaware Tribe and the Cherokee Nation are not new but a continuation of a history in which the ambiguities of the 1867 Cherokee-Delaware Agreement have been constantly rehashed. The legacy of such cases that began before Oklahoma statehood and continue today reveals, on a more public level, the very real tensions that have existed between the Delaware Tribe and the Cherokee Nation for over a century. Such strained politics are most clearly the result of an unworkable resolution that was reached almost 150 years ago that neither party has been able to uphold. The federal government promised the Delaware Tribe the opportunity to preserve their tribal organization if they removed to the Cherokee Nation and purchased land and citizenship in the Cherokee Nation. The Delaware thus expected to be made Cherokee citizens and landowners while also sustaining their own tribal sovereignty in a new Delaware homeland. On the other hand the Cherokee Nation was assured that the relocated "civilized Indians" such as the Delaware would not remain organized in a way that violated the laws of the Cherokee Nation. A separate tribe asserting independent sovereignty would certainly not be consistent with Cherokee law. From the outset then, the Delaware Tribe and the Cherokee Nation have held competing interests while claiming ownership of a shared territory and membership that would require outside resolution by the federal courts. As has been demonstrated, however, such court decisions have lacked consistency and have both confirmed and denied Delaware federal recognition. While the 2004 Denver court ruling has provided the most recent interpretation of the Delaware Tribe's status in the Cherokee Nation, it is not an interpretation that has allowed for the Delaware Tribe to preserve its tribal organization in the Cherokee Nation as originally intended in the 1867 Cherokee-Delaware Agreement.

CONCLUSION

The Delaware and the Cherokee are thus historically and culturally
unique and have only been in relative contact since 1867. Prior to
removal the Delaware and the Cherokee organized and relocated to
Indian Territory for the purpose of preserving their tribal identities.
Both tribes entered into the 1867 Cherokee-Delaware Agreement
by which the Delaware Tribe sought to preserve their tribal sovereignty while the Cherokee Nation made sure that their authority
would not be compromised with Delaware removal. Once in Indian
Territory, however, the Delaware Tribe and the Cherokee Nation
repeatedly clashed over their competing interests with recourse
being found only in the federal courts. Although the Delaware
were provided all rights as native Cherokee in the 1867 Cherokee-
Delaware Agreement, the agreement did not specifically terminate
the federal government's relationship with the Delaware Tribe. This
nineteenth-century inclusion of the Delaware as native Cherokee
has been of central importance in the interpretations made by the
federal courts. While it is clear that the clause gives the Delaware
full rights as Cherokee citizens, it remains unclear whether having
such rights contradicts the Delaware Tribe's right to full and separate
federal recognition.

This chapter presents the timeline of removal and subsequent
court cases to reveal the contrasts between Delaware and Cherokee
history and to lay out the long list of Delaware legal efforts to remain
independent from the Cherokee Nation while working to protect
their paid-for interests as occupants of lands in the Cherokee Nation.
Subsequent chapters describe Delaware persistence on deeper social,
cultural, and political levels that exist beyond such judicial settings.
The next chapter demonstrates that the Delaware did not merge with
the Cherokee upon removal to Indian Territory. On the contrary, the
Delaware established their own settlements far removed from the

Cherokee settlements on the Ozark Plateau. The Delaware brought and maintained their own tribal government, rural communities, culture, language, and religion and continued their daily lives in the prairie plains region of the Cherokee Nation. The social dynamics of the late nineteenth-century Delaware society remain today and constitute the foundations for the contemporary diversity in Delaware society. These dynamics are outlined in chapter 3.

3 Delaware Country

The Cherokees . . . agree to sell to the Delawares
for their occupancy, a quantity of land east of the
line of the ninety sixth degree of west longitude.

1867 CHEROKEE-DELAWARE AGREEMENT

The region of Oklahoma that lies to the north and northeast of Tulsa is not unlike any other prairie plains environment in
the midwestern United States. Thick but narrow groves of oak and
cottonwood trees line the rivers and streams that dissect the relatively flat fields and pastures. Here the urban centers of Bartlesville
and Nowata stand out to those passing through, but much of the
region is filled with small rural communities and family farms tucked
away from the busy traffic of the major cities. Despite its lack of
distinction, this territory drained by the Caney and Verdigris rivers in Oklahoma is also the homeland for the Delaware Tribe and
is bounded by Osage County to the west, the Grand River to the
east, Tulsa to the south, and the Kansas state line to the north.[1] The
Delaware's historic presence in this area of Oklahoma has given a
uniquely Delaware sense of place to a region that would otherwise
appear unremarkable to some observers. While the cultural geography of Delaware Country lacks distinction separate from Oklahoma's
midwestern landscape, this chapter seeks to bring out the veiled Delaware cultural geography and in so doing reveal the cultural diversity

and sociopolitical persistence of the Delaware Tribe that has yet to accept its incorporation into the Cherokee Nation.

As presented in chapter 2, the terms of Delaware removal to the Cherokee Nation included a provision that the relocated Delaware would become members of the Cherokee Nation. This Cherokee membership clause is one that has never proven acceptable to the Delaware people and has remained a controversial issue that has affected the Delaware Tribe since removal. This same membership provision also allows the Delaware people to enroll as members of the Cherokee Nation, an option that some Delaware chose out of economic necessity and others openly resist. The Cherokee membership provision remains particularly problematic for the Delaware Tribe and has given the Cherokee Nation considerable influence over Delaware acknowledgment decisions in the present.

The relationship that the Delaware Tribe holds with the Cherokee Nation has thus been the subject of an important political debate among the Delaware since removal and remains a divisive element in modern Delaware society. The stances taken toward membership in the Cherokee Nation were first established in 1867 and were then divided by family groups who each followed different religious faiths. While on the Delaware Reservation in Kansas, Delaware families associated themselves with either the traditional Big House faith or with different Christian missions. Such kin-based religious divisions were subsequently entrenched in the landscape when those Delaware of different sentiments and faiths settled in distinct regions of the Cherokee Nation. The Big House followers who were generally resistant to the membership provision settled along the upper Caney River while the Christians, who were more accepting of the terms for removal, established their own settlements to the south. The Methodists moved to a settlement along the Grand River, and the Baptists established settlements along the lower Caney and Verdigris rivers. A divided cultural geography would later emerge by the time of Oklahoma statehood as specific families were established in distinct settlements associated with certain religious institutions and political beliefs toward inclusion in the Cherokee Nation. Family and settlement names thus became an important component of the removed Delaware society. The family names associated with particular Delaware settlements throughout the prairie plains landscape of the Caney and Verdigris River valleys came to signify the differences that existed within the Delaware Tribe, and such markers continue to serve as understood signs of internal group diversity in the modern Delaware Tribe that is still divided over the issue of how to sustain Delaware sovereignty while resident in the Cherokee Nation.

The divided cultural geography of Delaware country thus provides a source for contemporary constructions and expressions of Delaware group and individual identity that help to shape political views in the present. A subtle geographic boundary crosscuts Delaware Country and separates two identifiable but overlapping Delaware worlds. The places of northern Washington County are most commonly associated with the families once active in the uniquely Delaware Big House Ceremony that resisted the Cherokee membership provision and sought to preserve Delaware religious and cultural practices into the mid-twentieth century. The sites of southern Washington County and the Verdigris River valley, on the other hand, were associated with the families whose representatives served on the recognized Delaware government during and following removal to the Cherokee Nation. Such governing families were generally less resistant to removal and the Cherokee membership provision and sustained a uniquely Delaware form of Protestant Christianity until soon after Oklahoma statehood. Two regionally tied and religiously and politically separate sets of kin-based groups established distinct settlements following removal, and the persistence of such internal differences continues to inform Delaware society today. Family surnames and the rural Delaware settlements thus act as emblems that convey a range of meanings in a community that is internally diverse, and the relevance of such important differences would be missed by those unfamiliar with Delaware society and the local cultural geography. Described here is the unique cultural landscape of Delaware Country, its removal origin and the continued relevance that such century-old geographical divisions have for understanding the diversity in modern Delaware society and the way such historical differences inform Delaware acknowledgment debates in the present.

BIG HOUSE AND CHRISTIAN WORLDS

The cultural geography of Delaware Country today provides a blueprint for understanding the way in which the Delaware remain an identifiable, yet divided, Indian community. One of the most recent ethnographic works with the Delaware was carried out by anthropologist Sue Roark-Calnek, whose purpose was to explain Delaware group identity in the twentieth century. Roark-Calnek (1977:810) concluded, "we can learn from the Delaware experience how a people may draw upon a history rich in cultural form, pageantry and high drama as well as in vicissitudes, making selective use of that history to find value and meaning in their contemporary lives and in the process achieving, in their individually various and relative ways, collective survival." One such history rich in cultural form to which Roark-Calnek refers is the legacy of the tensions that existed between the Christian and Big House socio-ceremonial worlds that were aggravated with removal to the Cherokee Nation. Her conclusion is instructive of how the divided Delaware past is remembered, enacted, and made tangible in the present. The reality is that the religious institutions and rural settlements that once centered both the Big House and Christian worlds of the early twentieth century have long been put away or abandoned. The Big House Ceremony was last performed in 1924, with abbreviated ceremonies held in 1944 and 1945. The Christian Delaware churches in which prominent Delaware men preached in Lenape were similarly restructured or abandoned in the early twentieth century. The Big House and Christian settlements have all but disappeared from the Oklahoma landscape due to the disproportional loss of allotment land that occurred in Delaware Country following Oklahoma statehood and the subsequent construction of two reservoir lakes along the Caney and Verdigris rivers (Obermeyer 2003:70–71, 144–146). Although such Delaware institutions and settlements are no longer in existence, they are not forgotten and remain viable in Delaware memories as resources in the present that are used to define group and individual identity in a modern Delaware society that has never witnessed these important Christian and Big House observances or lived in the rural Delaware settlements. In the process of resurrecting the memories of the Christian and Big House worlds, however, the Delaware are able to connect with and assert a collective tribal identity that is rooted in a sense of traditionalism defined by association with one or both of these now past Delaware worlds. Thus, the Big House and Christian faiths and associated rural settlements continue today in the thoughts, practices, and performances carried out by members of the contemporary Delaware community.

The geographical division between Big House and Christian settlements within Delaware society has been described elsewhere, and thus my observations presented here merely add a present perspective to the literature (Haake 2002a, 2002b; J. Miller 1989:1–2; Roark-Calnek 1977, 1980; Weslager 1972:440–445). Roark-Calnek (1977) found that the memory of the Delaware Big House Ceremony was most often put forward and celebrated at grounds and events located within or near the rural Delaware settlements of northern Washington County. Roark-Calnek (1980: 135) identified the rural Delaware settlements established with removal as "line communities," which were composed of groups of families with similar political and religious sentiments that established linear riverine residential units along the Caney, Verdigris, and Grand rivers. Roark-Calnek's (1977:857–867) work also includes detailed and invaluable maps that provide the locations of the Delaware line communities in Washington County where Delaware socio-ceremonial events were hosted from 1867–1974. My experience with the Delaware confirms the findings of Roark-Calnek and others as it was clear to me that a sense of Delaware identity grounded in the memory of the Big House Ceremony and its last adherents has certainly remained most visible at or near the locations of the once active rural settlements of northern Washington County where events and practices performed in the spirit of traditionalism associated with this uniquely Delaware ceremony continue today.

Because the continuation of a Delaware Big House identity persists most notably among the descendants of the former Big House community, existing Delaware ethnography is replete with information from such northern Washington County families (Grumet 2001; Harrington 1913; Howard 1980; Michelson 1912; J. Miller 1980b; Obermeyer 2007; Petrullo 1934; Prewitt 1981; Roark-Calnek 1977, 1980; Speck 1931, 1937). Roark-Calnek's (1977:857–867) detailed maps, for instance, include the locations of socio-ceremonial events only in southern and northern Washington County and do not indicate whether, if any, similar events were hosted by Delaware living on the Verdigris and Grand rivers. While the focus of previous ethnographic work on the northern Washington County preservationists was necessary considering the goals of previous research, such a limited focus does not provide an adequate presentation of the Delaware Tribe in its entirety. Missing from Delaware ethnography is a detailed report on the historical and cultural differences that exist within the Delaware Tribe as a whole. Scholarly work on the structure and practices of the historic Delaware Christian churches along the Verdigris, Grand, and lower Caney rivers is sporadic, but it is certain that Lenape was used throughout the service, and hymnals were also printed in Lenape (Weslager 1972:444; Young 1958). Taking a broader focus here gives a better understanding of the importance that the memory of the Christian and Big House worlds hold in structuring and enlivening the political and cultural identities that comprise Delaware society in the present.

As the Big House and Christian worlds are understood to exist in identifiable regions, the geography of Delaware Country is an important component to Delaware identity. The unique Delaware cultural landscape that was first established with removal still remains evident today and is conceptualized as overlapping and sometimes complimentary Big House and Christian regions. As the home for the former Big House community, the settlements and family names of northern Washington County are most often associated with the memory of the now defunct ceremony. In contrast, locations in southern Washington County and the Verdigris River valley where the Christian Delaware families lived who were less resistant to removal are conceptualized as Christian. As a reflection of such sense of place, this chapter later describes that the administrative facilities of the Delaware Tribe today are located in the cities of southern Washington County and near the Verdigris River valley (Bartlesville, Nowata, and Chelsea). On the other hand, most of the events at which the Delaware interact socially as an identifiable woodland Indian community, such as the annual Delaware Powwow and frequent stomp dances, take place in northern Washington County. An unconsciously held boundary thus continues to exist socially, politically, genealogically, and geographically that separates the world of the Delaware Big House families located in northern Washington County from the Christian world embodied in the Christian spaces and families of the Bartlesville, Nowata, and Chelsea vicinities.

Another important component associated with the Delaware sense of place is that family names as well as political views on the Delaware's relationship with the Cherokee Nation are often associated with particular places or settlement names. Though the existence of family-based political divisions within the Delaware Tribe and their connection to settlement places were reported to me on several occasions, the most concise explanation comes from an interview conducted by Katherine Redcorn with Fred Falleaf in 1969. Falleaf was a direct descendant of Captain Falleaf, a prominent member of the Big House congregation while still in Kansas and leader of the movement against removal. Captain Falleaf's great-grandson, Fred Falleaf, lived in northern Washington County, spoke fluent Delaware, and actively participated in the Delaware socio-ceremonial life that followed the end of the Big House observance. In the brief quote provided below, Fred Falleaf describes how locations within Delaware Country were connected with family name and political views toward the Cherokee Nation: "Nowata County over in there, over on Alluwe, now that's part of Delaware Country . . . Yeah, I even think that's where that Journeycake bunch was. Yeah, over in there . . . yeah, they bought in with the Cherokees. They give them the same rights that they've got. They've got the same rights of the Cherokees" (Falleaf 1969:16).

The pronoun usage in Falleaf's quote reveals well the relationship between family names and settlement-based political boundaries that exist within Delaware society. What the Delaware refer to as their family or "bunch" is a social unit that can also be conceptualized as a lineage. A Delaware family or lineage is an extended family in which the members can trace descent to a known apical ancestor. Although membership in a Delaware lineage was once traced by descent through the mother, contemporary lineage membership can be defined by descent through either the mother or the father or both. While Fred Falleaf regards the Journeycake "bunch" and the town of Alluwe as part of Delaware Country, the use of "they" indicates a degree of social distance between the Journeycake and Falleaf lineages that stems from the tensions surrounding removal.

The Journeycake family of today either descends from or is in some way related to Charles Journeycake, an ordained Baptist Minister who served on the Delaware Council and was a signer of the Cherokee-Delaware Agreement in 1867. Journeycake would thus have agreed to removal as well as membership in the Cherokee Nation as a consequence. Journeycake continued to serve on the Delaware Council after removal to the Cherokee Nation and would later administer the Delaware payment house from his home in Alluwe where the Delaware annuities were distributed from within the Cherokee Nation until Oklahoma statehood.

The Journeycake and Falleaf families were therefore of clearly separate religious faiths and political positions toward membership in the Cherokee Nation during and after the time of removal. The fact that "they" is used by Fred Falleaf to reference the "Journeycake bunch" in the mid-twentieth century reveals that such kin-based political and religious divisions remained in the modern Delaware society even after the Delaware settlements were abandoned and the final observances of the Big House and Delaware Christian churches had passed. The Journeycake lineage was and continues to be perceived as associated with the now under-the-water town of Alluwe and agreeing to the terms for Delaware removal including the membership provision. The Falleaf lineage, on the other hand, is associated locally with the settlements of northern Washington County, Big House ceremonialism, and staunch opposition to membership in the Cherokee Nation.

Indeed the landscapes of tribal regions throughout North America are often transformed into culturally meaningful places through such histories, discourses, and social practices (see Feld and Basso 1996). A cultural geography exists in the minds and practices of Indian people who often refer to different regions as a tribe's country. Keith Basso's (1996) foundational work on sense of place among the Western Apache illustrates the way in which sense of place operates for some

American Indians while providing a contrast for viewing Delaware usage and understandings of Delaware Country. Basso discusses how certain places in the Apache homeland are associated with historic and sometimes mythic events and are used to communicate a uniquely Apache sense of morality and social control. Unlike the Apache way, the Delaware use of place is more akin to other Eastern Woodland groups such as the Lumbee of North Carolina. Karen I. Blu's (1996) work on sense of place among the Lumbee describes how the landscape communicates something about one's sociopolitical identity in Lumbee society, and such is also the case for the Delaware. As Fred Falleaf's quote indicates, place names such as Alluwe often serve as a potential reference for a Delaware person's lineage and associated position toward membership in the Cherokee Nation. Thus, Falleaf sees himself and his lineage as geographically distinct from the Journeycake lineage, and the settlement names to which each lineage is attached serve as a marker for that lineage's diametrically opposed political and religious heritage, although both lineages are undeniably Delaware. Tribal countries in eastern Oklahoma are somewhat more unusual in that each tribal region is defined by the area initially settled by a specific group following a nineteenth-century removal. Douglas Allan Hurt (2000), for instance, outlined how the Muscogee (Creek) Nation reconstructed a new homeland after being relocated to Indian Territory and how such geographic meanings continue to impact contemporary life. Tribal territories among displaced peoples of eastern Oklahoma such as the Muscogee (Creek) Nation and the Delaware Tribe are thus different from that of those who have remained on diminished portions of their traditional homelands, such as the Lumbee and Apache, because the tribal regions of eastern Oklahoma are constructed in response to a historic forced relocation as well as those internal tribal differences and external pressures that all American Indians have faced.

Divided groups within American Indian tribes, such as the one articulated in Fred Falleaf's interview, are sometimes referred to as factions. It is clear from the ethnology of factionalism, however, that defining boundaries between such competing groups is often difficult and problematic (Dickson-Gilmore 1999; Fowler 2002; Lewis 1991; Shimony 1994). Political divides in American Indian societies have commonly been represented along a progressive versus conservative divide, but such theories cannot encompass the actual diversity and fluidity of sociopolitical life in any society. Loretta Fowler (2002:293–294 n. 2) provides what I found to be a concise yet comprehensive review of the ethnology on factionalism and concludes with the position taken here. As Fowler (2002:294 n. 2) states, "Characterization of progressive-conservative conflict as ideological — by outsiders, observers or native participants — is problematic and should be a matter of investigation." Thus, it may be that such dichotomous positions constitute the perceived ideo-logical reality held by a tribal community or even by outsiders, yet the membership and the meanings associated with each position is socially constructed and constantly shifting in response to imme-diate pressures and personal preferences. In other words, simply because Fred Falleaf considers himself as politically separate from the Journeycake lineage does not also mean that he cannot take on political action or cultural beliefs consistent with the platforms associated with the Journeycake family name and Alluwe sense of place, depending on the circumstances present.

The internal diversity of Delaware society today is thus best out-lined by viewing individual action in the context of a polarized, yet idealized, political spectrum characterized by opposed platforms on the issue of Cherokee membership that are each associated with settlement names and their associated family lineages, both of which are associated with either the Christian or Big House worlds. Every Delaware with whom I am familiar regards complete independence from the Cherokee Nation as the ideal. However, the strategies for achieving such a goal are of primary dispute and often fall along existing cultural and genealogical lines. On one end are the advocates that adamantly resist inclusion in the Cherokee Nation; a position linked with the memory of the Big House community centered along the upper Caney River, the practice of Delaware ceremonialism, and historic opposition to removal. At the other pole is a more diplomatic posture toward the Cherokee Nation and Cherokee membership that is assumed to have a basis in the Delaware Christian heritage and the families of the Verdigris and lower Caney River settlements who formally agreed to the terms for removal.

For the purpose of generalization, I have chosen to highlight the Delaware Big House and Christian communities here to reference the internal diversity in the modern Delaware Tribe. The Delaware Big House world is marked by the symbols, ideals, and spaces of the former regions of the Big House community where contemporary Delaware preservationists continue to meet at the annual Delaware Powwow, periodic stomp dances, church events, and social gatherings. Though once opposed by the Christian Delaware families, the Delaware Big House world as I am describing it no longer excludes Christianity as a potential faith. Delaware Big House identification in the present is principally an orientation that seeks to uphold the ideals of the former Big House leaders and to preserve through practice certain unique Delaware ways. One ideal fundamental to the Delaware Big House world was the resistance to membership in the Cherokee Nation. The memory of the Big House world thus provides the foundation today from which staunch resistance to, and calls to action against, the Cherokee Nation are mobilized. It is from here that advocates seek complete and unconditional acknowledgment separate from the Cherokee Nation. The Christian Delaware world, on the other hand, was once characterized by the participation in one of four Delaware Christian churches and is embodied in the regions once populated by the Christian community. Christian worldviews do not automatically include Delaware people who are followers of Christianity, as most Delaware today practice some form of Christianity. What characterizes the so-called Christian Delaware world in the present is a political orientation that seeks to sustain Delaware sovereignty through diplomatic negotiations with the Cherokee Nation, if necessary, and an appreciation for Delaware heritage without the need for direct participation or involvement in the maintenance of uniquely Delaware cultural practices.

Despite my generalization, the political complexity that exists within the Delaware Tribe is difficult to grasp unless the model used allows for fluid, overlapping, and constantly shifting boundaries. What separates Big House and Christian worlds in Delaware society can have little to do with one's actual religious faith, family lineage, or cultural participation but can be the result of one's choice in a given situation to associate with the ideals embodied within what are perceived as polarized cultural and political postures. Recognizing human agency is thus a vital component to understanding Delaware politics, and it would be ideal to be able to describe the individual nature of Delaware political action. However, this is not a biography of Delaware political leaders but a descriptive account of the Big House and Christian dichotomy as it developed in Delaware society in order to provide a generalized context from which to view the important but idealized social divisions that continue to inform contemporary affirmations of Delaware identity and political action in the present. Because the divided Delaware positions described by Roark-Calnek and articulated by Fred Falleaf remain operative in Delaware society today, it is necessary to understand the genesis of such internal group boundaries in order to truly appreciate the diversity that exists within the Delaware Tribe and the role of abandoned religious institutions and rural settlements in contemporary assertions of Delaware independence from the Cherokee Nation.

The divide between those who "bought in with the Cherokee" and those who did not is shown here to have originated with the Delaware's removal and to have continued in the local geography of the Cherokee Nation and later Oklahoma. The lineages of those who most vehemently protested against the Cherokee membership clause established settlements in the Cherokee Nation as far apart as possible from those settlements already established by the signers of the agreement who formally accepted the membership terms that made way for Delaware removal. The signers of the 1867 Cherokee-Delaware Agreement represented the Conner and Journeycake lineages while the official protests against the agreement came from the heads of the Sarcoxie and Falleaf lineages. Although other families either supported or opposed the agreement, the previously named lineages were the most visible in the written record on Delaware removal. Thus, the Conner, Journeycake, Sarcoxie, and Falleaf family names are referenced here to represent the Delaware kin-based political spectrum although my usage is not meant to exclude other families who were certainly involved or to elevate the importance of these four named families. My emphasis on the four families should also not be misread to suggest that they are somehow diametrically opposed today. However, kin-based divisions do remain, and the association of the separate settlements that each lineage established provides an ideal spatial and historical reference from which to view Delaware politics in the present, which is still divided according to such generations-old disputes. This section outlines the history behind Delaware settlement in Indian Territory and the sociopolitical diversity such settlements continue to represent.

The cultural diversity of the modern Delaware Tribe can be traced to the 1830s when the Delaware were re-establishing themselves on a reservation in what is today Kansas. A good number of Delaware families converted to different Protestant faiths during the mid-nineteenth century, and even followers of the Big House religion would send their children to the Christian mission schools (Weslager 1972:384–386, 511). Following the precedent set in the Northwest Territory (the present state of Ohio) baptized Delaware were allowed to participate on the Tribal Council and soon became a permanent fixture in Delaware politics without any recorded objections from non-Christian Delaware (Weslager 1972:288–289, 387).[2]

While the influence of Christianity did not threaten the integrity of the Delaware political system, the federal agent assigned to the Delaware Agency possessed the power to approve and appoint new chiefs on the Delaware Council. The last three Delaware agents — Thomas Sykes, Fielding Johnson, and John Pratt — tended to favor the men who were leaders in the local Christian mission communities (Weslager 1972:385–391). Such favoritism, at times, did not follow the Delaware custom of tri-clan representation, and the agents' biased approvals became more evident as the removal to Indian Territory drew near. The final straw that would eventually cleave Delaware society over removal occurred when the Delaware agent disregarded the importance of clan representation on the Delaware Tribal Council in 1861. This significant appointment took place when Turkey Clan chief Kockatowha died, and Delaware agent Thomas Sykes brought the council together to name a new chief. Sykes nominated Charles Journeycake, who, according to the agent, was unanimously confirmed by those assembled (Weslager 1972:391).

A closer review of Charles Journeycake's lineage and religious background, however, reveals that his appointment probably required a degree of coercion on the part of the federal agent. According to the Delaware custom of matrilineal clan membership, Journeycake should not have been eligible to replace the Turkey Clan chief. While Journeycake may have been an accomplished and influential lineage representative, he was actually a member of the Wolf Clan because his mother was a member of the Wolf Clan (Weslager 1972:391–392). Although not a member of the clan he was appointed to represent, Journeycake was a prominent member of the Baptist mission on the Kansas Reservation under the parsonage of John Pratt. Pratt and Journeycake maintained a strong friendship on the Kansas Reservation and continued to do so after Pratt was appointed as the Delaware agent in 1864 and even after the Delaware's 1867 removal. Journeycake's daughter Nannie would later marry Pratt's son Lucius, and the couple ran the Baptist mission near Edwardsville, Kansas, during Pratt's tenure as Delaware agent (Weslager 1972:385–391).[3]

By the end of the Civil War, the Christian appointees held the majority influence on the Delaware Tribal Council, and a critical decision was soon to be made that would dramatically affect the course of Delaware history.[4] The 1866 Delaware Treaty provided for the Delaware to sell the remaining portions of their reservation to the Missouri River Railroad Company, a corporation that included Delaware agent John Pratt as a stockholder (Weslager 1972:422). In exchange for the remaining lands in Kansas, the Delaware were promised by the U.S. government another tract of land equal to 160 acres per tribal member as explained in the previous chapter. The signers of the 1866 Delaware Treaty were Principal Chief John Conner of the Turtle Clan, Assistant Chief Anderson Sarcoxie of the Turtle Clan, and Assistant Chief Charles Journeycake of the Wolf Clan but appointed to represent the Turkey Clan. In the 1866 Treaty the Turkey Clan was not adequately represented, and the Wolf Clan was only marginally represented because Journeycake was a Wolf Clan member who was appointed to what the Delaware would have considered the Turkey Clan position (Carrigan and Chambers 1994:A4). There were apparently no protests filed over the 1866 Delaware Treaty despite the inadequate clan representation.

A few months later agent Pratt led a Delaware delegation to Washington DC to negotiate the agreement with the Cherokee Nation in order to secure the Delaware Tribe's removal to Indian Territory (Weslager 1972:424). Pratt's selected delegation again overlooked the Delaware clan organization and authorized the Christians on the Delaware Council as signatories (Weslager 1972:424). The Turtle Clan chief, Anderson Sarcoxie, was not included as part of the delegation. The 1867 Delaware delegation included James Ketchum, James Conner, John Conner, Charles Journeycake, Isaac Journeycake, Big John Sarcoxie, Black Beaver (who later moved back with the Western Delaware in Anadarko), Henry Tiblow, Charles Armstrong, and John Young. Ketchum was a member of the Methodist mission while the two Conner brothers, the two Journeycake brothers, and as well as Big John Sarcoxie were prominent members of the Baptist Mission. There were only four Delaware signatories to the agreement that spelled out the terms for Delaware removal, and all four were members of the Baptist mission and had a relationship with the Baptist missionary and Delaware agent John Pratt. The signers were Principal Chief John Conner and three members of the Delaware delegation: Charles Journeycake, Isaac Journeycake, and Big John Sarcoxie (Carrigan and Chambers 1994:A21–A25; Haake 2002b:422).[5] However, all three clans did have representatives that signed the 1867 Cherokee-Delaware Agreement because Big John Sarcoxie, a member of the Wolf Clan, replaced his father, Anderson Sarcoxie of the Turtle Clan, in the delegation. The clan representation was likely accidental, though, for the clan names were not mentioned in the 1867 Cherokee-Delaware Agreement as they had been in the 1866 Delaware Treaty (Carrigan and Chambers 1994:A21–A25).

Chief Anderson Sarcoxie, who signed the 1866 treaty but was overlooked by Agent Pratt for the negotiations with the Cherokee, was a son of the former Delaware chief, William Anderson, and was the senior member of the Delaware government at the time. Anderson Sarcoxie was not only the leader of an extended lineage but also an aged and respected leader in the Delaware Big House Ceremony.

Sarcoxie must have felt somewhat undermined by the signatories of the 1867 Cherokee-Delaware Agreement, for two of the four were Christian members of Sarcoxie's matrilineage. Principal Chief John Conner was Sarcoxie's sororal nephew, and Big John Sarcoxie was his son. Upon learning from his relatives that the agreement included a Cherokee membership clause that ran counter to the terms in the 1866 Delaware Treaty, Anderson Sarcoxie held a General Council of all Delaware to discuss the outcome of the Washington delegation. The result was a petition against the 1867 Cherokee-Delaware Agreement that was drafted by Sarcoxie and included over seven hundred signatories out of the approximately one-thousand-member Delaware Tribe (Sarcoxie 1867; Haake 2002b:423–424).

Chief Anderson Sarcoxie was not the only one leading the opposition as another Big House adherent, Captain Falleaf of the Wolf Clan, also filed a petition with the commissioner of Indian affairs (Falleaf 1868). Both the Sarcoxie and Falleaf petitions reflect the mood of the vast majority of the Delaware at the time as each petition was signed by more than two-thirds of the tribe. The petitions emphasized that the language of the 1867 Cherokee Delaware Agreement was not consistent with either the 1866 Delaware Treaty or the 1866 Cherokee Treaty. Specifically objectionable to both petitioners was the clause that the Delaware would be incorporated with and become members of the Cherokee Nation (Carrigan and Chambers 1994:A28–A34, Haake 2002b:423–425). Sarcoxie's petition stated rather directly, "The Delaware will never give up their nationality and become mixed in the Cherokee Nation" (Sarcoxie 1867). The Delaware petitioners stated that they had agreed to purchase land and citizenship in order to preserve their tribal organization and rejected the notion that they were to now consolidate with the Cherokee Nation. The petitions appealed against the 1867 Cherokee-Delaware Agreement and urged the federal government for any recourse to preserve Delaware sovereignty as was the original intent of the 1866 Delaware

Treaty (Sarcoxie 1867; Falleaf 1868). Agent John Pratt begrudgingly forwarded the Sarcoxie and Falleaf petitions on the behalf of the Delaware leaders but included his own commentary on the petitions adding, "it is not therefore surprising that before this great change should go into effect the most strenuous efforts should be made by the less enlightened portion of this tribe and other tribes, to postpone the time, interpose objections or create dissatisfaction" (Pratt 1867). Agent Pratt's vested interests in Delaware removal were clear. Pratt stood to gain financially from the sale of Delaware lands to the Missouri River Railroad Company, and he was not willing to see his investment fail simply because the vast majority of Delaware people were unwilling to accept membership in the Cherokee Nation.

While Captain Sarcoxie and Captain Falleaf led the opposition to removal and remained on the Kansas Reservation in protest until 1868, a minority of families that included the Conner and Journeycake lineages removed to Indian Territory and established settlements along the Verdigris River. Unable to convince the protestors to remove, agent Pratt resorted to withholding rations from the resistant Delaware. Eventually, the commissioner of Indian affairs arrived at the Delaware Reservation and negotiated with Sarcoxie and Falleaf to relocate to Indian Territory and convince their followers to do the same (Carrigan and Chambers 1994:17–18). By the summer of 1868 the resistant majority acquiesced and began the trip to Indian Territory but established their settlements along the Caney River. Most of the Christian families established or joined settlements along the Verdigris, Grand, and the lower Caney rivers while the Big House followers established their own communities along the upper Caney River and its tributaries (Haake 2002a, 2002b; Weslager 1972:441–445). A number of deaths occurred while the Delaware were en route to Indian Territory, and others happened once they arrived (Weslager 1972:427). Those who made it to the Cherokee Nation were not welcomed by the resident Cherokees, who apparently made life miserable when the Delaware attempted to rebuild (Haake 2002a:23–24). In general, the Christian Delaware tended to be more supportive of removal and Cherokee membership while the Big House adherents were generally opposed, but such attitudes toward the Cherokee Nation did not seem to have an effect on the ways in which different Delaware families were treated after arriving in the Cherokee Nation. Thus, two geographically separate groups defined by political and religious beliefs established settlements in Indian Territory following removal.

The Christian Delaware world established in Indian Territory was centered at four churches located within predominately Christian settlements with smaller and more religiously diverse communities located in the vicinity. The founders of the Christian churches were either signatories or delegates at the negotiations surrounding removal. At the time of Oklahoma statehood there were three Delaware Baptist churches and one Delaware Methodist church. The Baptist churches were established in the settlements of Alluwe and Silverlake and along California Creek while the Methodist church was at Ketchum. Reverend James Ketchum, who was a Delaware leader present at the removal negotiations and an ordained minister since 1860, built his home along the Grand River near the present town of Ketchum, where the Delaware Methodist church was later established (Young 1958:176–177). Other Delaware communities in which both Christian and non-Christian Delaware families settled were Hogshooter, Fish Creek, Coody's Bluff, and Mormon Creek.

The settlements at Alluwe and Silverlake provided the regional centers for the Delaware Christian world. Alluwe was located along Lightning Creek, a tributary of the Verdigris River. This small rural settlement was established by Charles Journeycake, who was also a founding member of the First Baptist Church at Alluwe, where he was later ordained as a minister. John Connor settled in the town of Alluwe, where he continued to hold the Delaware Council and where Journeycake continued to serve as assistant chief. Further west along the lower Caney River, Big John Sarcoxie and Charles Journeycake established a Baptist church near the Sarcoxie home at the settlement that later became known as Silverlake (Cranor 1991:79; Weslager 1972:427, 445–446). Journeycake initially served as the pastor for the Silverlake church until Big John Sarcoxie was ordained as a minister. Big John Sarcoxie's father and leader of the earlier protest against removal, Captain Sarcoxie, would ultimately live with his son and family at Silverlake, where he passed away a few years after moving to Indian Territory in 1876 (Cranor 1991:96). The relocated Delaware Council, now restructured to consist of a principal chief and two assistant chiefs, continued at Alluwe under the leadership of John Conner and later Charles Journeycake. Such Christian leaders who had originally signed the 1867 Cherokee Delaware Agreement and were now the representatives on the newly re-organized Delaware Council apparently revoked their original support for removal and Cherokee membership after arriving in the Cherokee Nation. The Delaware Council repeatedly petitioned the Department of the Interior and Congress for a Delaware district separate from the Cherokee Nation throughout the late nineteenth century although no Delaware reservation was ever established despite the council's best efforts (Haake 2002b:425–427).

The original protestors to the 1867 Cherokee-Delaware Agreement tended to be followers of the Big House faith and relocated along the upper Caney River. Some of those opposed to removal were even more dissatisfied with the treatment they received upon arriving in the Cherokee Nation, and approximately three to five hundred Delaware moved to Peoria lands along the Neosho River during 1869–1871 (Haake 2002a:24–25). After they returned to the Cherokee Nation in 1871 the resistant Big House followers also moved their Xingwikaon from Bismark Grove (six miles east of Lawrence, Kansas) to a site along the Little Caney River in Indian Territory (a few miles west of

Copan, Oklahoma) (Weslager 1972:419). There were two subsequent Big House structures built in roughly the same location along the western bank of the Little Caney River, and the Big House Ceremony was carried out in this location until the ceremony was discontinued in 1924 (J. Miller 1980b:109; Prewitt 1981:2). It appears that the Big House adherents continued to recognize their own leadership separate from the Delaware Council in Alluwe. Those opposed to removal continued to base their political structure on clan membership and ceremonial competence and thus rejected the authority of the predominately Christian Delaware leadership who were now assuming tribal office through popular election (J. Miller 1994; Obermeyer 2007; Weslager 1972:441–443). The first Big House building was associated with Colonel Jackson, a Wolf Clan leader who was not included in the delegation to Washington. The Big House adherents continued to recognize their own leadership under Colonel Jackson as separate from the Christian-dominated Delaware Council in Alluwe. Since Jackson was a member of the Wolf Clan, he would have replaced Big John Sarcoxie as conductor of the Wolf Clan ceremonies after Sarcoxie became an ordained minister (Grumet 2001:73). Conceivably, Colonel Jackson would have also been the favorite to serve as the representative on the Delaware Council during the negotiations with the Cherokee if the Delaware agent had not intervened and appointed Charles Journeycake. The second Big House, which was built after the structure associated with Colonel Jackson was abandoned, was associated with Charlie Elkhair, the last headman to hold the Delaware Big House Ceremony in 1924. He is remembered as the most respected leader and spokesman for the Big House community of the early twentieth century, although he was never elected to a tribal office (Prewitt 2001:8).

The Big House adherents settled in four distinct settlements along the upper Caney River basin, with some taking up residence with family members or spouses in the more diverse Delaware settlements mentioned above. The four distinctive Big House settlements were at

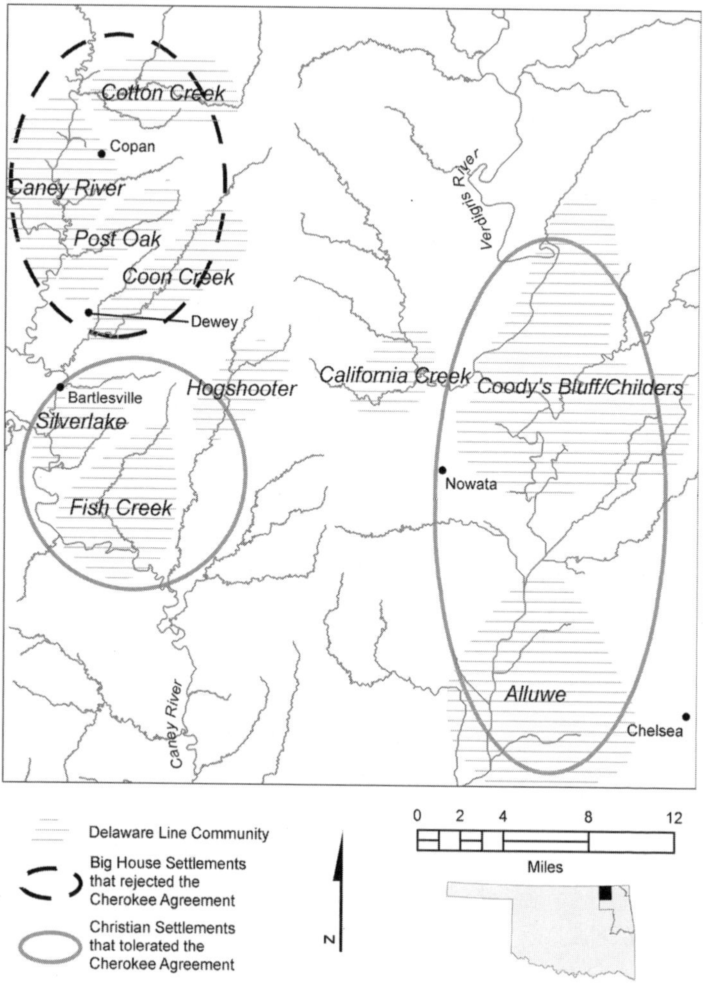
Cotton Creek
Copan
Caney River
Post Oak
Coon Creek
Dewey
Verdigris River
Bartlesville
Silverlake
Hogshooter
California Creek
Coody's Bluff/Childers
Fish Creek
Nowata
Alluwe
Chelsea
Caney River
Delaware Line Community
Big House Settlements that rejected the Cherokee Agreement
Christian Settlements that tolerated the Cherokee Agreement
N
0 2 4 8 12
Miles

4. DELAWARE LINE COMMUNITIES: The locations of the different politically aligned Delaware line communities as they were established in the northwestern portions of the Cherokee Nation following removal. Map by Rebecca Dobbs.

Coon Creek, Post Oak Creek, and Cotton Creek and along the banks of the upper Caney River. Captain Falleaf took up residence along the upper Caney, and Colonel Jackson lived along Cotton Creek. The other Big House lineage representatives that called such rural agrarian spaces home were active in the Big House Ceremony and the religious observances associated with the Big House faith. The Big House structure along the upper Caney provided the nucleus for the Big House community where congregants would gather annually. Throughout the year the Big House families would also meet periodically at ceremonial and social observances that were held at the homesteads of local leaders living in one of the four Delaware communities. Although other families living in the settlements along the lower Caney River hosted ceremonial and social events, such instances were either held less frequently or were relatively fewer in number (Prewitt 1981; Roark-Calnek 1977). The core of the Big House world thus rested along the banks of the upper Caney River and the settlements located along its tributaries far removed from the Christian-dominated Delaware world centered in Alluwe.

Although religious belief and political orientation helped to define the diversity that existed among the Delaware, the boundary between Christians and Big House families was never absolute. It is more instructive to conceive of Delaware regional diversity in the past and present in terms of two separate possibilities for cultural, political, and religious expression within which individuals and families could (and did) operate and move between. The Christian and the Big House leaders were the ones considered responsible for each religious and political orientation, with Delaware socio-ceremonial observances continued in northern Washington County and Christianity practiced in the southern regions of Delaware Country. This model constituted an ideal structure for Delaware identity within which individuals traveled freely as events and circumstances dictated. In practice, then, the ideal binary oppositions were not mutually exclusive or confining but were recognized as separable cultural and political realms embodied in specific locations, family lineages, religious orientations, and leadership. Thus, a split among Delaware religious leaders over removal created a uniquely Delaware sense of place in Indian Territory that conflated politics, religion, and lineage membership with particular agrarian settlements and regional spaces. The continued existence of the rural Delaware settlements and the important religious institutions around which each were centered would come under tremendous pressure with the dawn of the twentieth century until ultimately dissolved as a consequence of Oklahoma statehood and non-Indian encroachment.

The allotment of Indian Territory that preceded statehood significantly reshaped the landscape of Delaware Country. In the process of divvying up land allotments, small city townships or municipally held land was established and identified, yet the very obvious existence of the Delaware line communities was overlooked and was not codified on the allotment maps (Bays 1998:124–179). The lands allotted for the new towns that came with statehood were identified with a town name while the line communities were divided up into individually owned land allotments. Even though the Delaware line communities were not officially recognized on the allotment maps, such important Delaware residential units persisted in the way that allotments were selected. An investigation of the allotment distribution in Delaware Country revealed that the Delaware settlements were continued through the allotment process as was the Delaware settlement pattern of kin-based agrarian settlements strung along the major rivers and tributaries. If there is one redeeming quality to the allotment of Delaware Country, it is that the distribution of Delaware allotments outside the townships seemed to follow as closely as possible the pre-existing Delaware line communities. Thus allotment did not initially disrupt the integrity of Delaware society. Map 5 indicates the persistence of the Delaware rural settlements during

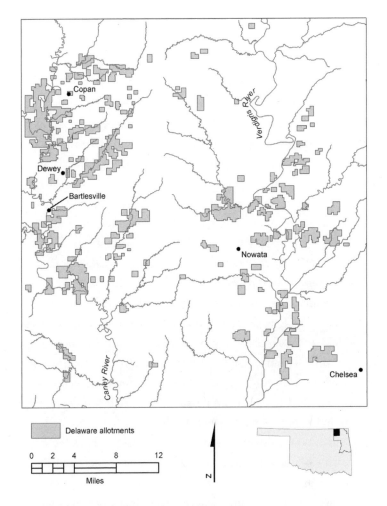

Copan

Verdigris River

Dewey

Bartlesville

Nowata

Caney River

Chelsea

Delaware allotments

0   2   4   8   12

Miles

N

5. DELAWARE ALLOTMENTS: The distribution of Delaware allotments in the northwestern portion of the Cherokee Nation at the time of Oklahoma statehood. Map by Rebecca Dobbs.

the early years of Oklahoma statehood as manifest in the locations of the tightly clustered allotments.

The influx of non-Indian settlement that came with Oklahoma statehood in 1907 disproportionately affected the existing Delaware Christian line communities. Since the immigrating non-Indian population followed the same religion as the Christian Delaware, the newcomers gravitated to such communities. Also, most of the Christian communities were in closer proximity to the newly established municipalities surrounding the major railroad stops at Bartlesville, Dewey, and Nowata. Intermarriage between whites and Christian Delaware thus increased exponentially with Oklahoma statehood. Increased non-Indian participation at the Delaware Christian churches also meant that fewer Lenape speakers filled the pews, and the Delaware pastors were obliged to incorporate English into their sermons to ensure wider comprehension by the early twentieth century. The transition from Lenape to English services in the Delaware churches was difficult to pinpoint for each church, but in general this process began with Oklahoma statehood in 1907 and was completed at some point during the 1920s.[6] Most Christian communities either provided the foundation for or were eventually consumed by the developing towns in Delaware Country after statehood.

When oil was discovered in the Alluwe area in 1905, the Journeycake Church found itself in the center of the increased Euro-American settlement that lasted until the 1920s. The large number of immigrant English-only speakers meant that while the town of Alluwe remained, the church service could no longer be performed in Lenape. The city of Alluwe was later condemned by the construction of Oolagah Lake, and the residents re-established the town of New Alluwe on its banks. Delaware sermons at the Silverlake Baptist Church also ceased around the turn of the century when a new church was built on the south side of the growing city of Bartlesville. The Silverlake Cemetery is located in the middle of the Hillcrest Golf

Course and marks the former location of the Silverlake Church. In 1910 a third Delaware Baptist church, originally founded in the California Creek community, was moved to the town of Delaware. The church building was moved again in 1920 but remained in the town of Delaware. The California Creek community remained in existence until the mid-twentieth century when the last residents moved or passed away. Today the California Creek community, located northwest of Nowata, is marked by a rural but well-cared-for cemetery that is listed on the National Register of Historic Places.

While the Christian communities accommodated the non-Indian world, the Big House communities remained somewhat more elusive. The religious life of the Big House community was distant from the immigrant non-Indian population. The Delaware Big House adherents frowned on white participation in their ceremonial life, and there were incidents when Delaware participants would refuse to perform observances if intermarried non-Indians were present. Although Copan and Dewey were also expanding towns established near Big House settlements, the non-Indian settlers primarily interacted with the Big House community socially and economically but not on religious terms. Thus, the urban areas of Dewey and Copan, even though they were located near the Big House communities, were not a part of the Delaware ceremonial world, which took place in the rural Delaware settlements and allotments and was attended by Delaware followers and those from neighboring tribes. Despite the reluctance of the Big House community, the impact of Oklahoma statehood was profound and resulted in land loss as well as the abandonment of important religious and cultural practices following statehood.

Terry Prewitt's (1981:71) demographic analysis of the Delaware Big House community relies heavily on the oral histories of the last generation of Big House followers living in the 1970s. Prewitt concluded that increased extra-tribal marriages coupled with the impact of English-only boarding and public schools during the early twentieth century created a Delaware population that matured to adulthood without adequate vision experiences to continue the performance of Big House rites. Because this was a twelve-day ceremony, the children of the early twentieth century were often unable to participate in the service while enrolled in school, and the boarding school instruction forbade the expression of Delaware culture and denigrated non-Christian beliefs. Contemporary oral histories collected almost twenty-five years later during my fieldwork reinforce Prewitt's conclusions while expanding his conclusion about the loss of the Big House to the abandonment of the Lenape language and the Delaware Christian churches.

Delaware elders today recall the social context of the early-twentieth century as one in which a Christian-believing and English-speaking dominant society pressured parents and grandparents to give up their non-Christian religious practices and Lenape language usage. They remember the difficulties that their families experienced when trying to perform the ceremonies that they held so dear or to speak in their native tongue. There was pressure against the Big House Ceremony from the general public, who considered any non-Christian practice to be a controversial religious expression. In some cases outsiders were openly hostile to the Big House Ceremony, and a few elders today remember stories about the U.S. marshal who was invited to the ceremony in the later years to protect the congregation from protestors. Delaware elders also remember stories about certain Delaware Christian preachers who would sometimes disrupt the Big House Ceremony with fire-and-brimstone sermons, telling those assembled that the ceremony was an abomination (Prewitt 1981:66). The use of Lenape was also under attack and was denigrated by the non-Indian public. It was nearly impossible then to pass on the knowledge needed to perform the Big House ceremony or even conduct a Delaware Christian service when the Delaware language could only be freely spoken in the home and only few elderly Big

House leaders had the knowledge and experience to continue such an important religious observance that was demonized by the larger society.

Today's elders strongly believe that their parents and grandparents put away the Big House Ceremony because they were concerned about the integrity of the performance. A few remember that their ancestors wanted the observance to continue only if it was done for the right reasons. The absence of a generation raised with the service thus convinced the last Big House followers to abandon the ceremony rather than to pass on the observance to a generation without an adequate experience to develop a true commitment to its performance. In order to protect the sanctity of the ceremony, tribal elders today warn of the danger that would result if the Big House was ever revived and used for anything other than the original purpose of the service. As one descendant of a Big House family explained to me, "You know, the Big House was lost, it shouldn't have ever been started back up again because many of those old Delawares, you know, they, just like, the Big House when it falls to the ground that's it. You can't revive anything like that . . . it would be foolish." Reviving the Big House is considered a foolish idea because many recall the reverence with which the old Delaware, their parents and grandparents, held the ceremony. Also remembered is the attitude that the Big House adherents had toward reviving the ceremony. Once the ceremony was reluctantly abandoned, the Big House faithful cautioned their children not to take up the observance for fear that it would be carelessly performed and would ultimately upset the supernatural. The message against revival as a measure of protection and respect is one consistent among Delaware elders. The descendants of the Big House families are clearly very proud of the ceremony and the traditional religious beliefs held by their ancestors. Care is taken not to spoil the legacy of this most important Delaware observance and to protect its memory by adamantly opposing revitalization. Thus, the Big

House Ceremony remains an important element of the Delaware's past where the observance is destined to remain in order to protect the wishes of its last followers, who sought not to upset the Creator and who put away the ceremony.

Today the Big House site remains vacant and stands unmarked on the western bank of Copan Lake, an Army Corps of Engineers reservoir completed in the 1980s that condemned many of the remaining allotments held by members of the Caney River community. The Big House Ceremony is not performed by the Delaware, and most of the relics of the last Big House building and observance are curated in museums.[7] Although I have been fortunate to view the items once used in the Big House and the Delaware are aware of the locations of such items, there has been no effort to repatriate the Big House ceremonial objects under NAGPRA, nor would attempting to do so be considered appropriate unless the objects could be properly cared for by the Delaware Tribe. Although it would be inappropriate to revitalize the Big House Ceremony, most know of its performance and unidentified location along Copan Lake. It is this important memory of the Big House Ceremony that continues to provide a source of inspiration and pride for many in the contemporary society. It is through such memories that contemporary Delaware elders recall their parents and grandparents fondly as individuals deeply committed to Delaware heritage while struggling with the harsh realities of the forced assimilation efforts of the early twentieth century.

Delaware oral histories also indicate that the abandonment of the Big House Ceremony occurred at about the same time that the transmission of Lenape declined. The loss of Lenape as a first language, now lamented by tribal members, was a choice that an entire generation of Delaware families were collectively forced to make in order to avoid conflicts with, and allow their children to be better prepared for, the Anglo-American-dominated world of Delaware Country in the twentieth century. Below is one woman's story outlining the generational changes that took place, and it is suggestive of a crucial period in the mid-twentieth century during which the Delaware acquiesced to avoid the adversarial posture taken against the outward use of Lenape:

CONSULTANT: My grandmother, she just refused to be like everybody else. She was traditional Delaware, and so it was very hard for her. She spoke Delaware and she knew English, but she wouldn't speak it. Even when she went to town, went shopping, she took somebody with her that was an interpreter. . . . She was just stubborn about it. . . . But when [my mother] went to school she had to learn to say everything in English. Kids, Indian kids were punished, and if the teachers heard them talking to each other they were told that they weren't to do that.

OBERMEYER: Did you learn to speak?

CONSULTANT: No, when I was little mom taught us how to count to ten and names of animals and names of different things, you know, like eat and thank you, and those are the only words I really learned, those that I learned when I was little. But I could understand Grandmother when I was little, but I was never allowed to try to learn, to try to speak.

This story of three generations of Delaware women and their different language proficiencies reflects the general way in which many families implemented a method for dealing with an Oklahoma society that discouraged, at times with force, the use of their native language. As a young girl, the narrator recalls that she "was never allowed to try to learn, to try to speak." She could understand the language, and it was obviously spoken in her home, but there was an acknowledged family prohibition against her learning the language. This woman's family story is not uncommon and in fact exemplifies the trajectory of language loss in many Delaware families. Delaware language usage was actively contested by the dominant society at the time, making fluency in Lenape an act of defiance as reflected by the narrator's memory of her stubborn grandmother. A majority of Delaware families were thus forced to simply drop the transmission of the language to the next generation rather than have their language spoiled by the dominant attitude at the time that degraded anything Indian.

Though the Big House and the Lenape language were abandoned, contemporary elders tell how the old Delaware strengthened their resolve in other areas that were much more difficult for outsiders to challenge. In their homes and among close family circles, Delaware parents and grandparents impressed upon their children and grandchildren a reverence and pride in Delaware ways, a pride that required some accommodation to a non-Indian dominated society. As one Delaware woman explained, "We were never taught the Delaware language and should've been. But, Grandma and Grandpa said: 'We live in a white man world; we have white man ways. So we don't need to learn.' But one thing they did teach us; and that was hold your head up high and be proud of who you are and what you are. You're a Delaware Indian girl and be proud of it. . . . And that, I think, the way I was raised, more or less, it made me strong." This woman's memory is a testament to the fact that while many Delaware parents refused to teach their children the Delaware language and traditional faith as a way to protect such important practices, Delaware families did not also abandon a commitment to a Delaware identity that was embodied in such performances. Her memory reveals the complexity of culture change as a phenomenon that can exist along with the maintenance of a sense of tradition and identity. A profound respect for Delaware heritage also meant letting go of important practices that were becoming controversial in order to protect the sanctity of such events. While important practices were certainly lost, such realities did not preclude the loss of a distinct and proud Delaware Indian identity. The story of their grandparents' decisions is far from evidence of assimilation, although it is clear that culture change did take place. Even though some Delaware elders feel slighted for not being taught the Delaware language and the Big House faith, they remain glad that they were taught to be proud of their Delaware heritage. In fact, the woman above cites the pride in her Delaware identity that her grandparents instilled in her as the reason why she is able to take on the more strenuous obstacles that confront her everyday life. Having the strength to be Delaware in a world that had no need for Delaware people was the lesson learned from her grandparents, and the woman's recollection quoted above is one with which many Delaware can relate.

The strategy implemented in order to sustain a sense of Delaware identity alongside the practice of "white man's ways" that continues to be practiced today is an ability to compartmentalize and live in two worlds. As one Delaware elder explained, "I guess I still believe in the old ways, you know, and I think that, you know, if you're going to live as an Indian, you know, you're always have that within you, something that you can't take away and, you know, for a lot of us, you know, we live two lives. We live the white man's way, you know, which a lot of white people can't live, and an Indian life." Separating the Indian life from the white man's way while remaining participants in both allows the Delaware to sustain their own group identity and social practices while living as everyday members of the non-Indian dominated world. In the process, accommodations are made, but always with the goal of sustaining a sense of traditionalism founded in the memories of the now abandoned Delaware practices or contemporary participation in Delaware and other Indian events. While the Big House Ceremony and Lenape language were abandoned, a strong sense of pride remains protected in the Indian lives and heritages of Delaware people whose participation and identities are inspired by the collective memories of such moribund but important practices.

Being a Delaware Indian today is thus a unique cultural identity characterized by the fond memories of the Big House Ceremony and distinctly Delaware-speaking Christian churches, practices in which no one alive has ever participated and should never attempt to revive. The Delaware hold that the Big House Ceremony and the Delaware Christian churches should appropriately remain with those who held such practices sacred enough to be able to let them go. Protecting the integrity of important Delaware traditions is a practice shared by the contemporary community and acts to mobilize and inspire collective action in the present. The commitment to Delaware Indian identity in the present is thus firmly grounded in these teachings of previous generations, and their legacy provides contemporary Delaware with a collective strength to not let the memories of the past be tainted by today's challenges. The pursuit for federal recognition, although far removed in time from the last held Big House Ceremony or Delaware Christian observance, is not so distant from the teachings of such followers in the minds of Delaware people. Federal recognition for some is as much about sustaining tribal sovereignty as it is to correct a federal system that mislabels their very real and proud sense of Delaware heritage. Although the Delaware have no desire to use federal recognition to help revive abandoned religious observances, federal acknowledgment will provide the formalized recognition needed to protect the memory of the ceremonies and the sense of Delaware identity embodied in them from being glossed as a Cherokee practice and lost from the minds of subsequent generations. For the Delaware, the struggle for federal recognition is an effort in which the Delaware hold their collective heads up high and are proud of who they are, just as their parents and grandparents instructed. They are Delaware Indians and proud of it.

Both Big House and Christian Delaware line communities alike were thus abandoned by the mid-twentieth century with only the remnants of a few remaining today in rural locations where one or several Delaware allotments remain clustered. What remains of the Delaware line communities are difficult to identify through casual observation and are often interspersed with non-Indians and filled with active and abandoned oil wells. However, the surviving line communities are visible to the Delaware. The Delaware line communities of the twenty-first century exist as small clusters of family allotments, an old abandoned church on a back country road, an inundated community at the bottom of a reservoir lake, or a dutifully manicured rural cemetery. The communities that have been long abandoned have not disappeared completely but continue to reside primarily in Delaware memories and social interactions. Today, Delaware people can place one another with reference to the previously active line communities of their youth or the youth of their ancestors. References to intangible communities that were once associated with the Big House or a Christian church, like Alluwe, Caney River, California Creek, Silverlake, and Coon Creek, still mean something to the Delaware although such communities cannot be found on a map or might be missed when passing through them. While the early years of Oklahoma statehood destroyed the physical integrity of the Delaware communities and their associated religious institutions, the Delaware still see important places and meanings in the locations of remnant, condemned, and abandoned Delaware settlements.

DELAWARE COUNTRY TODAY

Although modern Delaware society postdates Delaware removal by over a century, the Delaware Tribe's built environment in the present reflects the continued importance of the removal-forged cultural landscape of Delaware Country. The construction and maintenance of a unique cultural landscape in Delaware Country remain evident today in the ways in which the Delaware continue to mark particular spaces with their own unique qualities. An outline of the locations of important events, institutions, and tribal facilities reveals the sig-

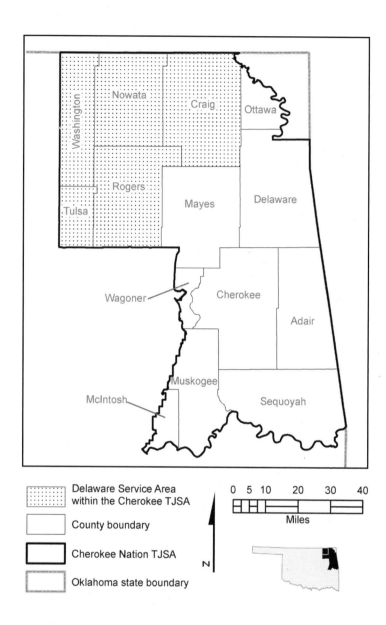

6. CHEROKEE NATION AND DELAWARE TRIBE SERVICE AREAS: The modern boundaries of the Cherokee Nation Tribal Jurisdictional Service Area and the Delaware Tribe's Five County Service Area. Map by Rebecca Dobbs.

nificance of the local cultural landscape to Delaware identity as well as how the Delaware Country of today continues to be informed by the social and spatial divisions first established with removal.

Primarily through the successful administration of the Housing and Child Care programs from the Delaware tribal headquarters in Bartlesville, the Delaware Tribe has tangibly asserted its regional presence in the modern era. The Delaware Business Committee first established the Delaware Service Area with the development of the Delaware Housing Authority in 1977 under the Oklahoma Housing Authority Act. A five-county region (Washington, Nowata, Craig, Rogers, and North Tulsa counties) was included in the Delaware Housing Authority Service Area. Not surprisingly, this service area included the counties that encompass the region first settled by the Delaware following removal. Housing and facility construction has been primarily focused in Bartlesville, Nowata, and Chelsea and has effectively marked the locally understood southern border of Delaware Country. The Delaware Tribe's Child Care Program followed the establishment of the Delaware Housing Authority and has remained consistent with the Housing Authority's practice of making visible the Delaware's territorial claim. Administered from the tribal headquarters in Bartlesville, the Delaware Child Care Program has its own service area that includes the Five County Housing Authority Service Area as well as two adjacent counties in Kansas for a total of seven counties. This ability to provide homes and childcare for American Indians living in Delaware Country has thus served as an important institutional way for the Delaware Tribe to make material their claims to their own jurisdiction within the Cherokee Nation in the modern era.

While the Delaware Housing Authority and the Child Care Program have formalized the boundaries of Delaware Country, the buildings that served as the headquarters for the Delaware Tribe have been located in Bartlesville for over thirty years. In 1973 a small tribal headquarters was purchased in Bartlesville, and the headquarters was later moved to a much larger building in the same town in order to house the central offices of the Delaware Housing Authority and the Delaware tribal government. The Delaware Tribe later purchased an eighty-acre tract of land on the east side of Bartlesville during the years of restored recognition. There the Delaware Tribe has built a substantial tribal complex complete with a community center, a child care facility, a housing addition for the elderly, and a wellness center. For the past few years (2001–2008) the Delaware General Council has continued to meet annually on the first weekend of November at this new community center in Bartlesville. The tribal complex now serves as the headquarters for the Delaware Tribe.

The locations of the administrative facilities established by the Delaware Tribe have consistently been focused in the towns of Bartlesville, Nowata, and Chelsea while recognizing a service area that encompasses a much larger region. Delaware-sponsored housing construction, child care facilities, and the tribal headquarters are located almost exclusively in the regional cities identified with the Christian Delaware world. One interpretation is that the facilities are distributed in such a way in order to be centrally located to the Delaware Service Area. Bartlesville, Nowata, and Chelsea are indeed located in central locations within the service area, with Nowata being the most central location. Another equally plausible interpretation is that the administrative elements of the tribal government (housing, child care, etc.) are commonly associated with the Christian world of Delaware governance and are thus placed in the appropriate contexts. Either way the Delaware have established a five-to seven-county service area that encompasses a region commonly understood as Delaware Country and have built competent administrative facilities to service the needs of the resident Indian population in the cities locally associated with the Christian Delaware families preceding their 2004 judicial termination.

While the administrative capacities of the Delaware Tribe have been focused in the local cities, Delaware cultural events and social institutions associated with the Delaware Big House world have been most prominent in northern Washington County. The Dewey Fair Building has been the locus for exhibition dances and social events among the Delaware since the early twentieth century (Roark-Calnek 1977:870–872). The legacy of Delaware social gatherings in Dewey continue at the powwows, stomp dances, and wild onion dinners sponsored by various groups that are commonly held at the fairgrounds. For instance, the Intertribal Indian Club of Bartlesville (IICOB) dances were held in Dewey before the organization's discontinuation in the late 1980s, and the powwows and events sponsored by Operation Eagle and the Bartlesville Indian Women's Club are held at the Dewey Fairgrounds as well. In the mid-twentieth century the town of Dewey was also selected as the site for the Delaware General Council when it was convened (Carrigan and Chambers 1994:A89-A90). Because of Dewey's location along Coon Creek, the events in Dewey continue to be understood as Delaware events regardless of which organization is the host.

Two Christian churches in northern Washington County are considered Delaware churches because a large majority of the church organizers and congregants are members of the local Delaware community. The New Hope Indian Methodist Church is the older of the two Delaware churches and is located in Dewey. The founding of this church exemplifies how the first Delaware generation without the Big House Ceremony adopted new religious institutions to sustain a degree of cohesion among the descendants of the Delaware Big House faithful. One Delaware woman recalled the story about her mother's role in helping initiate the Indian Methodist church.

> The Big House, that was really important to her, and the last time they had it then was during the war, and they quit after that . . .

at the time we were going to stomp dances at Bill and Thelma Pace's . . . down from their house to the south is Coon Creek. . . . Well, they fixed a stomp area, and we'd have to go to stomp dances down there, and it was just, it would be just packed. I mean, there would be a hundred Indians down there, and they'd be, you know, having a good time and everything. And Mom was, she talked to Bill Pace and told Bill, said, 'Bill, we should have a church for all these people,' said there is no church for them, and they'd go [to] different churches, some of them did, and he said, 'Well, we'll see about it,' you know, because Bill had been a minister at one time.

The stomp dances held at the Paces' house were hosted by Thelma (Elkhair) Pace's brother Ray Elkhair, and the location of the stomps was also recorded by Roark-Calnek (1977:872). Thelma's husband Bill Pace was non-Indian but supportive of Delaware cultural practices. Bill Pace helped establish the New Hope Church by contacting the Methodist church, and after some time a representative returned with a new preacher. Eight original members, who included Delawares, Cherokees, and non-Indians, established a charter and began holding services in the Dewey park until they could secure a proper building, which was built on the west side of town just outside of Dewey. A former attendee of the Big House Ceremony, Anna Davis, named the church "New Hope," and the church soon attracted Indian families from the Dewey area. Today the predominately Delaware, Cherokee, and non-Indian congregation has grown to include Osage and Shawnee families as well. The Indian Methodist church has thus become an important unifying institution within which Delaware families from northern Washington County can interact socially as Christians while also coming together in the spirit of traditionalism embodied in the memory of the Delaware Big House Ceremony.

The other northern Washington County church with a predominately Delaware membership is the Rose Hill Baptist Church. Rose Hill was first built in the early 1990s and is located on a Delaware allotment along Coon Creek. The owner of the allotment was Rose (Jackson) Hill, thus the name of the Church. Rose Hill's daughters retain possession of the allotment and were the primary founders of the church. The non-Indian husband of one of the Hill daughters is a well-respected pastor for the northern Washington County Delaware community and also serves as the preacher for the church. Although the church at Rose Hill does not openly support Delaware events such as stomp dances and powwows, the congregation includes many who are active participants at such Delaware events held in Washington County.

The Delaware Powwow also began as a significant social gathering to allow for the affirmation of a distinctly Delaware community in the context of a Delaware Indian celebration. Although it is included in Roark-Calnek's study, I have added here an extensive account of the Delaware Powwow's founding and continued importance because the grounds on which the powwow transpires has become an important space for the continuation of a Delaware identity inspired by the memory of the Big House community. The powwow grounds used today are on the allotment of Numerous Falleaf's half brother, George Falleaf, where their father, John Falleaf, hosted stomp dances until his passing in 1963. In the early 1960s John had hoped to have a powwow, but was unable to arrange this before his passing. A few years later Numerous Falleaf enlisted the support of his champion powwow dancer friend, Don Wilson, to host the first annual Delaware Powwow at the Falleaf Stomp Grounds on Cotton Creek. Numerous and Don invited the local folks by word of mouth to get together for a few days of noncompetitive powwow and stomp dancing, and the two men slaughtered a steer to help feed the attendees. The intention of the organizers was to hold a powwow in memory of the former Big House community while using the Plains-derived powwow to encourage more participation among the younger generations.

Today the Delaware Powwow has grown to one of the premier powwows in northeastern Oklahoma and is the most highly attended Delaware event of the year. Delaware families maintain permanent camps at the powwow grounds and often spend four days to a week at the annual event. Most of the Delaware activity at the powwow, however, consists of visiting, hosting meals, playing Indian football, participating in the frybread competition, and holding family gatherings and ceremonies. Perhaps the most anticipated non-powwow event of the Delaware Powwow for the Delaware people is the nighttime secular stomp dances that are held on Thursday evening and following the Friday and Saturday nights of competitive dancing. Few Delaware compete in the competitive dance events and act more as hosts for the professional dancers and visitors who are the primary participants in the actual competition portion of the event. Delaware Powwow hosting plays a crucial role in helping to maintain the vitality of the larger powwow circuit, yet the Delaware generally serve as hosts and stomp dance and powwow dance participants rather than powwow dance competitors. Thus, although the Delaware Powwow is an event recently borrowed from the Plains peoples of western and central Oklahoma, the Delaware Powwow maintains a particularly Delaware quality because of the importance of those events that surround the competitive dancing.[8]

Secular stomp and social dances remain an important component of the Delaware Big House world, and such gatherings exist throughout Washington County and in various forms. The first and most visible is in September at the annual celebration of Delaware Days held at the same grounds as the Delaware Powwow. Delaware Days is a family reunion of sorts at which the camped participants enjoy nighttime social and stomp dances in the powwow arena on Friday and Saturday nights. Another venue at which social and stomp dances are performed is at the weekly stomp dances held on every Tuesday throughout the year at the Delaware Community Center in Bartlesville. Such weekly gatherings first began as monthly meetings but are now held more frequently. The Tuesday night get-togethers are indoor events that begin with an evening potluck meal followed by the practice of pow-wow songs, Delaware social dance songs, language classes, and stomp dancing. Individual families from northern Washington County also periodically host their own stomp dances. The most recently hosted stomp was held by a family at their home on Coon Creek. Such family-sponsored stomps usually begin near dusk and feature nighttime stomp and social dancing as well as a potluck meal and refreshments.

The Delaware also maintain their own dance ground on land leased from the Army Corps of Engineers on the western bank of Copan Lake near the site of the last Big House structure. There, Doug Don-nell, with the help of a handful of Delaware preservationists, built a new dance ground named Eagle Ridge in the mid-1990s. The outdoor dance ground is situated on a ridge above the lake and consists of a cleared area of mowed grass surrounded by tables, outbuildings, and thick stands of post oak trees. In the center of the clearing is a rectan-gular plaza framed by plank board benches on all four sides and with a place for two fires in the middle of the eastern and western halves of the rectangle. An entrance to the plaza is provided by an opening in the benches on the east and west sides. The plaza at Eagle Ridge is built like the floor plan of the Xingwikaon, although no attempt to revive the ceremony has ever been made at Eagle Ridge, nor would doing so be considered appropriate. Here at Eagle Ridge the Delaware have hosted various social events including stomp dances and infor-mal powwows in the spirit of the abandoned Big House Ceremony, although at present the interest in the site has declined.

In northern Washington County, Delaware people thus continue to meet and reaffirm their distinct tribal identity at intertribal and community events while doing so beyond the administrative or Christian Delaware world. Yet the Christian world is an important element to Delaware community maintenance as it has been through-

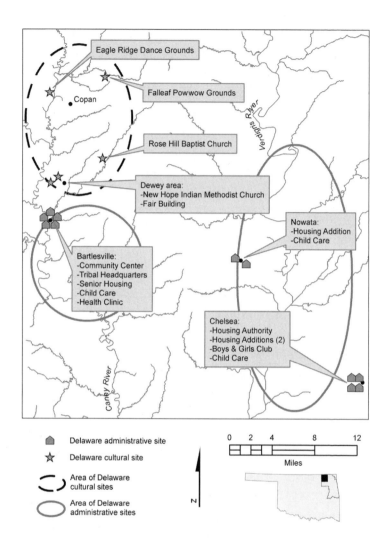

Eagle Ridge Dance Grounds

Falleaf Powwow Grounds

Copan

Rose Hill Baptist Church

Dewey area:
-New Hope Indian Methodist Church
-Fair Building

Verdigris River

Nowata:
-Housing Addition
-Child Care

Bartlesville:
-Community Center
-Tribal Headquarters
-Senior Housing
-Child Care
-Health Clinic

Chelsea:
-Housing Authority
-Housing Additions (2)
-Boys & Girls Club
-Child Care

Caney River

⬠ Delaware administrative site

☆ Delaware cultural site

⌒ Area of Delaware cultural sites

◯ Area of Delaware administrative sites

0   2   4   8   12
            Miles

N

7. DELAWARE ADMINISTRATIVE CENTERS AND CULTURAL SITES:
The modern locations of the administrative sites run by the Delaware Tribe and the cultural sites (grounds, buildings, and churches) important to the Delaware community that is active in the outward performance of Delaware songs, dances, dress, and language. The areas in which Delaware cultural sites and Delaware administrative sites range are also shown to reflect the spatial division between Big House and Christian Delaware regions that exist in the northwestern portion of the Cherokee Nation. Map by Rebecca Dobbs.

out the twentieth century. The participants of both Big House and Christian worlds combine efforts to claim jurisdiction over the territory within the Cherokee Nation that they both hold as important and do so in a uniquely Delaware way. Delaware Country has come to mean more than a region heavily populated by Delaware people. Delaware Country is a diverse and meaningful space from which the Delaware make evident their own unique sense of tribal identity as it is embodied in the local landscape.

The Delaware Service Area is therefore presented here as a codification of the Delaware Country that was established with removal. When understood in historical context, the Delaware Service Area is clarified as a region that exists as two overlapping worlds that reflect the once divided worlds within Delaware society. Delaware Country is bounded by an imaginary triangle with points at the tribal headquarters in Bartlesville, the Delaware Housing Authority in Chelsea, and the Delaware Powwow grounds near Copan. Delaware Country is further divided by an internal division that the Delaware understand to exist between the Christian and the Big House landscapes. These geographical distinctions have helped shape the distribution of the administrative and cultural sites in Delaware Country as well as reflect the unique history of Delaware removal to Indian Territory. The locations in which the Delaware administer federal services predominate in the urban regions first settled by the families who were less resistant to removal and exist in the landscape associated with a Christian Delaware identity. In contrast, the grounds and institutions associated with the abandoned Big House Ceremony are found in the rural regions first settled by the Big House families who were most opposed to the terms for removal. The distribution of place thus reflects the diversity as well as the complexity of Delaware identity in the past and present. The Delaware Service Area is merely an expression of a unified Delaware claim to a tribal homeland that is still cleaved from the removal experience.

1. DELAWARE TRIBAL SEAL: The Delaware Tribal Seal showing the Mesingw mask, fire drill, and peace pipe in the center surrounded at the cardinal directions by the symbols of the three Delaware clans and the Christian cross; twelve prayer sticks encircle the image. Reproduced with permission from the Delaware Tribe of Indians. Image courtesy of Jim Rementer.

THE DELAWARE TRIBAL SEAL: BIG HOUSE
AND CHRISTIAN WORLDS COMBINED

While distinctions can be made between the Big House and Christian Delaware worlds, the divided realms in Delaware society are not mutually exclusive but overlapping and are made potentially available for all Delaware people. Many Delaware people today belong to both Christian and Big House lineages and have some shared sentiments or attachments with both Christian and Big House heritages. Thus, Delaware identity is as much about the memory of the unique Big House community and their associated position against Cherokee membership as it is about a sense pride in those Christian leaders who continued to fight for their paid-for rights in the Cherokee Nation following removal. While the Big House and Christian Delaware worlds can be separated and each provides a perspective for dealing with the issue of Delaware membership in the Cherokee Nation, the reality is that both worlds often coincide in expressions of a collective identity as well as on a more personal and individual level. The symbols on the Delaware Tribal Seal further illustrate the identifiable but indivisible

Delaware worlds that exist in Delaware society. An explanation of the seal's origin and the symbols present on the seal make tangible the coinciding and complimentary Big House and Christian worlds.

When the Delaware Tribe held a contest to design the tribal seal in 1974, committee members were attempting to create a symbol that embodied Delaware sense of self as it was grounded in the tribe's unique heritage. They were looking for a seal that could be put forward as an emblem of Delaware identity. A number of entries were submitted by Big House and Christian descendants alike, and three of the entries were chosen. Instead of picking one entry over the others, the Delaware Business Committee decided to combine what they felt were the best aspects of each. Most of the entries submitted included different objects and symbols associated with the Big House Ceremony and clan totems as the Big House represented a heritage that only the Delaware possess. A few other entries emphasized Christian symbols such as the cross. The final draft chosen included a Christian cross situated at the top of the seal with the three Delaware clan totems encircling the seal. The Christian cross centered at the top placed the Delaware Christian heritage in a paramount position on the seal and provided a symbolic reminder of those Christian leaders who continued Delaware governance following removal. The three clan symbols below the cross are at the cardinal points and represent the three clans of the Delaware Tribe: Turkey, Turtle, and Wolf. Christian and Big House descendants alike are familiar with their clan membership, and clan totems often figure prominently in the material culture used to highlight one's Delaware identity. In the center sits the Mesingw mask next to a fire drill with a long peace pipe across both, and on the edges are twelve prayer sticks. The Mesingw, a central figure in the Big House Ceremony, was a deity known only to the Delaware. Thus the Mesingw is generally put forward as a symbol of the Delaware Big House Ceremony and the unique Delaware tribal heritage that the ceremony represents. Situated in the center of the seal, the Mesingw thus stands as a testament to the Delaware's cultural uniqueness. As Roark-Calnek (1977:828) wrote, "all Delaware are, retrospectively, Mesingw people." Symbols from both the Christian and the Big House communities are thus present on the seal and accurately represent the diversity of being Delaware in the modern era. All symbols are integral to Delaware group identity, and for many in the Delaware Tribe the inclusion of both the cross and the Big House symbols were not only representative but imperative.

The combination of two sets of seemingly oppositional religious symbols in the tribal seal expresses well the concurrent realms that exist within the Delaware tribe, and such a dichotomy also potentially resides within the sense of self held by each Delaware person. The symbols and spaces of both the Christian and Big House worlds are conceptualized as an aspect of Delaware individual and group identity. Some Delaware consider a Christian Delaware heritage and its associated political posture to be fundamental to their contemporary group identity, while others regard the memory of the Big House faith and the resistance to Cherokee membership as the most salient; still others see no contradiction in making selective use of both.

Jason Baird Jackson's (2003a:279) definition of tradition can help to facilitate an appreciation for how contemporary Big House and Christian identities can exist simultaneously among the Delaware while both are perceived as a potentially traditional form of Delaware Indian identity. Jackson (2003a:279) defines tradition as "a symbol (a meaning, a feeling, a construction) that people form in the present about the nature of themselves and their beliefs in light of a particular understanding of a significant past." The significant pasts associated with the Big House and the Christian Delaware ancestors are remembered and appreciated by contemporary Delaware for different reasons and in multiple ways. For some, the remembrance of a community that did not accept their membership in the Cherokee

Nation and preserved their indigenous faith is of central importance to contemporary constructions of being a Delaware Indian in the twenty-first century. Such memories provide the platform for a more assertive posture that maintains the historic and continued Delaware independence separate from the Cherokee Nation. For others, the recollection of those historic Christian leaders who saw removal as the Delaware Tribe's best option for survival in the late nineteenth century provides a source of empowerment when attempting to sustain the Delaware Tribe's acknowledgment through concessions and negotiations with the Cherokee Nation. For most Delaware, the ability to selectively take hold of both memories depending on the situation is what defines Delaware traditionalism in the present. The world of the Delaware Big House and that of the historic Delaware Christian churches collide in the present to provide foundational and potential sources of comfort, conflict, resistance, and ultimately self-identity in the Delaware Tribe while symbolizing two potential political positions on the Delaware Tribe's relationship with the Cherokee Nation. Thus, Big House and Christian worlds forged with removal and continued in the landscape of Delaware Country remain viable and alternative components of Delaware society as well as dual sources for individual, family, and collective expressions of Delaware identity and tribal sovereignty.

CONCLUSION

The built environment of Delaware Country and the Delaware Tribal Seal thus reflect a history of political and religious differences in the Delaware Tribe. Such diversity remains salient for contemporary Delaware identity and sociopolitical life as tribal members debate alternative routes to maintain federal acknowledgment. Although the Big House Ceremony is no longer performed along the upper Caney River and the Christian churches have long since ceased in Delaware Country, both the Big House faith and Delaware Christianity continue to serve as important symbols of Delaware traditionalism in contemporary Delaware society. As explained here, Delaware group identity is structured by lineage and settlement names, both of which continue to serve as markers of a distinct religious and political heritage. The importance of abandoned religious institutions and rural settlements for Delaware group identity is thus revealed through an in-depth understanding of the Delaware cultural landscape that was established with removal and that continues to inform the composition of the modern Delaware built environment and the contemporary tribal seal. It is evident from this account of Delaware society that a sense of tribal identity and traditionalism remain with the Delaware Tribe as they collectively maintain their independence from the Cherokee Nation while doing so in an often contested way that was first established with removal. Demonstrated by the state of affairs in Delaware society is a dynamic sense of traditionalism that allows for cultural change while also remaining an important identity concept rooted in a historic, yet divided, past. It is clear that dramatic cultural changes have taken place among the Delaware as significant cultural practices and settlements associated with the Big House and Delaware Christianity have been put away. The Delaware experience thus reminds us to consider the importance of long abandoned, but deeply meaningful, cultural practices and historic social boundaries in shaping modern tribal identity and political action. Subsequent chapters echo and affirm the importance of location and lineage for guiding Delaware views on the issue of Cherokee membership. Before moving on to contemporary Delaware debates about membership in the Cherokee Nation, however, chapter 4 examines the Delaware Tribe's long-standing government-to-government relationship with the United States and describes the resulting impacts on Delaware society.

Government to Government

We leave for another day what effect, if any, the
post-1867 legislative and executive dealings with the
Delawares had on their alleged status as a tribe.

CHEROKEE NATION V. NORTON, 2004

In November 2004 the Tenth Circuit Court of Appeals
issued the opinion against the Delaware Tribe's status as a federally
recognized tribe. As explained in chapter 2, the court's position was
based entirely on the language of the 1867 Cherokee-Delaware Agreement and the accusation that the Department of Interior violated
its own procedure for acknowledgment. The court's decision did
not take into account previous treaties or the established record of
the government-to-government relationship between the Delaware
Tribe and the United States. A judicial ruling that admittedly did not
rule on the basis of a government-to-government relationship would
be difficult for any tribal government to understand, especially considering the consistency with which the Delaware Tribe maintained
such an association. It is indeed curious that the federal court based
its opinion on the 1867 Cherokee-Delaware Agreement that actually
makes no specific provision dissolving the Delaware Tribe's federal
recognition and overturned a lower court's decision that the DOI
did not violate its own administrative procedures when it granted
recognition to the Delaware Tribe. From the Delaware perspective

this judicial termination was a crippling blow that forced an end to most tribal programs and federal grant projects.

The twentieth-century relationship between the Delaware Tribe and the federal government is presented here in order to give voice to Delaware history in response to the court's agreement-based decision. Emphasis is placed on the maintenance of a federally recognized Delaware governing system and the impact of the federal government's assimilation policy on the Delaware Tribe. The effect of continuous executive and legislative dealings with the Delaware Tribe, while ignored by the court, has resulted in the codification of tribal membership along with dramatic land loss, the breakup of the Delaware line communities, significant cultural modifications, infrequent per capita payments from land claims, and a relatively large tribal population living throughout Oklahoma and elsewhere in the United States by the early 1970s.

Despite the crushing impact of Oklahoma statehood and subsequent federal policy, the Delaware have dealt with each issue and historical event on their own terms. Continued throughout the years of Oklahoma statehood was the cultural division between the Christian and Big House worlds that proved particularly useful for dealing with the dual demands of local community maintenance and a sustained relationship with the federal government. As the federally recognized government for the Delaware Tribe, the Delaware Business Committee continued to push for land claims, establish tribal programs, and remain a tribal government in ways deemed legitimate by the federal government. Big House leaders, however, provided representation for those who did not feel adequately represented by the Christian-dominated Business Committee and sought to preserve Delaware cultural practices following the end of the Big House Ceremony that distinguished the Delaware from other tribes in Oklahoma as well as from the more dominant non-Indian Oklahoma population.

One of the most relevant outcomes of the Delaware's sustained relationship was the tremendous loss of land during the early years of Oklahoma statehood. During the allotment of Indian Territory, the federal government oversaw the redistribution of tribally held land to individual landowners. In the process Delaware-owned land and mineral resources purchased from the Cherokee Nation under the 1867 Cherokee-Delaware Agreement were systematically transferred to non-Indian immigrants, and a structure of federal dependency was artificially imposed on many Delaware families. As a result subsequent generations either sold or lost their land allotments and moved to the local cities and towns or out of Delaware Country in search of employment.

Another significant result of the Delaware Tribe's relationship with the federal government was the arrival of long-awaited land claim awards. The allure of per capita payments that resulted brought an increase in official tribal membership along with a bureaucratically regulated tribal membership application process. Rules for tribal membership were established with the aid of the BIA in which official inclusion was based on descent from a tribal roll, thus securing tribal membership on a federal level as separate from local forms of group identity. By the early 1970s the Delaware Tribe had become a federally recognized tribal government that consisted of a relatively large but dispersed population with all members holding the same tribal membership rights as those who continued to work within the Big House and Christian worlds of Delaware country.

OKLAHOMA STATEHOOD

Prior to Oklahoma statehood the Delaware had established an agriculturally based and rather successful frontier economy by the mid-1870s (Prewitt 1981). While starting over in a region in which they were clearly not welcome, the relocated Delaware developed substantial farms on land that had been purchased from the Cherokee Nation, and Delaware and intermarried white businessmen established small trading posts situated in locations central to the Delaware line communities. Jacob Bartles, a non-Indian who followed the Delaware from Kansas, married Nannie Journeycake Pratt (daughter of Charles Journeycake) after Lucius Pratt's death and is credited with playing a founding role in the origin of the major cities in Delaware Country (Weslager 1972:445; Teague 1967:116). Bartles's trading post operations in Indian Territory helped establish the cities of Bartlesville, Dewey, and Nowata.[1] By 1895 rail lines were built to the central trading posts at Bartlesville, Dewey, and Nowata to export cattle and agricultural goods to the Kansas City market. Increased rail service encouraged the economic growth of the Delaware trading posts and led to the further development of the regional market in northeastern Indian territory prior to Oklahoma statehood. The late nineteenth-century Delaware settlement of Delaware Country thus laid the foundation for the development of the regional economy that would flourish following Oklahoma statehood (Foreman 1942; Miner 1976; Bays 1998).

The passage of the General Allotment Act of 1887, or Dawes Act, was signed into law with the goal of implementing a federal policy of assimilation and opening up Indian reservations to non-Indian settlement. The Dawes Act broke up large communally owned tribal landholdings and redistributed the land to each tribal member for individual ownership while also providing allotment owners with American citizenship. A tragic outcome of allotment was that Indian tribes were disenfranchised from their land and large tracts of reservation property were sold to non-Indians. After each reservation member had obtained a land allotment, the surplus land that was not allotted was made available for sale to outsiders. The result was a checkerboard of Indian-owned land on what was once promised to be tribally held reservations.

After the Cherokee Nation was forced to accept allotment in 1902, the Delaware were allotted lands within the Cherokee Nation. As a consequence, the Delaware lost vast amounts of land, some suffered extreme poverty, and the traditional religion fell out of use by the late 1920s. This redistribution of land and resources ultimately caused the disintegration of some rather large Delaware landholdings including the rural Delaware settlements discussed in chapter 3 and a redefinition of land ownership rights that favored the vast number of non-Indians coming to Oklahoma. As a result of allotment the Delaware lost control over the thriving agrarian-based economy that they helped to develop following removal and many were forced into a state of federal dependency to sustain possession of their now diminished and individually owned land allotments.

Although Delaware allotments were chosen on lands within the line communities, influential Delaware landowners were obliged to substantially diminish their land base without compensation in the process. There were a few Christian Delaware and intermarried whites who owned land in or near the local trading posts now turned into rail depots and identified municipalities. These individuals did retain some control over the regional market but did so only by establishing partnerships with immigrant, non-Indian investors. The norm, however, was that Delaware landholders were forced to hand over large portions of property for the distribution to others. Individual land allotments issued with statehood ranged in size from 110 to 160 acres and were, at times, distributed in small tracts in scattered locations. Land allotments were not only small tracts of discontinuous lands but were divided into a 10-acre homestead and a 100-to 150-acre allotment. Thus, each dispersed allotment was often smaller and more spread across the land than most existing Delaware farmsteads.

Also imposed with allotment where new definitions for land ownership following statehood. In 1908 the U.S. Congress passed legislation defining different levels of land ownership rights among the allotment owners in the Five Civilized Tribes based on one's Dawes roll status. The first category included intermarried whites, freed-

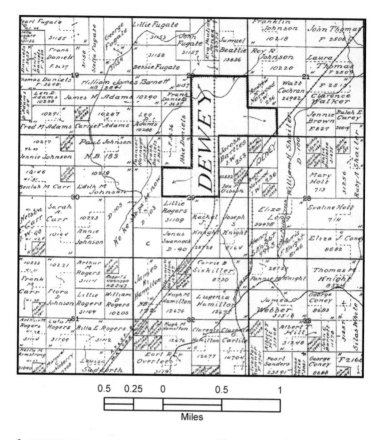

0.5 0.25 0   0.5   1

Miles

8. DEWEY AND DELAWARE ALLOTMENTS: The town site of Dewey and the surrounding allotments that are identified by the allotment owner's name at the time of Oklahoma statehood. The allotments given to intermarried whites are identified as I.W.; those given to freedmen are labeled as F; those allotted to the registered Delaware who were born before removal to the Cherokee Nation are identified as D; while all other allotments made to the Cherokee, Shawnee, and Delaware born in the Cherokee Nation were left unmarked. Reproduced from *Township Maps of the Cherokee Nation* (Washington DC: U.S. Government Printing Office, n.d.), located at the Washington County Assessor's Office.

men, and mixed-blood Indians of less than one-half Indian blood. Such defined landowners possessed their allotment and homestead in fee simple, giving them the right to sell or lease their land while also requiring the landowner to pay property taxes, which was a new financial obligation for most Delaware landowners at the time. Mixed-blood Indians of between one-half and three-quarters Indian blood constituted a second classification that owned their allotment in fee simple and were required to pay property tax on the allotment, but their homesteads remained under restricted status. Holding restricted land meant that the federal government held the land in trust for the property owner, which gave the Bureau of Indian Affairs the ultimate oversight over the sale, lease, or use of the land, and the land was exempt from taxation. The final category included full-bloods with three-quarters or more Indian blood who were given a land allotment and a homestead but not clear title to either. Full-blood allotments and homesteads were both placed under restricted status (Kappler 1913:351). The BIA, not the individual allottee, thus had the final authority to negotiate any sale or lease on restricted land and homesteads as long as the terms were considered to be in the best interest of the allotment owner. Thus, the new, paternalistic definitions for land ownership essentially created second-class citizens of those defined as mixed blood and all full-blood Delaware residing on lands that the Delaware believed were rightfully purchased from the Cherokee Nation.

As an example of how the allotment process impacted Delaware landholders, consider one Delaware man's story about his grandfather's experience with allotment. This Delaware man remembers that his grandfather always carried a leather book that contained information about all of the land that he was forced to turn over in exchange for his allotment. The allotment was not only significantly smaller than the original family holdings but also less productive. Some of his grandfather's land was allotted to his children, brothers, and sisters while other portions were given to other Delaware and non-Indians. Most of the family were full-blood Delaware and thus could not sell or lease their land without federal approval. As a result the once substantial landowner and his children were encouraged by the federal government to lease their allotments to an immigrant cattle rancher who had taken up residence nearby. Eventually the Delaware family allotments were sold to the rancher, and today only a small strip of this once substantial Delaware-owned property remains in the midst of one of the largest cattle ranches in northeastern Oklahoma.[2] It is on this small strip of property in far northwestern Washington County that the Delaware man who related his grandfather's story to me continued to live in the memory of his grandfather and much to the chagrin of his cattle-ranching neighbor.

The real catalyst for land loss was thus such new definitions for land ownership that placed immigrant non-Indian investors in an opportunistic position following Oklahoma statehood. Wealthy immigrants could easily purchase mixed-blood allotments if the owner was willing to sell and not take on the burden of property taxes. Other lands were purchased by non-Indians by paying for delinquent property taxes at the county courthouse and taking possession of the unpaid-for allotment. Non-Indians also had access to some mixed-blood and all full-blood allotments and homesteads through the auspices of the federal government. Since the federal government had the authority to negotiate the sale and lease of full-blood land in the best interests of the allotee, the agents representing the U.S. government would enter into contracts with local capitalists who were most often interested in procuring grazing rights and mineral resources. In exchange for using the allotment the capitalist would pay the federal government a certain agreed-upon sum, and a portion of the payment would be mailed to the allotee in the form of a royalty check. The allotment owner never received the full amount of the lease and in some cases was unaware of the actual terms of the agreement. Although the Delaware were provided allotments with Oklahoma statehood, the rules in place for land ownership essentially gave control over Delaware-owned raw materials to the federal government as well as wealthy and often non-Indian investors.

When oil was discovered in Delaware Country at the beginning of the twentieth century, non-Indian encroachment on Indian allotments only accelerated. Oil speculators discovered that Delaware Country was right on top of a large pool of oil that sat just below the surface. Mixed-bloods with less than one-half Indian blood soon found themselves with fee simple property that gave the allotment owner full land rights including the burden of property taxes. Many of the younger Delaware without the means to pay the annual property tax could do nothing while investors legally took possession of the allotment by providing the unpaid land taxes. Others simply sold their allotments to interested oil companies for cash.

Full-bloods and some mixed-bloods were even further marginalized from the emerging agricultural and oil industries of Delaware Country. Since those with three-fourths or more Indian blood were not able to obtain title to their own land allotments, they had to undertake transactions involving their allotment through the federal government. In some cases a guardian was named to assist in the oversight and administration of certain Delaware allotments. However, the guardian appointed was not usually impartial and often had a vested financial interest in the property. The best example of a guardian with a vested oil interest in Delaware Country was Iowa native Frank Phillips, who was also the founder of Phillips Petroleum Company. One of the allotments over which Phillips was named the guardian was owned by Anna Davis, a young Delaware girl in the early twentieth century who would later become one of the founders of the New Hope Indian Methodist Church in Dewey. It was on her allotment that the future oil giant would drill his first producing well, and Phillips was later given guardianship of the allotment by the BIA. Phillips apparently handled all of the money generated from the allotment, and Davis did receive a large royalty payment from the land, which prompted the local media to promote her as the richest Indian girl in Washington County (Cranor 1991:84–85). Phillips was subsequently able to obtain a tremendous amount of oil from the Davis allotment and reportedly worked with local Delaware community leaders, such as Willie Longbone, to gain access to the oil from other Delaware allotments. The bulk of the profits and discretion over the use of the oil, however, remained with the federal government and Frank Phillips. As a testament to the personality possessed by Frank Phillips, he is not remembered with disgust by Delaware people but rather as a very giving and charismatic but powerful businessman who was always willing to put the Delaware allotment owners first. Phillips also had a similarly successful relationship with the Osage and was very proud of his status as an adopted member of the Osage Nation. Thus, although Phillips's position as a guardian provided him access to a rich source of oil, he did not appear to allow his privileged position to get in the way of his strong ties with the Osage and Delaware from whom a major portion of his wealth originated (Wallis 1988).

The allotment of Indian Territory thus created an economic structure in which those with three-fourths or more Indian blood were restricted from utilizing the resources from their own allotment and homestead to create wealth. Although some Delaware such as Anna Davis secured substantial royalties from oil leases, the Delaware remained a class rich in raw materials with few holding the ability to access or control such resources. The restricted conditions faced by the Delaware were in turn exploited by non-Indian entrepreneurs. Non-Indian capitalists were free to secure leases with full-blood landowners through the federal government and often purchased land from those with less than three-quarters Indian blood.

The non-Indian exploitation of Delaware resources thus slowly eroded away most of the Delaware allotments and settlements. As a number of mixed-blood Delaware sold or lost their allotments to local investors, there was a subsequent increase in the number of Delaware families moving to the local towns or migrating out of Oklahoma (Roark-Calnek 1980:136). The Delaware with full-blood allotments either lived on their rural lands in what remained of the line communities or moved to the city in search of employment. Many other allotments were condemned with the construction of Copan and Oolagah lakes, which were built in the heart of the Big House and Alluwe communities, respectively. Some managed to hold onto their allotments and passed the ownership to their children and grandchildren until the acreage inherited by each generation became too small to be productive, and the land was eventually sold. A few still reside on their parents' and grandparents' allotments as a home place for large extended families or as a memorial to the memory of their departed loved ones. Such is the Delaware experience with Oklahoma statehood, and the story is not unlike those experienced by many other tribes in Oklahoma.

What makes the Delaware experience with allotment so tragic is the accelerated and near complete loss of land as a consequence of Oklahoma statehood. The explanation for such rapid land loss is most clearly the result of the location of the Delaware residential units in one of the most productive regions in Oklahoma. Previous research has shown that the productivity of the land is directly related to the disintegration of Indian settlements in Indian Territory (Warhaftig 1968). As the productivity of the land increased, so did the degree of settlement disintegration. Albert Warhaftig's (1968:517) study of the traditional Cherokee towns found that those communities located on fertile flat agricultural land dissolved more quickly after Oklahoma statehood than those communities in the less agriculturally viable hills and hollows that predominate in the Ozark Plateau. Unlike the Ozark topography, Delaware Country is in the Prairie Plains environment characterized by a relatively flat topography with fertile soils irrigated by two substantial river systems. Most of Delaware Country is thus a highly productive environment for agricultural development, and the discovery of easily accessible oil only accelerated non-Indian penetration of the region. Because Delaware Country possessed such productive agricultural and mineral resources, the Delaware were faced with much more intrusive pressures from non-Indian economic interests than the other less productive regions of the Cherokee Nation and Oklahoma (Bays 1998:178). Thus, while a good number of Cherokee towns remain in the Ozark hills of the Cherokee Nation separate from the agricultural and oil-based Oklahoma economy, no distinctly Delaware line community or town is still inhabited because such rural Delaware settlements were located on exactly those resources and environments most desired by the immigrant non-Indian population.[3]

The allotment of Indian Territory may have accomplished the physical breakup of Delaware communities, but it did not also put an end to the Delaware Tribe's political organization nor do away with the important differences that exist within the Delaware Tribe. Ironically, the legislation that brought about the allotment of Indian Territory also abolished the federal government's recognition of the Cherokee Nation. The Curtis Act was passed in 1898 and effectively destroyed the tribal governments in Indian Territory. A few years later, in 1901, the Dawes Act was amended to grant U.S. citizenship to all Indians living in Indian Territory (Prucha 1975:197–199). The following year, the 1902 Cherokee-Dawes Agreement provided for the termination of the Cherokee Nation on March 4, 1906 (Carrigan and Chambers 1994:28). With this legislation Congress effectively provided for the termination of the Cherokee Nation. The Delaware Business Committee, however, was not as affected by such legislation, nor were the Delaware forced to terminate their tribal organization, so the committee continued its own independent and long-standing collaboration with the federal government. Although the Five Civilized Tribes Act of 1906 later provided for the continuation of the Cherokee Nation's tribal government, the congressional actions surrounding the allotment of Indian Territory had severely limited Cherokee sovereignty in the process (Carrigan and Chambers 1994:28–30; Sturm 2002:173).

THE BUSINESS COMMITTEE AND THE BIG HOUSE COMMITTEE

A review of recent Delaware history clearly indicates that a continuous government-to-government relationship between the Delaware Business Committee and the U.S. government was maintained after Oklahoma statehood (Carrigan and Chambers 1994). Although somewhat disenfranchised as a consequence of Oklahoma statehood, the Delaware remained remarkably distinct as a separate Indian tribe with their own acknowledged tribal government and socio-ceremonial life. A dual system of Delaware governance that emerged with removal remained in place even after Oklahoma statehood and continued to serve the needs of the Delaware Tribe. This section presents the early history of the two political bodies that served the dual interests of the Delaware Tribe. An outline of the Delaware Business Committee's organization and dealings with the federal government into the early twentieth century is given first, followed by a review of the leadership in the Big House community. It is shown that the Delaware did indeed continue to rely upon two political bodies each with their separate but necessary purposes and political positions.

Once removed to Indian Territory, the Alluwe-centered Delaware Council adopted an election format to select representatives. From removal to 1889, the Delaware government consisted of a principal chief and an assistant chief. During some years the Delaware Council had two elected assistant chiefs while during others there was only one. The men who served on the Delaware Council were principally selected from those families associated with the signers of the 1867 Cherokee-Delaware Agreement aligned with the Christian communities. After Principal Chief John Conner's death in 1872, an election was held to name his successor. Reverend James Ketchum of the Methodist community in Ketchum won the election. The validity of the election was contested by Charles Journeycake, and the election was subsequently recalled. The recall election for principal chief was won by James Conner, the brother of former chief John Conner and member of the Alluwe Baptist community. Charles Journeycake and James Simon were elected as the assistant chiefs. Four years later James Connor passed on, and Charles Journeycake was elected to fill in as principal chief. The following year, in 1878, another election was held, with Charles Journeycake reelected as principal chief and Big John Sarcoxie elected as the sole assistant chief (Carrigan and Chambers 1994:22). The Alluwe-Silverlake alliance under the leadership of Journeycake and Sarcoxie thus remained in political office during the late nineteenth century and would continue to do so until the Delaware Council was reorganized eleven years later.

In 1889 the Delaware abandoned the system of principal chief and assistant chief and again restructured their tribal government to more adequately deal with the federal government. The Delaware instituted a committee structure headed by a principal chief that could more effectively handle the U.S. Supreme Court cases against the Cherokee Nation described in chapter 2. Delaware voters elected six delegates to represent them on the newly organized Delaware Business Committee, and those elected were almost exclusively chosen from the families in the Christian enclaves in the Silverlake and Alluwe vicinities (Carrigan and Chambers 1994:124). Committee members were generally well-educated lawyers, businessmen, or preachers who participated in the social network that revolved around the local Christian churches. The first Delaware Business

Committee consisted of Big John Sarcoxie, Andrew Miller, John Young, Henry and Arthur Armstrong, and Fillmore Secondine. Charles Journeycake was elected as the first principal chief of the newly organized committee and remained in the position until his death in 1894 (Carrigan and Chambers 1994:22).

Following Journeycake's passing, the DOI helped reorganize the Delaware tribal government in a way that mirrored the existing committee structure. Five members instead of six were elected to serve on the DOI-sanctioned Delaware Business Committee. There were apparently no term limits, and a chairman rather than chief was then selected from the five elected delegates. George Bullette, a member of the Alluwe community, served as the first chairman from 1895 to 1921. During his tenure Bullette moved the location of the Delaware Business Committee meetings to Dewey, where the seat of tribal governance remained for some time, and the town now serves as the understood nucleus of Delaware Country (Carrigan and Chambers 1994:125). The four other members of the first Delaware Business Committee were Little John Sarcoxie Jr., John Secondine, Henry Armstrong, and John Young (Carrigan and Chambers 1994:22). After Bullette, John Young served briefly as chairman in 1921 and was later replaced by Joseph Bartles, the grandson of Charles Journeycake and son of Bartlesville-Dewey founder Jacob Bartles and Nannie Journeycake. Joseph Bartles served as chairman of the Business Committee from 1921 to 1951 and continued to hold meetings in Dewey throughout his tenure (Carrigan and Chambers 1994:125).[4] The Delaware Business Committee thus followed the Delaware Council that was organized following removal, and it remained organized and staffed with representatives from the Christian families. The Business Committee also existed as the recognized body of the Delaware Tribe in all transactions with the federal government following removal and throughout the first half of the twentieth century.

Much of the Business Committee's work involved cooperating

with the federal government on various issues and working with the Cherokee Nation to ensure that the 1867 Cherokee-Delaware Agreement was upheld. The Business Committee's continued to pursue ongoing land claims as well as to look after certain needs of the Delaware Tribe. The Business Committee very rarely included members from the Big House community and did not consider itself responsible for encouraging the practice of Delaware ceremonies and language as was the primary concern of the Big House leadership. The Delaware Business Committee did, however, develop a diplomatic relationship with the Cherokee Nation. Some Delaware and Cherokee leaders, especially those Cherokee who called Delaware Country home, formed political and familial alliances with Christian Delaware leaders. W. W. Keeler is the most remembered example among Delaware elders. When President Eisenhower appointed Keeler as the chairman of the Cherokee Nation Executive Committee in 1948, Keeler was already a powerful economic force in the Bartlesville area. As the chief executive officer of Phillips Petroleum Company, Keeler either owned or leased most of the Delaware allotments and also employed many Delaware people, including some of the attorneys who served on the Delaware Business Committee. A strong partnership thus existed between Keeler and the members of the Delaware Business Committee during the mid-twentieth century.

While the Christian presence was represented on the Delaware Business Committee, the Big House followers who protested the 1867 Cherokee Delaware Agreement continued their own separate political organization into the twentieth century. Once relocated to Indian Territory, those opposed to the 1867 Cherokee-Delaware Agreement shunned the Delaware Council in Alluwe and sought to extend their social network to include neighboring Indian communities. In Indian Territory the Big House community settled in close proximity to their former enemies, the Osage. As an act of friendship, the Delaware hosted annual smokes to establish and maintain an alliance with the Osage (Weslager 1972:429). Delaware elders remember stories about joint Osage and Delaware social gatherings that would take place near the Delaware Big House grounds or at a community member's home. Roark-Calnek (1977:869) indicates that the Osage-Delaware Smokes continued to be hosted by Sam Flint along the upper Caney River into the early twentieth century. War dances, social dances, horse races, and giveaways were common events held at such Osage-Delaware gatherings. The Osage were reportedly also fond of Delaware-style clothing and often patronized particular Delaware artisans for the design of Osage dance regalia.

The Big House adherents also relied more heavily on their existing ties with the Shawnee living in the White Oak and Bird Creek vicinities. The Delaware have counted the Shawnee as friends and relatives ever since their shared occupation of refugee villages along the Susquehanna and Ohio rivers in the eighteenth century. The Delaware and Shawnee have also lived in close proximity throughout removal, and the Delaware refer to the Shawnee as their sister tribe (Weslager 1972:440; Howard 1981:40). It is this tradition that continued in Indian Territory and later Oklahoma where the Delaware remained particularly close to the Shawnee. Leaders from the Big House community frequently attended Shawnee events at the now defunct Spybuck grounds on Bird Creek and the active White Oak grounds near Vinita, and some Shawnee families in turn attended the Big House and other Delaware ceremonial events in northern Washington County. Many Delaware from both Big House and Christian families were also intermarried with Shawnee families. Frequent Shawnee-Delaware interaction continues today, and some traditionally oriented Shawnee-Delaware (individuals with both Shawnee and Delaware heritage) and a few Delaware identify with and participate at the Shawnee ceremonial grounds at White Oak and the nearby Native American Church hosted by a Delaware-Shawnee family.

The Big House leaders also maintained a separate political organization to help perpetuate their unique religious and cultural beliefs. Information exists that suggests the existence of an informal political organization among the Big House followers that lasted into the mid-twentieth century. It is clear from oral history and documented accounts that the Big House and Christian families alike recognized some Big House leaders as chiefs whose function was to attend to the political, social, emotional, and spiritual needs of both communities. As Nora Thompson Dean remembers, "the Chief does much more than function as a political leader. He might even go and stay with a family in grief or help them and encourage them. The last chief of this type was Charlie Elkhair. . . . In my young days, we had a chief that I recall very well. He performed all the functions and, of course, he couldn't speak English. He would always have to engage an interpreter to tell the congregation what was to take place at the various councils we had" (Dean 1978:16–17). Charlie Elkhair thus performed certain tasks not considered appropriate for the Business Committee to handle, but the tasks were expected of leaders in the Big House community. Chiefs such as Elkhair were responsible for conducting important ceremonial observances like the Big House Ceremony and other family-sponsored rites. Big House leaders were also asked to offer prayers at family gatherings and officiate during funerals while also attending to the emotional needs of the sick and grieving. However, documents suggest that Big House community chiefs were more than just religious specialists and were, at times, organized as a political body.

The most visible evidence of the Big House community's political organization appears in the Delaware's collaboration with ethnologist Frank Speck.[5] Speck's unpublished correspondence with the Delaware casts the last Big House adherents as recognized authorities within the community who were formally organized and in search of ways to preserve or continue the Big House Ceremony. With the passing of the Big House Ceremony and associated practices, Delaware ceremonialists did not apparently wholeheartedly abandon the observance but considered a number of possibilities to obtain the financial resources necessary to continue the service. With the goal of preserving and perhaps revitalizing the Big House Ceremony, James Charlie Webber was the first to approach Speck in 1928, and by 1929 the Pennsylvania Historical Society had donated $500 to help revitalize the Big House Ceremony (Obermeyer 2007:189–190). The Big House leaders subsequently met at Joe Washington's home in northern Washington County and established the Big House Committee on June 15, 1929 (Washington 1929). The nine recognized community leaders of the Big House community were present as a separate body, and none of those serving were also on the Business Committee. The nine members of the Big House Committee were James Thompson, George Falleaf, John Falleaf, Willie Longbone, Charlie Elkhair, Frank Frenchman, Samuel White, Jack Longbone, and Fred Washington. Fred Washington's father, Joe Washington, served as the secretary (Washington 1929).

In his published work, Speck (1931:9) identified his primary consultant, James Charlie Webber, as Chief War Eagle, who was "elected to the Council of the Fowl or Turkey division of this tribe in 1902, and re-elected secretary of the Delaware executive council by the combined Delaware and Munsee tribes in 1921." Since there is no record that Webber ever served on the Delaware Business Committee or that the Business Committee was referred to as the Executive Council, Speck's work and unpublished correspondence provide clear evidence that a second political organization existed within the Delaware Tribe.

The Delaware Executive Council cited by Speck did indeed exist although the body was never formally recognized by the Bureau of Indian Affairs. The Executive Council was staffed by the Big House leadership and provided a voice for those not satisfied with the

Delaware Business Committee. Webber was among those on the Executive Council, a body that was also identified as the Delaware Indian Councilors. In 1932 the Delaware Indian Councilors organized a petition to "abolish the Delaware Business Committee, and appoint or elect an executive Council in their place, by direct vote of the Delaware people" (Falleaf 1932). George Falleaf signed as the principal chief, Charlie Elkhair signed as the assistant chief, and James Charlie Webber signed as the secretary. The signers of the petition against the Business Committee included eight other Big House leaders who signed as members of the Delaware Executive Council with James H. Thompson listed as the chairman. A total of seventy-seven Delaware petitioners signed the petition, and most came from those families associated with the northern Washington County Big House community (Falleaf 1932). Although the petition was unsuccessful, it does provide clear evidence for the formal continuation of a Big House leadership that remained opposed to the Delaware Business Committee.

In their efforts to continue support for the Big House leadership, a few younger visionaries later revived the Big House Ceremony during World War II (Newcomb 1956a:110). Reuben Wilson and some former participants in the Big House Ceremony held the observance a couple more times in a semipermanent shelter near Julius Fouts's home north of Dewey. Although the ceremony was not performed for political reasons and was primarily intended to expedite the end of World War II, the connection between the revitalized observance and the formal political organization of Big House descendants should not be overlooked as a possible way to reinvigorate support for the culturally conservative leadership at midcentury (Newcomb 1956a:110; Obermeyer 2007).

The Big House leadership and the Business Committee are thus best understood as two organizations that represented the overlapping but divided interests of the two Delaware worlds in the years before and after Oklahoma statehood. The Business Committee remained organized to deal with issues pertaining to the Delaware Tribe's political and economic interests. The Big House Committee, or Executive Council, on the other hand, also existed as a tribal authority organized according to the leadership rules within the Big House community, whose task was to look after the tribe's social and ceremonial needs and, in some cases, to challenge or check the actions taken by the Business Committee. The two distinct Delaware political bodies that existed in Indian Territory remained separated by religious and political sentiments as well as kinship constituencies. The families living along the Verdigris and lower Caney rivers staffed their political organization around the local Delaware Baptist churches. The pastors and church leaders from the prominent extended families in the Christian settlements were those chosen to serve on the restructured Delaware Business Committee. The Big House adherents, on the other hand, looked to the men who had leadership roles in the Delaware Big House community and who held ceremonial competence. Leaders from the Big House Church were recognized for their role as both spiritual and secular leaders in the community. Religious sentiment thus helped structure governing bodies in both the Christian and Big House communities. The two complimentary Delaware governments that existed before and after statehood were thus different in faith and scope, but their constituencies were potentially overlapping.

OIWA AND THE INDIAN CLAIMS COMMISSION

The Oklahoma Indian Welfare Act (OIWA) of 1936 represented a new direction in federal policy that provided Oklahoma tribal governments with the opportunity to reorganize according to federal guidelines. Both the Delaware Business Committee and the Cherokee leadership initially passed on reorganization. The Delaware maintained the divided political organization discussed previously until a new constitution was adopted in 1958. Prior to this the Business Committee held the government-to-government relationship while the Big House leadership attended to the needs of the local Indian community. The Cherokee Nation followed as well and remained as the Executive Committee appointed by the president of the United States until substantial modifications were made beginning in the late 1960s (Sturm 2002:90–94).

The Big House leadership cited in the previous section and their descendants were very much opposed to the Delaware Business Committee's decision not to organize under the OIWA. The descendants of the Big House leaders recall the push by their parents and grandparents to reorganize the Delaware Business Committee in order to be consistent with the OIWA. The Business Committee, however, remained steadfast against the OIWA and the Big House leadership even though the BIA declared the Delaware eligible to organize under the legislation (Carrigan and Chambers 1994:35–37). Dissent against the Business Committee over the issue of OIWA reorganization remained into the 1950s as the meetings were reportedly attended by Big House and Christian leaders alike and were never harmonious (Newcomb 1955:1041). In the end the Delaware Big House leaders were not able to reorganize under the OIWA, and the Business Committee continued largely unchanged as the recognized governing body.

The Cherokee Nation also did not organize under the OIWA and would not emerge in its modern form until the passage of the Indian Claims Commission Act of 1946. As the appointed chairman of the Cherokee Nation, W. W. Keeler handpicked the nine-member Executive Committee with the principal purpose of bringing land claims before the Indian Claims Commission. Although a committee appointed to represent the corporate interests of the Cherokee Nation, Keeler and his Executive Committee were separate from the federally recognized United Keetoowah Band of Cherokee Indians and remain so today. In the 1940s a separate Cherokee tribal government consisting of Cherokee Nation Dawes enrollees and their descendants organized under the OIWA. The United Keetoowah Band of Cherokee Indians drafted a constitution according to the OIWA charter and created their own tribal membership roll consistent with federal regulations. The Keetoowah Base roll was created in 1949, and the tribe received official federal recognition in 1950.

The Delaware Business Committee eventually altered their tribal government in order to sustain their position as representatives of the Delaware Tribe and more actively litigate ongoing land claims under the Indian Claims Commission (Weslager 1972:457–463). Horace McCracken, of both Cherokee and Delaware descent and from Nowata, was elected chairman of the Delaware Business Committee in 1951. McCracken replaced Jacob Bartles, who had served as chairman for over thirty years. McCracken continued Bartles's tradition of holding Business Committee meetings in Dewey, and the town continued as a shared middle ground for the Big House and Christian Delaware families to meet (Carrigan and Chambers 1994:A91–A92). The Delaware adopted a revised constitution and bylaws in 1958 to define the legal structure under which the Delaware Business Committee was to operate, and the governing document was later approved by the BIA in 1962 (Carrigan and Chambers 1994:38–40). Not surprisingly the 1962 Delaware Bylaws and Constitution were consistent with the OIWA but did not specify organization under it, a result that was certainly due to the cooperative work with the BIA as well as the influence of the Big House leadership who pushed for organization under the OIWA.

The reorganized Delaware tribal government was similar to the previous structure of the Business Committee with some modifications. The 1962 Delaware Bylaws and Constitution formally recognized the bicameral nature of Delaware governance that had been in existence since removal. A five-member grievance committee was added for the purpose of investigating complaints of misconduct against members of the Delaware Business Committee, likely a concession made to satisfy the Big House leadership's desire to more closely check the actions of the Business Committee. Tribal elections were standardized under the new constitution and held every four years for each committee member. Term limits were not imposed, and there still are no term limits for elected Delaware representatives. Tribal membership was codified as including only those individuals who could document that they were Delaware by Blood. There was no mention of blood quantum in the 1962 constitution, and the Delaware Tribe still does not recognize blood degree as a requirement for membership. The Delaware by Blood requirement was not yet tied exclusively to the 1904 Delaware Per Capita Roll, and Delaware membership was an inclusive stipulation that potentially included anyone who could demonstrate descent from a Delaware Indian (Delaware Constitution and Bylaws reprinted in Carrigan and Chambers 1994:A46–A49). Such a tribal membership criterion makes sense since the Delaware Tribe were the descendants of the main body of Delaware, and thus the possibility was left open for those Delaware groups scattered in other locations throughout North America to rejoin the tribal fold. The reorganized Delaware Business Committee as established by the 1962 governing documents thus continued to operate as the recognized Delaware tribal government until termination in 1979.

As the Delaware Tribe was reorganizing in the 1960s, an unprecedented growth in the American Indian population was taking place that was caused by changes in health care, public policy, and racial self-identification on the U.S. census (Snipp 1989:64–72). The American Indian population grew by 72 percent and expanded following a substantial migration of American Indians to urban centers during the first half of the twentieth century as a consequence of allotment, termination, and relocation policies. As a result roughly half of the American Indian population in 1980 was living in urban centers often far removed from reservations or tribal communities (Snipp 1989:82–83). Similar demographic trends had taken place among the Delaware Tribe by the 1970s, causing a dramatic increase in tribal membership with a considerable portion of the rise coming from members who lived in cities in Oklahoma and outside the state. The land loss and exploitation of Indian people in the early years of Oklahoma statehood caused many families to leave Indian Territory in search of opportunity. The desperate poverty of the Depression Era in Oklahoma exacerbated the existing poverty initiated with allotment and forced many Indians and non-Indians alike to move to California and elsewhere. Delaware participation in the military, out-of-state Indian boarding schools, and the urban relocation program in the 1960s also increased migration out of Delaware Country. Thus, by the time that the land claims were awarded in the late 1960s, many Delaware descendants were not living in Delaware Country, and today almost three-fourths of the Delaware population lives beyond the region.

In the context of such a rapidly expanding and nonlocal tribal population, identifying such a dispersed tribal membership required an even more formally regulated process. When the Indian Claims Commission finally awarded over 9 million dollars to the Delaware, the Delaware Business Committee was soon swamped with applications for membership (Weslager 1972:460–461). Working in conjunction with the BIA office, the Business Committee established more specific criteria for legal membership in the Delaware Tribe. The Delaware amended the 1962 constitution in 1974 to change the Delaware-by-blood requirement to those who met or whose lineal ancestors met the qualifications required to participate in the distribution of the land claims award (Carrigan and Chambers 1994:A50–A54). The revision restricted tribal membership to only those descendants of the 985 Delaware who were removed from the Kansas Reservation. The applications for membership slowed, but the Delaware tribal population still increased dramatically during the 1970s. Residence was not considered a factor when determining tribal membership, and the population living beyond Delaware Country grew in number while the locally active Delaware population remained relatively constant. The promise of per capita payments and the need to codify tribal membership with the criteria considered valid by the federal government required that the Business Committee define Delaware tribal membership more rigidly. In the shift to a more strict definition of tribal membership, local definitions based on lineage membership and local participation were eclipsed by a legally regulated process.[6]

The increase in Delaware tribal membership that came with successful land claims significantly altered the demography of the Delaware Tribe. Because residence in Delaware Country was not included as a requirement for tribal membership, one only had to demonstrate descent from a Delaware person who removed to the Cherokee Nation in order to be a member of the Delaware Tribe. Successful land claim awards provided a financial incentive to tribal membership at a time in history when the non-Indian public was taking a greater interest in American Indian culture and heritage (Nagel 1995; Thornton 1987; Snipp 1989). Although attendance at local Delaware tribal events rarely exceeded 300 participants, Delaware Tribal membership rose exponentially in the late twentieth century. The original removal roll counted 985 Delaware who came to Indian Territory, followed by the 1904 Delaware Per Capita Roll that counted 1,100 tribal members at the time of Oklahoma statehood. Thus the Delaware population was relatively stable during the forty years prior to Oklahoma statehood. By the time of the land claims awards in the 1970s, the Delaware population had risen dramatically, reaching over 6,000 by 1971 (Weslager 1972:460). Over the next thirty-five years the Delaware tribal population would almost double again in size, reaching almost 11,000 tribal members by 2006. In roughly a century, the population of the Delaware Tribe has grown to almost ten times that which existed at the time of Oklahoma statehood.

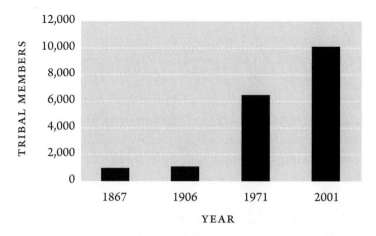

12,000

10,000

8,000

6,000

4,000

2,000

0

TRIBAL MEMBERS

1867   1906   1971   2001

YEAR

1. DELAWARE TRIBE POPULATION GROWTH, 1867–2001: The estimated
rate of population growth in the Delaware Tribe following removal to the
Cherokee Nation up until 2001. The graph is based on known population
amounts for the Delaware Tribe in 1867, 1906, 1971, and 2001.

As the Delaware Tribe's population grew, so did the distinctions
within the tribal membership based on residence and participation.
A significant portion of the Delaware Tribe does not live locally and
are not active in the local Delaware community. On the other hand
there is what can easily be identified as a Delaware community composed of Delaware tribal members who are active participants in the
local social and political life of the tribe. This Delaware community
is further subdivided by resident and nonresident members. The
resident Delaware community is defined as those active Delaware
who live in Delaware Country and who maintain tribal operations,
participate at the Delaware Powwow and stomp dance events, or
attend a Delaware church or institution. This small group comprises
representatives from several Delaware families, each of which is associated with at least one of the now abandoned Delaware line communities. There is also a large nonresident but active constituency
of Delaware tribal members who add a nonlocal component to the
Delaware community. The nonresident Delaware are a significantly

Government to Government ◄ 143

larger group than their resident cohort. Nonresident community members remain active in tribal elections and make frequent visits to Delaware Country for important social and political events. Such nonresident community members are often connected to the resident population through close kin members who live locally, and their participation marks them as active members of the local community though they reside outside of Delaware Country. Beyond the Delaware community there is an equally significant population of inactive Delaware tribal members who are not considered members of the Delaware community because they are not present at local social and political events and may not even participate in tribal elections. The Delaware community members consider this large but inactive group of tribal members as potential community members because each can trace descent to one or more Delaware families, and lineage membership provides the necessary link to the Delaware community. The possibility of participation in local events is always present for inactive members, and thus membership in the Delaware community is available as well. The line between the Delaware community and inactive Delaware tribal members, as is the case for most tribal communities, is one based on a degree of participation, and thus it is a status that can change throughout one's lifetime.[7]

Population shifts and migrations that have occurred as a consequence of federal policy have thus reshaped the demography of the Delaware Tribe, yet the removal-forged political structure has remained remarkably consistent. While the bicameral system of Delaware governance has certainly undergone significant change since removal, it is clear that the United States has maintained federal recognition of the Delaware Tribe throughout such changes. First identified as eligible to reorganize under the OIWA, the Delaware Business Committee was later reorganized under a federally approved constitution in 1962 and remained the acknowledged tribal authority as it had since Oklahoma statehood. In the process the definition of tribal membership shifted from a locally understood phenomenon to a bureaucratically regulated process based on descent. The result was the codification of a federally recognized Delaware governing body that was achieving significant land claims awards and a growing tribal constituency seeking to join in on the eventual per capita distribution. Thus it is clear that by the mid-1970s the Delaware Business Committee was a federally recognized tribal government whose formally established bicameral structure was influenced by the demands made by the Big House leadership and with whom the BIA dealt as the representatives for the over six thousand Delaware constituents who were recognized as members of the Delaware Tribe in the years prior to their 1979 termination.

CONCLUSION

Both positive and negative results have thus come from the Delaware Tribe's ongoing relationship with the federal government. The encouraging outcomes have been a record of government-to-government relations and significant land claims awards. The discouraging impacts are those shared by other Oklahoma tribes: tremendous land loss and dislocation, a significant population that is dependent on federal Indian programs and services, a bureaucratic definition of tribal identity, and a widely dispersed population. Despite such a shared history with other tribes, the Delaware Tribe was judicially terminated in 2004 without any consideration or deference given for such a history. The historical similarities between the Delaware and other federally recognized tribes including the Cherokee Nation provide the basis for the Delaware Tribe's doubts about the Tenth Circuit Court's termination. This outline of Delaware governmental history points out why the court's decision was so shocking to the Delaware as they recall the sometimes good but all too often tragic results that came from the ongoing relationship between the Delaware Tribe and the U.S. government.

5 Self-Determination

It is admirable to consider how powerful the kings are,
and yet how they move by the breath of their people.
WILLIAM PENN, *WATSON'S ANNALS OF
PHILADELPHIA AND PENNSYLVANIA*

On my first visit to the Delaware Powwow I had been invited
to the Thursday night gathering that takes place at the grounds before
the actual powwow begins. Known simply as Family Night, this event
features potluck suppers offered by camps throughout the grounds
followed by an evening of social dancing after sunset. The informal
get-together provides both local and visiting family and friends the
opportunity to gather and reestablish community bonds in the comfortable atmosphere of the Falleaf allotment that sits along Cotton
Creek just a few miles northeast of Copan. Most families stay for the
long weekend at the family-specific camps located on the north and
west sides of the powwow arena. My host for the event had offered
to let me to stay at his camp, and I gladly accepted the invitation.
Living space was a valuable commodity at this most crowded of
Delaware events, and I was grateful to my host for giving me a space
to set up my tent.[1]

Although I thought that I would never find my destination in the
maze of small drives and courts that led to the various family camps,
the directions I had been given were exact, and I pulled right up to

the correct lot. After some conversation my host showed me where I could set up my tent for the long powwow weekend. With my tent put up, I returned to the camp's main shelter, took a place at one of the picnic tables, and was soon engaged in conversation. Friends and relatives from all over the country were reuniting, unpacking, and setting up tents of their own. As each visitor arrived at my host's camp, the newcomers were deluged with food to the point that many often left with covered paper plates full of fry bread, meat, and cookies. Sometimes people arrived with food from other camps, but they were reminded that they had to eat something before they left the current camp.

That night after the sun went down I accompanied my host to the large open arena that now serves as the location for the dance events of the Delaware Powwow. On the way to the arena we passed other family camps as they were concluding their own meals and cleaning up for the night. Conversations, stories, jokes, and bursts of laughter were common as we said our hellos to the different families at various camps along the way, each lit by the glow from campfires and sixty-watt bulbs. It was a soothing atmosphere of hospitality and camaraderie on what had become a comfortably warm late spring dusk, and I began to understand why so many folks looked forward to this highly anticipated Delaware event.

With the scent of fires heavy in the air and the muffled voices of reuniting friends and relatives audible in the background, my host and I approached the central arena that was to be the location for the upcoming social dances. I found my seat at one of the folding chairs on the outside of the arena that had been set out earlier by my host camp. In the waning twilight I watched as a handful of men dressed in cowboy boots, blue jeans, button-up shirts, and straw hats converged on the middle of the arena. Among the men were the chief of the Delaware Tribe, my host, and other prominent leaders within the community. They carried wood shavings, a few logs for firewood, and a flint in order to prepare a fire for the upcoming social dances. As the men lit the fire, families from the surrounding camps responded to the cue and began gathering around the arena in their own folding chairs set just outside the arena. With the fire lit, the chief gave an invocation in Lenape, which he then translated into English for those assembled. Everyone stood during the prayer, the men removed their hats, and we all bowed our heads. On a still night with a chorus of crickets providing the background, that rural space and the Delaware audience that filled it seemed to welcome back the nearly forgotten words and intonations of the Delaware language. Though few in the audience could speak or even understand the language used in the prayer, it was as if everybody was comforted by a familiar voice from their collective pasts as both young and old remained attentive to every word.

Following the prayer, everyone returned to their seats while a few singers who had helped with the fire now ablaze in the middle of the arena took their spots on a lonely wooden bench set at the edge of the arena. As the singers began tuning the water drum for the upcoming dance, a man seated to my right leaned over to me and offered his own commentary on the night's events. In a hushed tone he whispered, "That's neat to have a chief that can speak the language. It's not often that you see that these days; most chiefs can't speak their own language." I agreed and shook my head with a smile. It was indeed moving to hear Lenape spoken in such surroundings. The social dances soon commenced, and most everyone gathered around the arena joyously participated. The laughter and conversation that had spilled into the arena from the camps was muffled only by the resonant beat of the water drum, the rhythmic shuffle of the shell shakers, and the captivating voices of the singers.

Even as an outsider it was not difficult for me to sense the importance that such endeavors had for the Delaware. Everyone in attendance wanted Delaware practices to remain a part of the contemporary world and looked eagerly to a select group of Delaware leaders who were willing to take on such an ominous responsibility. As my familiarity with the Delaware increased, it became evident that leadership and governance for the Delaware was a complex phenomenon that could not simply be equated with election victories or holding a tribal office. As I look back on my first experience at Family Night, I realize now that the men in that arena who were both elected and non-elected leaders were tasked with a tremendous responsibility that had not been taken lightly. That select group who were seated on the edge of the arena just outside of the fire's glow was attempting to continue and complete a monumental task. Not only were they the primary performers of Delaware song, dance, and prayer at tribal events, but those few men were also active participants in the effort to maintain federal recognition for the Delaware Tribe that was then being challenged by the Cherokee Nation.

Accomplishing and sustaining independence from the Cherokee Nation has long been a primary goal of the Delaware Tribe. Since removal to Indian Territory, Delaware Big House leaders, the Delaware Business Committee, and today the Delaware Tribal Council have asserted their sovereignty and right to self-determination while remaining attentive to the needs and desires of their Delaware constituency. As documented in chapter 4, earlier forms of Delaware government accomplished such a task with a bicameral structure consisting of the Delaware Business Committee working in conjunction with the federal government while the Big House leadership focused on attending to the needs of the local Indian world. By the 1960s both the Big House and Christian lineages looked to the newly organized Delaware Business Committee and Grievance Committee for leadership and thus expected that the needs of both worlds would be met by the newly elected government. Those men who had prepared the fire and were taking on the leadership role at Family Night were the next generation of elected Delaware leadership and were now looked to for shouldering the burden of providing guidance in the effort to maintain federal recognition.[2]

The history and unique qualities of Delaware tribal government in the modern era are thus explored in this chapter. The first section describes the leadership expectations from the Delaware perspective. I begin with an interpretation of the Delaware ideal for leadership by which contemporary leaders are judged. Delaware leaders are expected to be attentive to the needs of the group that they were chosen to represent and move only after receiving collective approval. While tribal leadership comes with certain expectations, prospective candidates must also consider the contemporary structure and voting behavior of the tribal constituency. Obtaining and remaining in tribal office is the second issue explored as getting elected to tribal office has required potential candidates to win what has become the increasingly significant absentee vote as a consequence of the demographic shifts described in the previous chapter. While most absentee voters do not live in the immediate vicinity of Delaware Country, the absentee vote is not divorced from local-level politics as most voters are linked by one or more lineage representatives who remain active in the Delaware community. Thus getting elected requires the support of a select group of locally active lineage representatives who possess a large absentee voting kinship network. Since support from the local lineage leaders is needed, such local backing requires candidates and elected leaders to try to uphold the ideals of Delaware leadership. The third section of the chapter provides a history of the significant restructuring done to the Delaware tribal government during the self-determination era in order to remain independent from the Cherokee Nation while continuing to have access to the significant land claims awards. The final section focuses on the history of tribal leadership and discusses the relatively recent balance between Christian and Big House representatives on the tribal government during the years of restored recognition, a coming together that can be traced to the shifts in tribal government that began with the land claims awards in the 1970s. It is argued here that the financial and political security allowed by control over the Delaware Trust Fund and later federal recognition brought into office more voices from the separatist-minded leaders whose views toward the Cherokee Nation were associated with the Big House community's opposition to removal and Cherokee membership. When such Big House–aligned leaders were unsuccessful in maintaining acknowledgment against Cherokee challenges, the absentee voters shifted their support and sided with the leadership that held a more diplomatic posture toward the Cherokee Nation, a political strategy associated with the Christian communities who were more open to removal and Cherokee membership. It is shown here that while the Delaware tribal government may have shifted in organization, leadership, and voting constituency over the past thirty years, community expectations for a leadership that can maintain Delaware independence have not changed.

VANQUISHING THE FISH

Leadership for the Delaware is a position that comes with certain expectations. The archetypical figurehead is a humble and thoughtful leader who possesses the ability to resolve problems while holding community approval. Chiefs are expected to conduct themselves differently, have a stable and agreeable temperament, and never show anger or impatience (Howard 1981:105). One story that is told only by the Delaware illustrates the way in which leadership is approached by the Delaware (Bierhorst 1995:8). This story was told by Charlie Elkhair, and his telling provides insight into the Delaware leadership ideal.

In "The Big Fish and the Sun," Elkhair tells the story about a young girl who gave birth to a fish (Bierhorst 1995:47–56).[3] Perplexed by the conceived fish but not wanting to cause a stir, the girl's mother found a small puddle and left the fish in the water. Over time, the fish continued to swim in an expanding circle, and soon the puddle and the fish grew to an enormous size. The problematic fish continued to get larger, and soon it started eating people when they came near. The chiefs held a council and decided that no one among them could kill the fish. So the chiefs offered a reward for whoever could kill the fish.

A very poor old woman heard of the reward and told her two grandsons. One of the grandsons assured her that he could kill the fish. The old lady took her grandsons to the place where the chiefs were gathered, and the chiefs agreed to follow the boy's plan. That night the boys returned home, and after waiting for their grandmother to go to sleep, one boy suggested that they enlist the help of their friend the sun. The boys agreed, and one boy turned himself into a raven and the other into a pigeon. Since the pigeon could not fly to the home of the sun, the raven had to periodically help him on their journey. Once at the home of the sun, the boys were given a pile of the sun's ashes to battle the fish. The boys returned with the ashes and continued counseling together while trying different options.

After seeing how the fish ignored the butterfly, one boy turned himself into a butterfly and flew to the middle of the lake while the other boy dove to the bottom. The butterfly sprinkled ashes over the middle of the lake, and the boy at the bottom of the lake released his ashes at the same time. After setting the trap of ashes the boys returned home and fell asleep in front of the fireplace. When the old lady awoke she assumed that the boys did not complete their chore, and she chastised them for their laziness. But when the boys showed her the parched fish in the middle of a dry lake, the old lady was pleased and informed the rest of the tribe of the slain fish. The boys were rewarded and later became great men in the tribe.

The mythical feat of vanquishing the all-consuming fish is metaphoric of the Delaware ideal for leadership on a number of levels and describes how such delicate issues should be resolved. First evident in the story is the Delaware ideal for conflict resolution. The fish represents an unfortunate problem that has beset the tribe, and the best way to deal with the issue is to put the fish in some remote location so that it can be ignored. However, when the fish grows so large and begins eating people, then it becomes a problem that can no longer be pushed aside and must be solved. This same story told almost a century ago could be metaphoric for the problem that the Cherokee Nation presents for the Delaware Tribe today. When the Cherokee Nation did not threaten the integrity of the Delaware Tribe, the issue of the Delaware's inclusion within the Cherokee Nation was largely ignored. However, the modern turn in federal policy has inflated the issue and is allowing the Cherokee Nation to challenge the very existence of the Delaware Tribe's federal acknowledgment. Thus, the Delaware are now faced with their own all-consuming fish and look to contemporary leaders to solve the problem.

When problems can no longer be ignored and must be solved, then there are ideal characteristics that are used to help identify leaders. First, everyone is a potential leader including even young adults. Most feel confident in their abilities to perform certain tasks, but the people who move in and out of leadership positions are those willing to step forward and take on the responsibility as illustrated by the boys' willingness to take on a task needed by the tribe. The potential for everyone to lead thus gives Delaware society a relatively egalitarian feel. Community leaders are those who shoulder and carry out the chores desired by the group. Whether the goal is a successful social dance on family night or the Delaware Tribe's federal recognition, the individuals in leadership positions are chosen because they are willing to take on a responsibility, not because they inherited the position. Leadership is not a birthright or an ascribed status but a position that is achieved through one's own actions. The chosen leader will be the person within the tribe who has a plan for completing a needed task. In the big fish story, the recognized chiefs did not have an answer but were willing to let the boys take on the responsibility because they had a plan. However, willingness is not the only requirement. Potential leaders must be considered capable of completing the goal before being allowed to perform such duties. Community sanction is vital to Delaware leadership, and potential leaders must be able to demonstrate to the membership that they have a competent plan for completing a particular task.

Another message within the story is that the best way to deal with problems that will not go away is by carefully considering all options before moving forward. The boys had an initial plan for vanquishing the fish but sat back and carefully observed the actions of the fish before attempting to complete the task. Likewise, Delaware leaders are expected to move and speak with care when dealing with important issues. Actions that appear too hasty or rash are highly criticized and can lead to the loss of community support. The etiquette for resolving conflict is always through careful consideration, and this approach continues to inform contemporary leadership in the Delaware community. The most respected individuals are those who are able to solve conflict either through thoughtful deliberation and working together or by finding innovative ways to fit the demands of all relevant parties. It is important for respected leaders to move slowly and always with humility. A sense of companionship among leaders is also important. The two brothers' coordinated efforts in planning, getting to the sun, and vanquishing the fish were cooperative efforts. The willingness to learn from others is valued and exemplified in the chiefs listening to the boys and in the boys seeking help from the sun and then watching the butterfly for clues. Cooperation is an important quality for Delaware leaders to possess and can help bring consensus on what can be important issues that are creating divisions within the tribe.

A final interpretation that can be inferred from the story is that once the boys accepted the responsibility, it was their task to accomplish. When the grandmother suspected that the boys were neglecting their duties, it was her rightful action to chastise her grandsons even though no one else in the tribe had a plan for dealing with the fish. Because group approval is considered critical to Delaware sensibilities, the group also feels that when a person is not doing what he or she promised, the failing leader should be replaced or simply not supported. At cultural gatherings such disapproval is voiced through lack of participation and support. In formal contexts such as on the tribal government, perceived low-performing leaders are formally removed from office although such extreme measures are rare. In most cases elected officials who face informal social controls such as avoidance and gossip remove themselves from the tribal government on their own accord rather than continue to work for a disapproving constituency.

One man in particular exemplifies the ideals of informal community leadership, and a description of his leadership qualities concludes my comments on Delaware tribal leadership expectations. The Delaware leader whom I use as an example first introduced himself to me as "Chief of the Delawares." Although the introduction was in jest as the man was not the chief, his greeting was typical of his good-humored personality. He is a man who is always ready with a firm handshake, a funny story, and a sincere lecture. He loves his mother, his family, his tribe, and his country (I would assume in that order) and participates in every Delaware event that his work schedule allows. On more than one occasion he single-handedly brought consensus on the Delaware Tribal Council simply by choosing one side or attempting to find a middle ground on which all could agree. He was often recognized at family events and was usually asked to speak. His was a power inspired and guided by the community he served. He was elected to the Tribal Council during the years of restored federal recognition, but as a result of family and work obligations he was later forced to resign his position.

The events that took place during this community leader's resignation from the Tribal Council, however, illustrate well the degree to
which the Delaware look to such individuals for leadership. A resignation from the Tribal Council can only take place with a formal motion
from someone on the Tribal Council. The resigning council member
was not present at the Tribal Council meeting but asked that the chief
introduce his motion to resign on his behalf. After reading a letter
of resignation, the chief asked for someone to second the motion
so that it could go to a vote. None of the council members wanted
to accept the resignation and second the motion. After a long and
uncomfortable silence, one of the members begrudgingly seconded
the motion but indicated that the Tribal Council should send the
man a note of appreciation and thanks. The resignation passed so
that the meeting could proceed, but the motion was accepted with
an unspoken disapproval.

Leadership is thus influenced by such norms in Delaware society
and takes the form of elected representatives as well as informal community leadership. Not all recognized leaders are elected to a tribal
office, and some local leaders have chosen not to participate on the
tribal government at all. Non-elected prominent individuals in the
Delaware community are identifiable because of their charismatic
personalities and substantial social and kin-based support. Such non-
elected individuals are generally present at most tribal functions and
are important to political action in the Delaware community as they
are often looked to by their kin group for direction on important
issues. Although such informal leadership positions are not inherited
and may not even be sought, it is an informal office that everyone
recognizes and respects. Such local leaders can hold tremendous
influence on political decisions because of the socio-familial networks
that look to such leaders for guidance. Unfortunately for some in the
Delaware community, informal forms of leadership recognized by
the Delaware are not recognized by the federal government unless

the respected individual seeks and holds an elected position. Getting (and staying) elected in the Self-Determination Era, however, introduces a new dimension to Delaware political life.

GETTING ELECTED

As explained in the previous chapter, demographic shifts in the Delaware Tribe during the 1970s brought about a much larger and nonlocal Delaware population. The Delaware Tribe's enrollment director reported (e-mail to author, May 31, 2001) that in 2001 the Delaware population was over 10,000 tribal members with 2,077 living in the Delaware Five-County Service Area, another 1,517 living in Oklahoma beyond the service area, and 6,488 outside the state. The largest number of those members not resident in Oklahoma live in California, Kansas, or Texas, but the Delaware Tribe does have members living in almost every state (Weslager 1978:251).[4] The dispersed nature of the Delaware Tribe's membership means that approximately 80 percent of the potential voting constituency lives outside of the Delaware Tribe's home region.

Because the Delaware Tribe is so widely distributed, the governing documents allow absentee voting and vest supreme authority in the adult voting membership, a constituency that includes all adult members of the Delaware Tribe regardless of residence. The adult voting membership is also referred to as the General Council, and every year a General Council meeting is held on a Saturday during the month of November, but special General Council meetings have been convened in order to address emergent and time-sensitive issues. A General Council is defined as any meeting during which the voting members of the Delaware Tribe of Indians assemble in one geographic location to conduct tribal business. General Council meetings are held in Delaware Country and are commonly convened either in Bartlesville or Dewey, although some councils have been held in Tulsa. While tribal elections and referendums do not have to take place in the General Council meeting, they have consistently been held simultaneously in smaller rooms adjacent to the large conference room in which the General Council is held.

As the adult voting membership, the General Council is therefore potentially composed of both resident and nonresident members of the Delaware Community as identified in chapter 4. The daily operations of the tribal government and programs as well as important social and religious institutions and events are the responsibility of the core resident group. The local residents are more likely to benefit from tribally run programs as well as to be impacted when the same programs are lost, moved, or discontinued. Most resident Delaware community members vote in person at tribal elections and referendums, and thus their votes are tallied as walk-in votes. The nonresident Delaware community members who live outside of Delaware Country either in other regions of Oklahoma or in another state may or may not attend the General Council meeting. Individuals living beyond Delaware Country are often not immediately affected by the loss or attainment of tribal programs although they possess the same political and economic rights as local community members. The kinship relationship between the local residents and their nonresident Delaware relatives can be a persuasive force. Usually an elder member of a large extended family remains politically and socially active in the resident community, and the members of the national kinship network attached to the individual are encouraged to vote in ways consistent with the locally active family member. Nonresident voters are more likely to vote using the absentee ballot system. Absentee voters simply request that an absentee ballot be mailed to them, and then they return the completed ballot to the Delaware Election Committee. Thus, one person in the resident group can potentially hold considerable electoral power if he or she has the support of a vast and reliably mobilized nonresident absentee kinship network. While the two groups differ proportionately, with there being fewer local community voters than nonresident absentee voters, there is a balance of power in that members of the resident group hold considerable influence among the absentee nonresident population.

The need for backing from the local lineage leaders is thus very important to Delaware politics and is taken into account by tribal leaders and constituents when campaigning for office. It is general knowledge that members of extended Delaware families tend to vote in common blocks and are heavily influenced by those family members in the resident community. Support from a resident group member with a large, active family constituency is thus important for potential candidates as such local support translates into a much larger number of votes that can be activated by the recommendation from a locally active family member. Campaigning for tribal office is thus undertaken with the consideration of the connection between local community members and their extensive nonresident kinship networks.

Beyond soliciting the approval of active lineage leaders in the local community, candidates also employ three different campaign strategies in hopes of gaining support among the dispersed Delaware constituency. One popular medium for reaching the widespread Delaware voting membership is to campaign through the mail. Candidates often mail out profile fliers that include the candidate's picture and positions on important issues such as federal recognition, economic development, and cultural preservation. Another mailed campaign form is the quarterly published *Delaware Indian News*. Candidates choosing to announce that they are running for tribal office can purchase advertisement space (the cost for a one-page advertisement was $300 in 2003). Mailed-out fliers and campaign ads in the tribal newspaper often include a list of Delaware families from whom the candidate has received support. One Delaware chief's newspaper ad, for instance, listed three families supporting his re-election, all of whom were the families of a former chief or Business Committee chairman of the Delaware Tribe. The Internet is another important means through which candidates and supporters seek to inform resident and nonresident voters of current issues and their bids for candidacy. Several online forums and lists exist to keep interested members up-to-date and provide the space for lively debates between those who would otherwise not have the opportunity to do so.

The absentee vote is thus gained when a potential candidate can obtain the support of local family leaders or is able to persuade nonlocal residents through mailings, newspaper ads in the *Delaware Indian News,* or online campaigning. As one long-time Trust Board and Tribal Council member explained to me, "I don't have any support in Bartlesville; all of my votes come from absentee voters, most of which are family or friends of the family." Securing the absentee vote has become increasingly important in recent years and has emerged as the crucial factor in recent elections in the twenty-first century. More absentee votes have been cast each election, and the importance of the absentee vote continues to grow. In the most recent elections of 2002 and 2006, there were far more absentee votes than walk-in votes. More than 2.5 times the number of absentee voters participated in the 2006 election compared with the 2002 election. During the same time the number of walk-in voters decreased by more than 50 percent yet remained within the range of 100–400 voters, reflecting the stability in the size of the resident Delaware community. Thus, the percentage of absentee versus walk-in ballots increased from 66 percent of the vote in 2002 to 86 percent of the vote in 2006. In both elections the winner of the absentee vote was also the winner of the election, yet the absentee vote was a much more important factor in the 2006 election. Gaining the support of the absentee vote either through a few local leaders with large, nonresident extended families or through the newspaper, fliers, and the Internet has become the key to winning an elected position in the Delaware Tribe.

Although the absentee vote represents the vast majority of the voting membership, the local family members hold the most influence over their large kin-based electorates. Getting elected may require the candidate's ability to persuade local opinion, and remaining in office once elected also requires the support of the same local leaders. Thus, elected leaders must sustain local support in order to remain in office and hold influence with the absentee vote, which often obliges the candidate to be attentive to Delaware leadership ideals that may or may not be consistent with the requirements imposed by the BIA.

DELAWARE TRIBE AND SELF-DETERMINATION

Detailed in the following section are the recent shifts in the structure of the Delaware tribal government as the tribal leadership continued to push for the right to self-determination under the new federal policy. Such movement within the tribal government has been the result of the changes in the Delaware Tribe's ongoing relationship with the federal government, while the alterations made have remained consistent with Delaware's existing political practices. The Delaware felt the most pressure to change from the Cherokee Nation, which influenced the BIA to terminate the Delaware Tribe in 1979 and subsequently sought control over the remaining portions of the Delaware's land claim awards. Thus, the shifts in the Delaware Tribe's government explained below were carried out in order to preserve the Delaware Tribe in response to the Cherokee Nation's challenges while moving forward in a way consistent with community expectations.

The Delaware Business Committee's efforts under the Indian Claims Commission brought an unforeseen dilemma as to how the money awarded would be spent, invested, and administered; an issue that allowed the struggle between the Delaware Tribe and the Cherokee Nation to resurface. Amid the decisions to award the Delaware Tribe more than 12 million dollars for their unsettled land claims,

Delaware tribal members were called to a series of General Council meetings from 1970 to 1972. The meetings took place at the Dewey Fairgrounds, and the primary issue was to adopt a plan of action for the distribution of the funds from the awarded land claims (Carrigan and Chambers 1994:41–42; Weslager 1972:462). Two opinions existed among the General Council over how the award should be spent. Some favored distributing all of the money to tribal members through per capita payments, while others supported a plan to save 10 percent for the operation of tribal government and distribute the remaining 90 percent through per capita payments (Weslager 1972:462–463). The 10 percent plan, as the latter strategy would be called, was eventually passed, and the U.S. Congress divided the money accordingly in their appropriation (Carrigan and Chambers 1994:40). In 1977 the BIA finally distributed 90 percent of the award to the Delaware on a per capita basis and kept the remaining 10 percent in trust for the Delaware Business Committee. The 10 percent of the judgment fund withheld would be identified as the program fund or Delaware Trust Fund and would later include other pending awards. The 10 percent plan was not without opposition, and those who did not support the plan turned to the Cherokee Nation. A Delaware tribal member employed by the Cherokee Nation appealed the 10 percent plan and challenged the Delaware Business Committee's ability to protect the tribe's interests (Carrigan and Chambers 1994:62–63; Seneca 1979).

It was at this point that Cherokee claims to authority over the Delaware Tribe and the Delaware Trust Fund surfaced as the stakes of recognition increased in the late 1970s and a new Cherokee chief was elected following the Keeler administration. Consider, for instance, this Delaware elder's recollection of the origins of the current struggle with the Cherokee Nation:

CONSULTANT: You know, when we started the CHR program, Committee Health Representatives program, that I worked in, you
   know, when it came about, we . . . I forget now who wrote the first

proposal for a CHR program, but anyway, I know that I wrote one from then on until we've . . . until Ross Swimmer, you know, he was responsible for taking away our programs that we had and federal recognition and everything else, you know. But at the time, when we had the first CHR program was going, W. W. Keeler, he was Cherokee, chief of the Cherokee Nation at that time.

OBERMEYER: And his family is from around here, right?

CONSULTANT: He would ask about that program, operating a program with the Cherokee Nation, you know, he said, it didn't make any difference to him, as long as the people were being served, you know. But uh, Swimmer, when he became chief, he didn't feel that way about it. He thought everything should belong to the Cherokee, that it was under Cherokee Nation, you know, programs and all, you know, whoever ran those programs, you know. And he didn't go for that, this contracting for the same programs that they had over there, you know, at the Cherokee Nation.

OBERMEYER: And you did that until Ross became the chief.

CONSULTANT: Until Ross Swimmer put a halt to it.

OBERMEYER: So it sounds like, and I've never heard this, but before Ross, the Cherokees and the Delawares politically got along pretty well?

CONSULTANT: Before, you know, when Keeler was chief of the Cherokee Nation, everyone got along.

From this consultant's memory we are introduced to the origins of the pivotal role that health care seemed to play in the modern Cherokee-Delaware dispute. Providing adequate health care services to the local Indian population was and continues to be of primary concern for both the Delaware Tribe and the Cherokee Nation. As early as 1974 the Delaware Business Committee was operating a Community Health Representatives (CHR) program as well as seeking to establish a health care center in Nowata to provide medical and dental service from a central location in Delaware Country (Carrigan and Chambers 1994:44). The man quoted above served as the director for the CHR program, and he explains the collaboration that existed with the then chief of the Cherokee Nation, W. W. Keeler, who was not concerned about which tribe ran the CHR program as long as it was providing the needed services. The quoted passage is clear, however, on the shift that took place in the relationship between the Delaware Tribe and the Cherokee Nation after Ross Swimmer was elected principal Cherokee chief in 1976. The CHR director's recollection is indeed accurate as Chief Swimmer did petition the BIA and demand that the Delaware not be treated as a separate tribe (Swimmer 1977). Swimmer's position was quite clear and spelled out in correspondence and meetings with the Indian Health Service (IHS) and the BIA (Swimmer 1977, 1978; Farring 1978). Swimmer's position was that the Delaware Tribe was not entitled to recognition as a tribe and thus was not eligible to contract for services under the Self-Determination Act (Swimmer 1977). Furthermore, Swimmer considered the Cherokee Nation as responsible for the administration of such self-determination program services to the Delaware and should hold oversight on the operations of the Delaware Business Committee (Swimmer 1978). Chief Swimmer even went so far as to insist that the Cherokee Nation, not the Delaware Business Committee, should hold oversight on, and administer the trust fund from, the Delaware's successful land claims awards, and he was apparently willing to take the BIA to court if his position was not met (Swimmer 1978; Carrigan and Chambers 1994:56).

Swimmer's ability to influence the BIA's stance toward Delaware recognition did not disappear after he stepped down as Cherokee chief in 1985. Swimmer was subsequently appointed as assistant secretary of Indian affairs by Ronald Reagan from 1985 to 1989 and later appointed by George W. Bush as a special trustee of American Indians in 2003 following his work with the Office of Indian Trust Transition that began in 2001 (Results.gov 2007). Ironically, as assistant secretary, Swimmer would have had the final authority to halt Delaware acknowledgment through the BIA's Federal Acknowledgment Process, and his service on the issue of Indian trust moneys would have also given him oversight on the Delaware Trust Fund. Considering that Swimmer would later hold such high-ranking positions within the Department of Interior, it is indeed understandable that the Delaware Tribe was and remains hesitant to pursue acknowledgment through the FAP or executive branch.

Influenced by an appeal from those Delaware opposed to the 10 percent plan and facing the mounting pressure from Swimmer, the BIA terminated the Delaware Tribe's government-to-government relationship by leaving the Delaware off of the first list of federally recognized tribes (Carrigan and Chambers 1994:40–41). The Delaware Trust Fund thus remained in the hands of the BIA, and the now-terminated Delaware Business Committee could not access the money awarded to them. The BIA informed the Delaware Business Committee that because of termination the Delaware would have to define their membership in relation to the Cherokee Nation in order to hold acknowledgment and thus have access to the Delaware Trust Fund. The Delaware Business Committee refused to adopt such incorporative language and remained unrecognized and without access to the substantial Delaware Trust Fund (Carrigan and Chambers 1994:70–71).

While most Delaware supported the 10 percent plan, they also understood the implications of the BIA's position. If the Delaware defined their membership in relation to the Cherokee Nation, such a redefinition would give the Cherokee Nation ultimate jurisdictional authority over Delaware constituents. However, the 10 percent plan was adopted to provide the tribal government with a financial base in order to operate at a minimal capacity. Faced with a difficult decision, Delaware leaders explored different possibilities that would allow them to access the Delaware Trust Fund while remaining independent of the Cherokee Nation. The Delaware Tribe eventually adopted a unique form of tribal government in order to survive financially as well as remain responsive to the Delaware's long-standing resistance to Cherokee membership.

During the self-determination era, the Delaware undertook a significant restructuring in the tribal government that continued the Delaware tradition of two governmental bodies principally organized to meet separate yet overlapping positions on Cherokee membership. The first step was to reform the Delaware Business Committee, which was restructured and replaced with a tribal council form of government in 1982 that lacked a separate Grievance Committee. The Delaware Tribal Council consisted of seven members including a chief, assistant chief, secretary, treasurer, and three additional members. All positions were to be filled by voting members of the Delaware Tribe and elected by secret ballot. Each member including the chief served four-year terms, and there were no term limits. Elections were held every two years, with the chief and three members elected during one election and the three other members elected at the subsequent election. The Delaware Constitution establishing the Tribal Council defined Delaware tribal membership as all persons whose names were included on the 1904 Delaware Per Capita Roll and their descendants. No mention was made of Delaware membership in the Cherokee Nation (Delaware Tribe of Indians 1982). The Tribal Council, however, continued to lobby for tribal acknowledgment, often at their own personal expense, but it was repeatedly denied because of their unwillingness to define the Delaware membership in relation to the Cherokee Nation; a position on Cherokee membership that was consistent with the post-removal Big House platform. Despite concerted efforts, it soon became clear that the BIA would not release the Delaware Trust Fund unless the Delaware defined their membership in relationship to the Cherokee Nation.

The Tribal Council thus moved to another option in order to remain separate from the Cherokee Nation while also gaining access to the Delaware Trust Fund. The Tribal Council dropped the possibility of changing the 1982 constitution and simply added an entirely new governing body whose organizing document would include language that would meet the requirements set forth by the BIA and would thus follow in the tradition of the post-removal Christian platform of tolerating the possibility of Cherokee membership in order to obtain political and economic resources that were rightfully theirs. The Delaware Trust Document, as it would later be called, was passed in 1991 and established the Delaware Trust Board for the purpose of administering the Delaware Trust Fund. By the time that the Delaware Trust Board was established, the trust fund from the 10 percent withheld totaled approximately 3.8 million dollars. The Trust Document defined tribal membership with the same language as in the 1982 constitution but added an extra line stating, "and who are also members of (or eligible for membership with) the Cherokee Nation of Oklahoma through the Cherokee Dawes Commission Rolls" (Delaware Tribe of Indians 1991). The Delaware Trust Board did not replace the Tribal Council but was created as a complementary governing body tasked only with oversight of the Delaware Trust Fund. The Trust Document provided the BIA with the membership language it required, and access to the Trust Fund was handed over to the newly organized Delaware Trust Board. The Delaware thus maintained the Tribal Council that sustained its position as completely separate from the Cherokee Nation while also being able to access the Trust Fund through the Trust Board that allowed for the possibility of Delaware enrollment in the Cherokee Nation.

The Delaware Trust Board consisted of a chairman and six members, all of whom were to be registered members of the Delaware Tribe. The chairman and each board member were elected by secret ballot and served four-year terms. Elections were staggered and were held every two years so that three board positions were open for each regularly held two-year election. There were no term limits for trust board members or the chairman. The Trust Board was responsible for the administration of the Delaware Trust Fund but was also subject to the authority of the Delaware General Council (Delaware Tribe of Indians 1990). Once the Delaware Trust Board was established, the elected representatives adopted a master plan for the distribution of the judgment fund in order to support tribal programs and services while maintaining a principal of 3.8 million dollars upon which interest would accrue annually. The annual interest would then be the principal Trust Board budget for each year in order to perpetually maintain tribal operations at a minimal level (a conservative 5 percent interest estimate gives a tribal budget of $190,000 annually). The program distribution included the establishment of the following tribal programs: Community Service (25 percent), Economic Development (25 percent), Education (20 percent), Tribal Operations (10 percent), Reinvestment (10 percent), Land Management (5 percent), and Cultural Preservation (5 percent) (Delaware Tribe of Indians 1991).

The Trust Board's establishment alongside what was then the nonrecognized Tribal Council, while a recent innovation, can also be set against an existing precedent of a bicameral governmental structure that dates to removal. The Trust Board was established through concessions to the Cherokee Nation for the singular purpose of access to the Delaware Trust Fund. The Tribal Council, however, remained independent of the Cherokee Nation and continued to work toward federal recognition in order to secure the independence of the Delaware Tribe. Thus the Tribal Council was able to hold to the stance against Cherokee membership and maintain a completely independent position while the new Delaware Trust Board was established with the possibility for Cherokee membership in order to look after the social and financial needs of the community.

Although the Trust Board had to adopt inclusive language, creating the new governing body to administer the funds also protected the Tribal Council's ability to function separately and gave the Delaware Tribe access to the interest from millions of dollars, a small portion of which was earmarked for cultural preservation.

In reality, the Trust Board was not much different in composition than the Tribal Council. Though completely separate in charter, the members of the Tribal Council were and continue to be elected to the Trust Board as well, making the two structures different more in scope than in membership. At times the chief of the Delaware Tribe has also served as the Trust Board chairman. Tribal Council members as well as Trust Board members can serve on both governing bodies at the same time, and some campaign to do so. The Trust Board and Tribal Council are so similar in representation that tribal members often speak of both as different sides of the Delaware tribal government. It is not unusual to hear tribal members speak of business or activities that take place on the Tribal Council side or the Trust Board side, or debate which body should handle a particular issue or program.

The Tribal Council continued to push for federal recognition after the establishment of the Trust Board, and its efforts were eventually awarded with federal recognition in 1996. It is important to point out that the Delaware Tribal Council was federally recognized in 1996 as a body separate from the Delaware Trust Board and with the membership criteria established in the 1982 constitution that did not specify the potential for Delaware membership in the Cherokee Nation. Thus, the Tribal Council was recognized as a federally recognized tribal government without defining its membership with respect to the Cherokee Nation. The 1996 recognition allowed elected leaders more security, and they moved forward with tribal programs as an independent tribe under self-determination policy. The Trust Board remained but was then a separate body organized within an acknowledged tribe. The two governmental bodies thus remained separate in purpose and positions on Cherokee membership, yet the Trust Board and Tribal Council would ultimately be subject to the review and oversight of the Delaware General Council.

The Delaware Tribe that was judicially terminated in 2004 was thus a political structure situated in a legacy of Delaware governance based on two overlapping and complementary bodies that represented the interests of the Delaware Tribe, which is still divided on the issue of Cherokee enrollment. The prospect of denying Delaware sovereignty and placing the Delaware Tribe under Cherokee jurisdiction in order to access the Delaware Trust Fund was not a route that most Delaware were willing to accept. Thus, a new governing body that allowed for Cherokee enrollment established alongside the existing Delaware Tribal Council in the early 1990s provided the Delaware Tribe with their rightful access to the Delaware Trust Fund without conceding the Tribal Council to Cherokee authority. Restored recognition of the Delaware Tribal Council subsequently allowed for the centralization of tribal government and provided the tribe with a more secure footing. Thus, Delaware tribal government in the self-determination era is a story of how the Delaware remained politically independent from the Cherokee Nation by sustaining a complex form of tribal government divided on the issue of membership but consistent with the governing system that had worked for the Delaware since before Oklahoma statehood.

TRIBAL LEADERSHIP

The more recent years under self-determination have also witnessed a historical shift in the composition of those elected to tribal office. Leadership on the Delaware Business Committee and later the Tribal Council was generally drawn from the Christian Delaware families throughout most of the twentieth century. An interregnum in Christian leadership has occurred since the early 1990s during which time

Chairmen and chiefs	Location/family	Tenure in office
John Conner, Chief	Alluwe/Conner	1856–1872
James Ketchum, Chief	Ketchum/Ketchum	1872
James Conner, Chief	Alluwe/Conner	1873–1877
Charles Journeycake, Chief	Alluwe/Journeycake	1877–1894
George Bullette, Chairman	Dewey/Conner-Bullette	1895–1921
John Young, Chairman	Caney River/Young	1921
Joseph Bartles, Chairman	Dewey/Journeycake	1922–1951
Horace McCracken, Chairman	Alluwe/Conner	1951–1970
Bruce Townsend, Chairman	California Creek/Miller	1971–1978
Henry Secondine, Chairman and Chief	California Creek/Secondine	1979–1982
Lewis Ketchum, Chief	Bartlesville/Ketchum	1983–1994
Curtis Zunigha, Chief	Dewey/Wilson	1994–1998
Dee Ketchum, Chief	Bartlesville/Ketchum	1998–2002
Joe Brooks, Chief	Bartlesville/Whiteturkey-Sarcoxie	2002–2005
Jerry Douglas, Chief	Alluwe/Ketchum	2005–present

1. CHAIRMEN AND CHIEFS OF THE DELAWARE TRIBE, 1856–PRESENT: A list of the chairmen and chiefs of the Delaware Tribe who have served since removal to the Cherokee Nation. The principal town and family affiliations for each chief and his years in office are also listed.

there was an increased representation from preservation-minded leaders active in the Big House–inspired events and social network of northern Washington County. While previous elected representatives have made cultural preservation a priority, it seemed that this issue became more central to the Tribal Council's work since the organization of the Trust Board and federal recognition. Explained here is the recent shift in leadership as well as a discussion for why the move took place.

Table 1 presents a list of past and present paramount leaders of the Delaware Tribe since removal. The chart clearly shows that the Delaware governing body recognized by the federal government was consistently led by those from the Christian family enclaves. The Journeycake-Conner families associated with the settlement of Alluwe steered the direction of tribal politics until shortly after World War II. Leaders from outside the Journeycake-Conner families were elected to the highest tribal office in the post-WWII era, but all were descendants of Christian families identified with either Nowata or southern Washington County. With the dawn of the self-determination era, the chairmen and chiefs representing such Christian families laid the foundations for future leaders to gain access to the land claims award and for re-establishing federal recognition. Chairman Bruce Townsend and Chiefs Henry Secondine and Lewis Ketchum were strident leaders who continued to push the BIA to recognize Delaware sovereignty and right to self-governance. It was under the guidance of Townsend, Secondine, and Ketchum that the significant Delaware land claims were awarded and the Delaware Tribal Council and Delaware Trust Board were established.[5]

The dominance of Christian families continued until recently when an interest in the political ideals and cultural practices of the Big House community were revitalized and spread among both Christian and Big House sympathizers in the 1990s. The establishment of the Delaware Trust Board under Chief Lewis Ketchum brought about the formal development of the Cultural Preservation Committee (CPC) in 1991. The CPC was given an annual budget based on the interest drawn from the Delaware Trust Fund and used the money to fund multiple cultural preservation projects including language classes, support for local social events, and the building of the Eagle Ridge Grounds. The CPC's organization came at a time in the Delaware

Tribe when the Delaware voters were beginning to look to leaders with platforms consistent with the Big House platform to serve on the Tribal Council. Chief Curtis Zunigha served from 1994 to 1998 and followed the tenure of Chief Lewis Ketchum. Zunigha's election marked the first time that a Big House descendant would hold the premier office since Delaware removal from Kansas. Chief Dee Ketchum, who followed Zunigha from 1998 to 2002, and Chief Joe Brooks, who succeeded Ketchum from 2002 to 2005, were also active in the social network of northern Washington County. Each of the last three chiefs had a decided interest in promoting Delaware cultural preservation and revitalization in the memory of the former Big House community.

The visibility of representation from the northern Washington County network on the tribal government has increased since the early 1990s and can also be inferred as an extension of the existing social trend in which Delaware from both Christian and Big House families were embracing Delaware cultural practices for the sense of traditionalism that such observances represented. The revitalized interest in Delaware cultural practices began in the midst of the land claims litigation in the 1970s as descendants from the Christian and Big House Delaware worlds began taking a more active interest in the songs, dances, and practices then sustained by a handful of Big House descendants in northern Washington County. One elderly Delaware man from a Big House family described to me the emerging interest in Delaware culture at the time. He explained, "It seems like these younger ones, you know, they didn't know much about their ancestry, you know, until later on in their life, you know. And most of them were mostly white, you know. And as soon as they found that, you know, they were part of the Delaware and whatever part that may be, they was proud of it. And I think that most of them feel that way about it, even till this day." Revitalization has thus expanded since the 1970s and has further accelerated over the past thirty-five years as the younger tribal members described by the elder above have since passed on their interest and pride to their children and grandchildren. Renewed interest continues to be characterized by more participation at local events such as the Delaware Powwow, formalized instruction in the Lenape language, and the reaffirmation of culturally unique practices such as dance, dress, and ceremonies at Delaware events. Such expressions of pride in Delaware Indian identity have remained in rural spaces of the less visible world of northern Washington County as discussed in chapter 3.

This shift toward a more preservation-minded leadership came at an important point in Delaware history and reflects the significant changes taking place in Delaware society at the time. By the early 1990s Delaware cultural preservationists had begun making their presence felt on the tribal government. Membership at the tribal leadership level became more evenly distributed between those supporting the ideals of the former Big House leadership while seeking federal recognition and economic interests. One Delaware man active in tribal government and cultural preservation efforts describes the shift in tribal leadership in the following way:

> I think it was just the base families, all the traditional folks realized that if something was gonna happen and we were going to have a part in it and we wanted to keep it the way we wanted it, then we better do something about it. So, really the power, the base shifted from the Christian side to the traditional side but today, it's kind of an amalgamation. . . . But that's what happened, a lot of the traditional folks, or I don't want to say traditional folks, maybe I should say the sons and daughters of those old traditional people, started taking positions and responsibilities in the tribe, but they had a different outlook on what should be saved and what should be cared for traditionally. That's when the shift came back to the traditional stuff.

The election of such preservation-minded chiefs and representatives thus took place in the context of the significant restructuring of the Delaware government explained in the previous section, which provided access to the Delaware Trust Fund followed by restored federal recognition in 1996. The affirmation of Delaware identity as culturally separate from the Cherokee Nation soon became an even more important aspect of tribal politics. Following renewed recognition, cultural preservation efforts were formally funded and organized through the tribal government and federal grants. It would seem that as the Delaware Tribe was achieving significant victories at the beginning of the twenty-first century, the Delaware people were becoming even more outwardly expressive of their unique tribal identity and were willing to take a more assertive position on the issues of Delaware independence and opposition to Cherokee membership.

The rising success of the Big House representation on the tribal government was delivered a difficult blow when the Cherokee appeal was successful in 2004, and Chief Brooks's administration came at a pivotal time in recent Delaware history. Chief Brooks bore the brunt of criticism for the Cherokee victory; he was removed from office and ultimately was replaced by his assistant chief, Jerry Douglas. Chief Douglas was later elected to serve as chief in 2006, and his election brought back into paramount leadership representation from the Delaware families associated with the Nowata and Chelsea regions. In the anxious years following judicial termination others sympathetic with the Christian platform were also elected to serve on the Tribal Council with the hope that they could bring back federal recognition even if doing so required negotiations with the Cherokee Nation. Today Chief Douglas and a majority of the Delaware Tribal Council and Trust Board represent the kinship networks of the Nowata and Chelsea regions, and their primary efforts are focused on the return of federal recognition as soon as possible, which at this point will likely require concessions to the Cherokee Nation. Chief Douglas's position is that the tribal government will have to fold financially if they do not work something out with the Cherokee Nation. Without federal recognition, the Delaware Tribe has relatively few resources and must use whatever energies it still has to try and regain federal recognition while dealing with the considerable resources and influence of the Cherokee Nation. Restoring federal recognition will indeed be a difficult problem to solve, and the leadership at present is poised to accomplish such a task by working with the Cherokee Nation, as it would appear that doing so will be the quickest and most efficient way to move forward.

The recent presence of representatives who were willing to take a more diplomatic approach toward the Cherokee Nation represents a move away from the less concessionary approach that characterized the years immediately prior to and during federal recognition. In retrospect, it appears that the more separatist leadership was supported when the voters felt a sense of economic security and the promise of complete tribal sovereignty that came with federal recognition. Judicial termination thus brought back to life the uncertainty of federal recognition and brought a set of representatives back into office on the basis that they could re-establish federal recognition through negotiations with the Cherokee Nation. Just as in the story "The Big Fish and the Sun," the newly elected Tribal Council has a plan to solve the Delaware's ongoing problem with the Cherokee Nation, and it is now the task of the newly elected representatives to achieve federal recognition and defeat the metaphoric all-consuming fish. However, the decisions of the contemporary Tribal Council and Trust Board are still regarded as subject to the will of the constituency that voted them into office. While the Tribal Council is now negotiating terms with the Cherokee Nation for federal recognition, such terms will still be required to meet the expectations of the local lineage leaders and the Delaware community. Therefore, current tribal leaders are fully aware that care must be taken when working with the Cherokee Nation on the issue of Delaware acknowledgment.

CONCLUSION

It is said that all politics are local, and such a statement has been shown here to certainly be true of Delaware politics. Delaware leaders recognize the importance of community sanction when in office while also trying to meet the requirements of the federal government. Local sanction for the Delaware is shaped by the Delaware ideal for leadership, and Delaware leaders are expected to be humble and thoughtful individuals who are willing to take on the responsibilities of office and have a plan for solving the issues at hand. Moving on important issues too swiftly and without proper consideration is viewed with hesitation and concern. Public service in the Delaware community has undergone alterations over the years, but certain guiding principles remain. Tribal leaders, both elected and non-elected, must gain their support from extensive kin networks and be willing to lead with deference and a cooperative spirit. The recent restructuring of Delaware tribal government was undertaken with such deference and has produced a tribal governmental structure that was able to exert complete Delaware sovereignty while also maintaining a financial base by allowing for the possibility of Cherokee membership.

Delaware leaders today who associate themselves with either a Christian-inspired platform or one inspired by the Big House tradition thus face a unique challenge as they search for ways to re-establish federal recognition while doing so in a way that is considered appropriate by the local constituency and legally acceptable by the federal government, and that can withstand challenges from the Cherokee Nation. The question that is on Delaware minds today is whether contemporary tribal leaders will be able to overcome such objections from the Cherokee Nation just as the brothers were able to vanquish the problems presented by the all-consuming fish. It remains to be seen just how the Delaware Tribe will deal with the big fish and restore federal recognition, but it is certain that the tribal leadership is dedicated to fixing the problems created by the Cherokee appeal.

While the Cherokee Nation's impact on the Delaware Tribe may be likened to the problematic fish, the most consuming aspect may not come from the court actions but from the Cherokee Nation's hold over Delaware enrollment. The most important dilemma that limited the Delaware Tribe's sovereignty from 1996 to 2004 was their constituency's dual enrollment in the Cherokee Nation, and dual enrollment continues to be a significant factor that limits the Delaware Tribe's ability to achieve complete independence as it has since removal. As enrolled members of the Cherokee Nation, the Delaware anticipate great difficulties if they pursue separate recognition according to the Federal Acknowledgment Process, and they have been told by high-ranking federal officials that they must pursue recognition through legislative action that maintains Cherokee support. The next two chapters explore this unique problem presented by Delaware enrollment in the Cherokee Nation and explain how Delaware leaders sought to solve the issue of dual enrollment during the years of restored recognition. Understanding the complexities of Delaware enrollment and why the Delaware continue to avail themselves for Cherokee enrollment when they do not see themselves as part of the Cherokee Nation is the subject of the following chapters.

6 Cherokee by Blood

The Delaware will never give up their nationality
and become mixed in the Cherokee Nation.
CHIEF ANDERSON SARCOXIE, 1867

At intermission during an afternoon Gourd Dance, I decided
to introduce myself to a Delaware family whose campground at the
powwow grounds had caught my attention earlier because of the
unique construction. The owners of the camp had taken great care
to give the appearance of a frontier-style cabin, which stood in contrast to the other camps. The standard picnic shelter format used by
everyone else had been altered into a plank board porch bordered by
a sagging cottonwood railing. I approached the cabin-style shelter and
introduced myself, naively describing that I was an anthropologist
interested in learning more about the Delaware and their relationship
with the Cherokee Nation. Laughter erupted at my introduction,
followed by some politically charged comments to which I should
have paid closer attention, but I was more interested in making sure
that I was not intruding into a family circle. To my surprise, the four
generations stopped their conversation, invited me onto the porch,
and agreed to visit with me. I was offered a chair next to the family
matriarch, who assured me that it was all right if I wanted to record
our conversation. I pushed "record" on the tape recorder and asked

how she first got her Certificate Degree of Indian Blood (CDIB) card. She responded rather frankly that she got it some time ago, "when they were signing everybody up back in Claremore. They registered me as a Delaware, because that is what I told them I was, a Delaware."

Her response confused me at first as I had already spent the past year talking with other Delaware and had yet to find any tribal member with a CDIB card that had *Delaware* listed under tribal affiliation. To my knowledge, all Delaware who enrolled through the Cherokee Nation's registration office were listed as Cherokee. So I asked, "Does it say Delaware on your CDIB card?" She responded, "On my card it had Cherokee-Delaware; Adopted Delaware." Recognizing the way in which the Delaware interpret the Cherokee CDIB label, I wanted to confirm that she did not have any Cherokee ancestors. I followed up and asked, "Are you full-blood Delaware?" She answered, "No, I am a quarter," to which her daughter immediately corrected, "You're a half, Mother." The matron agreed with her daughter, saying with some sarcasm, "I'm a half-breed, that's right. My dad was a full-blood [Delaware], and we always said we were half-breeds." As our conversation continued, it became clear that the family with whom I was talking had no Cherokee ancestry nor any desire to become Cherokee. It also became evident that the degree of blood listed on their CDIB cards was largely irrelevant to the family's kin-based identity. Like most Delaware, the matriarch and her family had Cherokee-issued CDIB cards that identified them as possessing a degree of Cherokee or Cherokee A.D. blood even though the family was not of Cherokee descent and did not equate Delaware kinship with blood degree. I soon learned that although their cabin-style camp was unique among the Delaware, their experience with the extraneous federal Indian identification process, and the Cherokee Nation's control over it, was not.

Given that the Cherokee CDIB card was essentially viewed by the

Delaware as meaningless and that the Delaware do not want to be members of the Cherokee Nation, it was indeed perplexing for me to learn that so many Delaware either owned Cherokee CDIB cards or continued to enroll for such cards even after federal recognition was restored to the Delaware Tribe. Because of the pervasiveness of card ownership and the importance of the CDIB card to the federal government's understanding of Delaware identity, it became necessary for me to explore the phenomenon of CDIB card ownership in the Delaware Tribe and the results of my work are presented here. Provided first is the history behind the CDIB card and a theoretical perspective from which to view the topic. A contemporary look at CDIB enrollment from the Delaware's experience follows to show that the CDIB has indeed become a document-based and routine process, yet the Cherokee Indian identity that comes with CDIB enrollment has not. An account of Delaware perceptions toward the Cherokee CDIB card and a discussion of the different ways in which the Delaware actually utilize the card are presented to provide a clear understanding for why the Delaware apply for and use federal Indian identification cards that mark them as Cherokee by Blood.

CHEROKEE BY BLOOD: A HISTORY

The history behind the federal Indian identification process and its impact on the legal status of Delaware people in the Cherokee Nation are outlined in this section, demonstrating that the modifications made to the federal Indian identification process during the self-determination era have actually worked against the sovereignty efforts of the Delaware Tribe while further buttressing the authority of the Cherokee Nation. Such Delaware disempowerment stems from the Cherokee Nation's administrative control over the CDIB card, which is the only identification card that provides eligible applicants proof of a federally sanctioned Indian blood quantum. The following discussion explains the origin and history behind this most powerful concept as it has been used to identify the Delaware by both the Cherokee Nation and the federal government in the modern era.

Indian blood quantum is a concept that is fundamental to the federal government's definition of Indian identity and was first developed in its present form during the late nineteenth century. The federal government maintains a variety of legal definitions for Indian identity, with most requiring that a person possess a certain degree of Indian blood or ancestry or that the person is a member of a federally recognized Indian tribe (M. Miller 2004:7, 11). Most federally recognized tribes require descent from a federally approved tribal roll or the possession of a degree of Indian blood for tribal membership, although the actual degree of Indian blood required varies from tribe to tribe (Snipp 1989:362–365; Strong and Van Winkle 1996:554–555). The concept of Indian blood is thus an important aspect of both tribal and federal definitions of Indian identity, and controlling the administration of such a central identity marker carries considerable power in the self-determination era.

The Cherokee Nation has attempted to establish Delaware citizenship through the concept of Cherokee blood for some time. As early as the late nineteenth century and before the allotment of Indian Territory, the Cherokee Nation was extending citizenship on an administrative level to all Delaware through the terms of *adoption* and *blood*. While still in Kansas, a federal roll was taken listing those Delaware who elected to relocate to Indian Territory (Weslager 1972:425–426). This 1867 Kansas Delaware Roll did not record blood quantum and listed those Indian and non-Indian tribal members who were either adopted or married into the Delaware tribe that intended to relocate to Indian Territory (Records of the Bureau of Indian Affairs 1871).[1]

According to the 1867 Cherokee-Delaware Agreement, the Delaware who were born in the Cherokee Nation were to be treated as Native Cherokees.[2] Thus, the Cherokee census of 1880 recorded those Delaware not listed on the 1867 Kansas Delaware Roll who were born in the Cherokee Nation as *Cherokee by Blood* while the older Delaware enumerated on the 1867 roll were enrolled on the 1880 census as *Cherokee by Adoption* (Records of the Bureau of Indian Affairs 1880). The distinction separated those identified as Cherokee by Adoption, who would eventually disappear with time, from the younger Cherokee by Blood children who would grow in size with each new generation. This distinction allowed the Delaware population labeled as Cherokee by Blood to increase with each Delaware child born following removal while the Cherokee by Adoption population inevitably ceased to exist. The differentiation between Cherokee by Blood and Cherokee by Adoption continued on subsequent Cherokee censuses and would become an important precedent used by the federal government during the allotment of Indian Territory and the establishment of the Cherokee Nation Dawes Roll.

The importance of quantifying the amount of a person's Indian ancestry, however, did not come from the Cherokee Nation but from the federal government. The idea of blood quantum initially developed out of a political compromise in the U.S. Congress during the implementation of allotment under the Dawes Act. The term *blood quantum* is actually an administrative fiction developed in the late nineteenth century as a crude measure of one's degree of Indian parentage and by extension presumed cultural assimilation. It was incorrectly assumed at the time that people with more Indian ancestry were also more culturally Indian and less competent to own land, while those with less Indian descent were also less culturally Indian and more competent to own land. Based on this erroneous assumption, advocates who sought to protect Indian interests and land holding saw blood quantum as a way to shield those with one-half or more Indian ancestry from the onslaught of non-Indian settlement that was sure to follow allotment (Sturm 2002:80–81). Unsympathetic legislators, on the other hand, saw that blood quantum would allow for allotment to proceed that would eventually expedite the formal assimilation of American Indians into Anglo-American society (Biolsi 1995:40–42).[3] Thus, blood quantum became the cornerstone of the federal government's legal definition of Indian identity primarily because the idea was one on which both sides of the non-Indian American political spectrum could agree.

The first time that the use of blood quantum appeared in what is today Oklahoma was during the allotment of Oklahoma and Indian Territories. The idea of blood quantum was initially introduced and had to be accepted by Indian people if they wished to individually retain a small portion of what was once tribally owned land during the process of Oklahoma statehood as outlined previously. A number of historical works have documented the allotment period in pre-statehood Oklahoma and describe how Indian residents were required to accept a blood quantum–based status in order to receive a land allotment and remain on the tribal rolls being completed at the time. Such works clearly indicate that allotment was largely unpopular among Oklahoma tribes and had very little support, but that tribal leaders were simply given no choice but to accept allotment and the blood quantum–based identities associated with it (Burns 1994; Carter 1997; Debo 1940; Hagan 2003; Holm 1979; McLaughlin 1996).

Although the issuance of blood quantum status was a universal component to allotment in Oklahoma, each tribe underwent its own specific enrollment and allotment procedures. In the Cherokee Nation the Dawes Commission was faced with the monumental task of enrolling all Cherokee citizens, including Indian and non-Indian citizens. The Cherokee Nation and the other Five Civilized Tribes refused to accept the terms of allotment, and thus Congress was compelled to terminate their recognition of the Five Tribes, including the Cherokee Nation, as described in chapter 4. With recognition terminated, the allotment of Indian Territory proceeded without delay. A collection of federal agents known as the Dawes Commission subsequently undertook the task of compiling a roll of all residents in Indian Territory to identify eligibility for allotment ownership. In 1906 the Dawes Commission completed the *Final Rolls of Citizens and Freedmen of the Five Civilized Tribes, Cherokee Nation* or the Cherokee Nation Dawes Roll as it is more commonly known (Records of the Bureau of Indian Affairs 1907), which listed the Cherokee, Shawnee, Delaware, Natchez, Creek, intermarried whites, and freedmen citizens of the Cherokee Nation. Allotment of the Cherokee Nation lands proceeded accordingly, and the Dawes Commission assigned each Indian person a land allotment and a blood quantum (Bays 1998:11; Sturm 2002:79). People identified as non-Indians such as the Cherokee freedmen and intermarried whites received land allotments in the Cherokee Nation but were not given an Indian blood quantum.

When compiling the Cherokee Nation Dawes Roll, the Dawes Commission simply borrowed the existing Cherokee protocol used for the 1880 census for enumerating the Delaware as either Cherokee by Blood or Cherokee by Adoption. Those listed as Cherokee by Blood in the previous Cherokee census were recorded on the Dawes Roll as Cherokee regardless of actual descent and were given 110-acre allotments like all other citizens of the Cherokee Nation. The Delaware who were listed as Cherokee by Adoption on previous Cherokee rolls and who were still living at the time of allotment were recorded as the 197 Registered Delaware and were given 160-acre "D" allotments as stipulated by the Supreme Court's ruling in *Cherokee Nation v. Journeycake* (1894) as described in chapter 2. The irony was that Delaware parents who were listed as Registered Delaware were enumerated on the Dawes Roll next to their Cherokee Nation-born children, who were identified as Cherokee (Records of the Bureau of Indian Affairs 1907). The Dawes Commission thus recorded Cherokee children who were born to Registered Delaware parents.

While the Dawes Commission was enrolling the Delaware for the purpose of distributing allotments, the Delaware Business Committee was also to receive a small payment for land claims against the United States. The Delaware Business Committee worked with the Department of the Interior to compile a separate roll of Delaware tribal members in order to have a list of those who were to share in the payment. The *Delaware Indian Per Capita Pay Roll* was completed in 1904 but not officially approved by the president of the United States until 1906. This 1904 Delaware Per Capita Roll, also called the Delaware Secretarial Roll, listed 1,100 tribal members, all of whom were descendants of the Delaware listed in the 1867 Kansas Delaware Roll compiled prior to removal to the Cherokee Nation. Unlike the Dawes Roll, the 1904 Delaware Per Capita Roll did not record blood quantum and made no mention of Cherokee citizenship (Records of the Bureau of Indian Affairs 1904).

The 1904 Delaware Per Capita Roll was used to verify Delaware membership and later eligible descendants for the periodic land claims that were awarded and distributed per capita to each tribal member. The 1904 Delaware Per Capita Roll only included Delaware tribal members and was not used by the federal government to determine Indian blood quantum because it did not include such a calculation. Thus, the Delaware Tribe has a separate tribal roll while the 1906 Cherokee Nation Dawes Roll is not actually a tribally specific roll, as it lists the citizens of what was once a reservation on which both Indians and non-Indians held membership rights. Tribal rolls often refer to rolls that list the members of a culturally and politically distinct organization such as the 1904 Delaware Per Capita Roll as would be required by current procedure according to the Federal Acknowledgment Process.

Regardless of this now important distinction between tribal rolls and reservation rolls, the Dawes Commission used the 1906 Cherokee Nation Dawes Roll to calculate and verify a Delaware person's Indian blood quantum following Oklahoma statehood because it was the only roll in existence at the time that identified a Delaware person's Indian blood quantum. As explained in chapter 4, blood quantum became extremely important following allotment because it defined an Indian person's land ownership rights. Indian enrollees and their descendants had to maintain a Certificate Degree of Indian Blood from the Department of the Interior in order to show their ownership rights for their allotment and formally sustain an acknowledged Indian status. Thus, the Delaware people born after removal were required to identify as Cherokee by Blood in order to own an allotment and hold an acknowledged Indian status following Oklahoma statehood. Access to land and services required that the Delaware accept a new blood quantum–based identity just as other tribes, but the difference was that the Delaware were now recorded as possessing a degree of Cherokee rather than Delaware Indian blood. Since all of the registered Delaware (previously Cherokee by Adoption) were deceased by the mid-twentieth century, all living Delaware today would thus possess, according to the federal government's redefinition as a consequence of statehood, a degree of Cherokee blood despite their actual Delaware descent and heritage.

Although federal Indian policy has changed substantially since the allotment period, the use of blood quantum to determine Indian identity has remained. Since Oklahoma statehood, the federal government has directly administered the federal Indian enrollment process until the passage of the Indian Self-Determination Act. Self-determination policy has subsequently allowed federally recognized tribal governments the ability to operate their own enrollment programs and administer CDIB registration cards. Tribal control over the federal Indian identification process has allowed greater flexibility for tribes to redefine their own membership criteria and protocol. Using blood quantum as a legal definition of Indian identity for over a century has given the concept a measure of acceptance. Most tribes today require that their membership be able to document at least some degree of Indian descent, and the most convenient way to determine such a lineage is through the existing CDIB protocol (Strong and Van Winkle 1996:554–555).

Some tribal governments, such as the Cherokee Nation, have reshaped the federal Indian identification criteria in ways that are more locally consistent or advance their own political and economic goals. In response to the Self-Determination Act, for instance, the Cherokee Nation adopted a revised constitution in 1976 and continued to use the Cherokee Nation Dawes Roll as their base roll. The Cherokee Nation also pursued the administration of a number of federal services previously offered through the BIA as stipulated under the Self-Determination Act. One of the contract services was the CDIB enrollment for the Cherokee Nation Dawes enrollees and their descendants. Cherokee administration of the enrollment process began in the late 1970s and was under complete Cherokee control by the mid-1980s. Because the Cherokee Nation Dawes Roll listed all Indians born in the Cherokee Nation as Cherokee by Blood, all Dawes Roll descendants were given some form of a Cherokee label regardless of actual descent. Legally recording the Delaware as Cherokee on the CDIB card was a practice consistent with the nineteenth-century Cherokee Nation census collected prior to allotment. However, the label was ignored by some Delaware who continued to see actual, not legally imposed, definitions of descent as operative, as was illustrated in the opening vignette.

Circe Sturm's (2002) ethnography of Cherokee identity focuses on the more empowering ways in which tribal governments have modified federal requirements to benefit their own political and economic interests. Sturm's analysis describes the advances realized by the Cherokee Nation as a result of handling their federal Indian identification process in the self-determination era. Her work explains how the Cherokee Nation successfully challenged the Indian Health

Service's quarter-blood degree requirement in the early 1970s and reconfigured tribal membership to be based on blood descent rather than blood degree. Although such a definition still required blood descent from someone labeled with Indian blood on the Cherokee Nation Dawes Roll, blood descent was reshaped as a form of identity that was more consistent with the relatively low blood quantum amounts of the leadership in the Cherokee Nation at the time. The new definition of Cherokee tribal membership successfully allowed for the Cherokee Nation to greatly expand in size; growing to more than two hundred thousand members by the twenty-first century. More tribal members also meant more federal funding for Cherokee administered contract services under Self-Determination, which further expanded the economic infrastructure of the Cherokee Nation in eastern Oklahoma(Sturm 2002:95–98).

Controlling the federal Indian identification process also allowed the Cherokee Nation greater claims to authority over Cherokee Nation Dawes Roll descendants. The ability to label Delaware and other non-Cherokee Indians as Cherokee created what appeared to be a larger and more uniform population. The labeling of all Indian citizens within the Cherokee Nation as Cherokee could have also encouraged a sense of cohesion among the culturally diverse Indian people of the Cherokee Nation. Such a move would help to direct the Cherokee Nation's newly created service population to look to the Cherokee Nation rather than the federal government for programs, aid, and services as well as for tribal leadership (Sturm 2002:95–98). However, my experience with the Delaware indicates that such an anticipated outcome has not yet arrived.

The CDIB labels issued by the Cherokee Nation Registration Department are listed in table 2. The labels *Cherokee* or *Cherokee (A.D.)* are the two used on most Cherokee CDIB cards issued to Delaware people. The A.D. was added by the Cherokee Nation to identify the cardholder as an Adopted Delaware. For most Delaware, the label

Labels	Tribal descent
Cherokee	Cherokee, Creek, Delaware, Natchez, Shawnee
Cherokee (A.D.)	Delaware
Cherokee (A.S.)	Shawnee
Cherokee (A.D./A.S.)	Shawnee–Delaware

2. CHEROKEE NATION CERTIFICATE DEGREE OF INDIAN BLOOD
LABELS: A list of the labels commonly used by the Cherokee Nation's
Registration Office and the tribal descent that each can be used to identify.

Cherokee (A.D.) is understood to mean "Cherokee, A. (Adopted) D.
(Delaware)," and thus some regard the card as an accurate identification card of Delaware identity. Others see the Cherokee (A.D.)
card as simply a bureaucratic category that has little impact on their
understanding of Delaware identity. Unfortunately, neither Delaware
interpretation of the Cherokee (A.D.) label is consistent with federal
policy. For purposes of federal enumeration, Cherokee (A.D.) may
be informally acknowledged as Delaware by some Delaware people
or simply ignored by others, but the label records such individuals
as possessing a degree of Cherokee, not Delaware, blood.

As blood quantum became a measure of tribal membership for
most tribes under the self-determination policy, the meaning of
blood quantum shifted from an indicator of racial identity to an
identifier of tribal identity. For the Cherokee Nation, such a shift
meant that those Delaware enrolled on the Cherokee Nation Dawes
Roll and their descendants were registered with a Cherokee blood
quantum even if they did not have any actual Cherokee ancestry.
Under federal control, CDIB identification as Indian was not speci-
fied by tribe. Thus, a person's Indian blood quantum could be the
combination of multiple tribal heritages. For example, a person whose
mother was full-blood Osage and whose father was full-blood Delaware would be considered a full-blood Osage and Delaware by the
BIA. When the Cherokee Nation began taking on the enrollment

process, the protocol was altered in ways that worked to establish Cherokee Nation authority over the descendants of those listed on the Cherokee Nation Dawes Roll. Cherokee ancestry was expanded to include any descendant from an Indian enrollee on the Cherokee Nation Dawes Roll. Descent from other tribes not enumerated on the Cherokee Nation Dawes Roll was not included in the blood quantum sum, and the Cherokee-issued cards only listed the blood quantum amounts calculated from the Cherokee Nation Dawes Roll. Thus the same person with a full-blood Osage mother and full-blood Delaware father would be labeled today as half-Cherokee, or half-Cherokee (A.D.) on the Cherokee Nation–issued CDIB cards.

The Cherokee Nation extended the usage of Cherokee by Blood to mean Cherokee tribal membership and included all Indian descendants of the Cherokee Nation Dawes Roll for pragmatic reasons in response to the self-determination policy. The Cherokee Nation had to establish an Indian service population that did not overlap with the service populations of other tribes in order to begin taking over the administration of federal program services as stipulated by the regulations from the Self-Determination Act. Like most Oklahoma tribes, the Cherokee Nation simply adopted their base roll and its descendants as their primary service population and re-asserted their former reservation boundaries as their Tribal Jurisdictional Boundary, or service area. Non-Cherokee Indian citizens who or whose ancestors were listed on the Cherokee Nation Dawes Roll were thus compelled to accept a Cherokee-issued CDIB card in order to continue to be eligible for federal Indian services that were then being taken over by the Cherokee Nation. Because the Cherokee Nation was the first to contract with the BIA to administer the federal Indian identification process for all Indian enrollees on the Cherokee Nation Dawes Roll and their descendants, non-Cherokee Indian Tribes within the Cherokee Nation today thus lack direct access to the federal enrollment process as originally intended under the

Self-Determination Act. The Delaware, Shawnee, and a small group of Natchez and Creek thus share the experience of having to accept a new form of Indian identity in return for limited economic security and a federally acknowledged Indian identity. With firm control over the CDIB enrollment office, the Cherokee Nation has imposed their own definitions of identity on non-Cherokee Indian tribes, who have no choice but to accept such forms if they are in need of federal services that hold a blood quantum requirement. However, the Cherokee Nation is not without sympathy for such issues and has indicated that the CDIB labels for Delaware people could be changed as long as the connection with the Cherokee Nation is recognized. As Cherokee chief Chad Smith explained, "I understand that a sense of identity is very personal and very real. That's something we'd be glad to look at, and I think we would have to agree to the language because it may have to be Cherokee-Delaware or something, but, focusing on their lineage as Delawares is something that I think we'd be delighted to, to try to work out."

Thus, the terminology used to formally identify Delaware people was once federally imposed and has recently emerged as an important issue in the current struggle between the Delaware Tribe and the Cherokee Nation. Michel Foucault's (1983:220–222) perspective on power is useful for framing the way that federal forms of Indian identity were introduced and remain operative among tribal governments today. Foucault states that the successful exercise of power lies in disciplining or guiding the actions of what appear to be free subjects. In other words, the most effective way to impose authority is to make it appear as though those subjected have the freedom to reject such authority when in reality those in power are able to guide individual choices to the advantage of the powerful. Presented with no other option, Oklahoma tribes at the beginning of the twentieth century were forced to accept a blood quantum-based Indian identity or forego the land ownership that came with allotment. Today, the Delaware are presented with a similar choice. They are forced to enroll as Cherokee by Blood or forego the marginal economic security provided by federally sponsored, but Cherokee administered, programs and services.

Extending Foucault's work to Native North America, anthropologists Pauline Strong and Barrik Van Winkle (1996) argue that Indian people have essentially been disciplined to think about their federal Indian identities in terms of blood quantum. The scholars contend that the prevalence of blood quantum among Indian tribes and communities is the result of over a century of federal policies and programs that have impressed the concept on Indian people through the census, economic coercion, land allotments, and Indian boarding schools. Strong and Van Winkle's position is further supported by Thomas Biolsi's (1992, 1995) ethnohistorical work on the Lakota. Biolsi shows how the federal policies resulting from the Indian Reorganization Act created a new identity for Lakota people. Drawing on the ideas of Michel Foucault as well, he concludes that the Lakota people accepted a new and externally imposed racial identity in exchange for marginal economic security in order to survive the artificial reservation economies of the late nineteenth and early twentieth centuries.

We can clearly see that blood quantum–based identities in the Cherokee Nation were imposed through a similar process. Delaware people were obliged to accept a blood quantum–based identity in exchange for a land allotment in the years leading up to Oklahoma statehood and continue to do so in the present, although in new forms. With self-determination and Cherokee control over enrollment, the Delaware are now given no other choice but to submit to a Cherokee by Blood identity in order to maintain an acknowledged Indian identity. Indeed, most Delaware do hold a Cherokee CDIB card and are familiar to some extent with their blood quantum amounts as well as their Cherokee by Blood labels.

Cherokee by Blood ◂ 193

The Delaware's experience with the CDIB card as brought forward by the camp matriarch in the opening vignette, however, reflects a more critical understanding of the enrollment process than would be available from a strictly Foucaultian framework. The woman's uncertainty concerning the blood quantum amount and the label listed on her CDIB card illustrates just how superficial such imposed blood quantum–based identities are seen by Delaware people and the ways in which such identities are often either simply ignored, reinterpreted, or reworked as a means of resistance. The fact that most Delaware hold a Cherokee CDIB card does not mean that the Delaware accept the idea of blood quantum as a meaningful expression of Indian identity, nor do they consent to their inclusion in the Cherokee Nation. As anthropologist James Hamill observed (2003:280), "In Oklahoma today, any claim of Indian identity cannot be sustained by the mere possession of a CDIB; it also requires participation in Indian life. In fact, many Indian people in Oklahoma today believe that the CDIB means nothing about Indian identity." As Hamill correctly concludes, CDIB enrollment in any Oklahoma tribe should not be misunderstood as consent to the labels and meanings associated with the card. Hamill's observations on Oklahoma Indian identity in general are true for the Delaware as well. In Oklahoma and for the Delaware in particular, Indian identity is not encompassed by CDIB ownership although most Delaware people do own a CDIB card.

CDIB card ownership was imposed and may now be universal, but it is more accurate to see the CDIB enrollment process as one grounded in imposition that is either ignored, tolerated, or selectively utilized as a form of empowerment and resistance. The Delaware's perspective on the Cherokee CDIB card, however, is better understood with reference to being both the subjects of Cherokee power and agents of resistance who do not passively accept their subordinate position. The Delaware of today are in a situation both similar to and unique from that which has confronted most Oklahoma Indian people throughout the twentieth century. Just as the federal government did with blood quantum, the Cherokee Nation now requires the Delaware to accept a new form of identity, Cherokee by Blood, in exchange for access to services sponsored by the federal government and the Cherokee Nation. As is shown in the next section, the Delaware have accepted the necessity of the federal Indian identification process to the point that CDIB enrollment has become routine. The Delaware, like other Indian people, have been disciplined to accept the political and economic expediency of the document-based CDIB enrollment process while rejecting the significance that the Cherokee-controlled card has on Delaware Indian identity, as Hamill describes.

Even though the Delaware may hold Cherokee CDIB cards, card ownership should not be mistaken for consent to an imposed Cherokee identity. The Cherokee Nation has effectively set the rules for CDIB enrollment by which the Delaware and other non-Cherokee Indian citizens must formally be classified as Cherokee by Blood or forego an acknowledged Indian status and the marginal economic security associated with such a status. The result is that the choice presented to the Delaware is one that ultimately forces individuals to enroll for a Cherokee CDIB and inadvertently give the appearance of consent to the Cherokee Nation's authority. The Delaware, however, reject the Cherokee Nation's control of the CDIB card but are presented with no other option for enrollment. Most Delaware simply ignore or reinterpret the implications of the Cherokee CDIB card like the woman in the opening vignette, yet the Cherokee Nation's control over the process effectively silences such subtle forms of Delaware resistance. While the Delaware do consider CDIB ownership as a necessary requirement for access to federal services and programs, they continue to search for ways to resist, challenge, rework, and ignore their mis-identification as Cherokee by Blood now conferred by the Cherokee-controlled federal enrollment process.

The following section presents Delaware experiences with the Cherokee CDIB card in order to highlight the commonalities that I found shared among most Delaware enrollees. The words of Delaware CDIB card owners show that CDIB enrollment is a document-based process that is considered routine by the Delaware, but the Cherokee by Blood identity that CDIB enrollment confers is not. Potential enrollees are required to compile written records to demonstrate descent to the Cherokee Nation Dawes Roll. Kinship and cultural participation, which are locally understood markers of Delaware identity, play no role in verifying a legal Indian status. Despite the irrelevance of CDIB cards to local Delaware identity, the ownership of such cards has been practiced for some time, and it has become standard to possess what is locally called an Indian Card. Yet, while CDIB card ownership is normalized, enrollment for the card is not pursued because the Delaware believe themselves to be Cherokee or that the Delaware Tribe should be placed under Cherokee authority. CDIB enrollment is undertaken primarily for access to Indian programs and services that hold a blood quantum requirement. Thus, the card is known to the Delaware as one's Indian or CDIB card and is not referred to as a Cherokee card. In fact, I found that the Cherokee labels on the CDIB card are not regarded with much support by non-Cherokee Indians.

The CDIB application process administered by the Cherokee Nation has retained many elements that were borrowed from federal protocol and remains an enrollment process that is regulated by federal guidelines in the Code of Federal Regulations (CFR). CDIB enrollment in the Cherokee Nation requires the applicant to compile documents such as birth and death records that establish a genealogical link with one or more lineal ancestors on the Cherokee Nation Dawes Roll. Self-identification does not make one eligible for a CDIB card. If an applicant cannot produce the documents required, the application will be denied regardless of locally understood markers that may indicate an Indian identity. As one Delaware woman proclaimed, "It's so hard, because you have to jump through so many hoops to get your CDIB card. There is plenty of people that can't actually make that hoop with a document. So they don't, they are unable to claim their CDIB card." Documentation thus plays a critical role in being able to get a CDIB card and is more important to the process than a person's actually genealogy and group identity.

In some cases finding the necessary documentation is a tedious process that involves research in local libraries and public agencies. For others, a family member who has already gathered this information owns the required documents and shares the documentation with the rest of the family, making this step less difficult. For example, one woman explained her mother's efforts when compiling the paperwork needed for CDIB cards for her family: "My mother took care of that for me when I was a little girl. I was probably eight when we got our CDIB cards. She had to collect a lot of paperwork. Like we had to trace back to our relative that was on the original Dawes roll. Then she had to get those certificates to show how those people were related to us, and then she sent off to Tahlequah and it took a long time for us to get them or to get mine . . . it was a lengthy process." This woman's experience is common for the Delaware: a recognized family genealogist conducts most of the preliminary work required. Often the family genealogist gains such documentation while performing research in order to enroll his or her own children or grandchildren. For example, when I asked a Delaware man how he obtained his CDIB card, he replied, "I can't do that . . . [pause] . . . my mother got it for me when I was going to school." Given that this kind of response was fairly typical among Delaware people, and in particular those from the younger cohorts (age forty and under), it was evident that a large number of Delaware tribal members have never actually applied for their own CDIB cards.

After the research is completed, the applicant either delivers in person or mails the completed application to the Cherokee Nation's Registration Department in Tahlequah. Mailing the application is the most popular option among the Delaware, which means increasing numbers of Delaware have never been to Tahlequah or the Cherokee Nation's' Registration Department. Some explain that they prefer the postal service because there is a strong animosity toward the Cherokee Nation in general and the CDIB process in particular. For instance, one Delaware woman habitually avoided Tahlequah because she considered the city as taboo and refused to enter the city limits. Others have chosen to apply by mail as a matter of convenience since Tahlequah is a two-hour drive from most locations in Delaware Country.

One interesting case highlights the document-centered nature of the enrollment process and shows how written evidence trumps even the most commonly held stereotypical views of Indian identity in the enrollment process. In the example quoted below, the Indianness of an applicant who applied in person at the registration office in Tahlequah was questioned because her phenotypical features were not as Indian looking as her brothers. As a result the enrollment agent was unwilling to enroll the Delaware applicant even though the necessary documents were presented.

> About my Indian Card? . . . Well, we tried to do everything through the mail, because it was a great big hassle. . . . We took off and we went over to Tahlequah. My mom was with me and I didn't take my birth certificate or anything. I just didn't because Mom had everybody's stuff already done. . . . So we went over there and they gave my brothers theirs. Apparently Mom had sent in some stuff . . . and she just went to pick them up, and they wouldn't give me mine cause they said that's not your daughter. They accused mom of me being adopted, and I said, "No, that's my mom . . .

and that's my brothers." We had to go all the way home, we had to get a death certificate and birth certificates and go through a lot more than what everybody else had to because I'm blonde. ... But see it's really weird because my brothers didn't have to go through all that, because . . . if you put me with them of course you are going to question it 'cause I don't look anything, I don't even have the same color eyes they do.

This woman's experience demonstrates the emphasis placed on documentation especially when the applicant lacks the expected outward markers of Indian identity. The woman's appearance indicated a non-Indian person to the enrollment agent, and thus the CDIB card was initially denied. However, the rest of the woman's family who had provided the same documentation apparently showed enough phenotypical markings of Indian identity to be approved. The clerk at the registration department eventually issued the Delaware woman a CDIB card but required overwhelming documentation beyond that provided by the woman's brothers before the woman's CDIB card would be approved.

After all of the documentation is provided and the application is successfully completed, then each applicant waits four to eight weeks before receiving the CDIB card. The card is usually sent by mail to the applicant's home, and only after the applicant obtains the card is he or she eligible for federal Indian services. The card is white and about the size of a driver's license. Next to the seal of the Department of the Interior, it states: "United States, Department of the Interior, Bureau of Indian Affairs, Tahlequah Agency, Certificate Degree of Indian Blood. This is to certify that *[individual's name]* born *[individual's birth date]* is *[Cherokee blood quantum]* degree of Indian blood of the Cherokee *[A.D., A.S., A.D./A.S. or Freedmen]* Tribe." At the bottom the card is dated and signed by the issuing officer in Tahlequah. The back of the card reads: "Department of the

Interior, Bureau of Indian Affairs, The degree of Indian Blood shown on the face of this card is computed from the final rolls of the Five Civilized Tribes closed March 4, 1907, by the act of April 26, 1906 (34 Stat. 137). Any alteration or fraudulent use of this Certificate renders it null and void."

While CDIB card ownership is common among the Delaware, the card is a form of identification from which many Delaware remain removed and distant. I argue that such distance kept between the Delaware and the Cherokee Nation illustrates the divide that is seen by the Delaware between them and the Cherokee Nation. The reality is that most Delaware own a Cherokee CDIB card out of necessity and are not comfortable with the implications of card ownership. The Delaware may see CDIB enrollment as normal, but they have not internalized that a connection exists between them and the Cherokee Nation despite the labels used in the process of Cherokee enrollment. Although the Cherokee CDIB card labels Delaware people as Cherokee, many Delaware remain ambivalent toward the Cherokee Nation because, as one woman explained, "I just don't know who they are." The Delaware have accepted that the federal Indian identification process is necessary to identify those eligible for federal Indian programs, but they resist the notion that such bureaucratic necessities also require their misidentification as a Cherokee by Blood. The fact that compliance is nearly universal is not because most people agree with the process but because the Delaware are inclined to overlook and ignore the inconsistencies in federal Indian identification in order to obtain the desired goal. The Cherokee Nation benefits from the accepted document-centered enrollment process, and thus it offers no other option or labels for Delaware CDIB enrollment at the moment.

The Delaware engage the CDIB card in multiple and overlapping forms, and such critiques can be classified into two general challenges. The first position identifies the inaccuracy and meaninglessness of blood quantum to Delaware identity. The second is a critique of the way that the Cherokee Nation mislabels the tribal identity of Delaware people on the Cherokee CDIB card. Such arguments posed against blood quantum and Cherokee citizenship were not mutually exclusive and were often difficult to untangle. An understandable slippage occurs in Delaware understandings of blood quantum and Cherokee CDIB card enrollment because both forms of identity are administered by the Cherokee Nation and appear side by side on the CDIB card. Thus blood quantum and the Cherokee label are often conflated when the Delaware voice critiques about the enrollment process and the Cherokee Nation's control of it.

Blood quantum and Cherokee citizenship are most often confronted when the Delaware illustrate how such imposed forms of identity are not consistent with local sentiments about Delaware identity. One former head man dancer of the Delaware Powwow expressed this generally held position rather eloquently:

Indian isn't a blood quantum, although a lot of people try to associate blood quantum with it; however, I think it is cultural. As long as you have an understanding of your culture and the history of your culture and your traditions associated with that and you know about it. You've been raised that way and you've been taught things like that and you can trace your ancestors — then, yeah, you're Indian! It's not up to the government to decide who's Indian. Just because I'm registered Cherokee, even though I don't have any Cherokee in me, that doesn't make me not Delaware or not Shawnee.

In this man's argument is seen the Delaware's critical perspective of the Cherokee CDIB card, which mislabels Delaware identity as Cherokee by Blood. First he begins by clearly separating local forms of Indian identity from the federal Indian identity understood in terms of blood quantum. He asserts that being Indian is not based on having an Indian blood quantum but rests in the possession of a unique cultural background associated with one's tribal heritage. Indeed, cultural performance and kinship are the two most important indicators of local identity in Delaware society. As can be read in the Delaware man's quoted passage above, cultural participation is paramount in his consideration of Delaware identity. The importance of culture is not recognized by the federal Indian identification process, and thus many Delaware reject the idea that Indian identity can be solely represented by blood quantum.

The Cherokee Nation's control over the enrollment process warrants even further critique from Delaware people. While blood quantum may not be seen as an accurate representation of Indian identity, one's tribal belonging is also seen as a birthright and thus an essential quality that is gained by descent and exists within an Indian person. Delaware identity is considered an inherited status as kinship, or being able to trace one's ancestors, is also included as an important aspect. The consultant quoted above is a member of a Delaware and a Shawnee family, and thus he asserts that he is Delaware and Shawnee by kin group membership. Since he does not belong to a Cherokee family, the head man dancer argues that he does not have any Cherokee in him, which means that he has no Cherokee descent. It is clear then that this man understands his Indian identity to be, on one level, a racial or an inherited status based on family membership as well as a group identity achieved through cultural performance in Delaware and Shawnee societies.

This Delaware man's testimony is repeated here because it is generally consistent with most Delaware perceptions of the Cherokee controlled CDIB enrollment. Like the head man dancer, Delaware people also commonly challenge the significance of the Cherokee label that appears on their CDIB card. Many Delaware report that although their card may say Cherokee, they are not Cherokee — they are Delaware. Others remember tearing up their CDIB card after they received it in the mail because the card had Cherokee listed under tribal affiliation. Some have even reported the error in labeling to the Cherokee Nation Registration Department in Tahlequah, thinking that the misidentification was a simple mistake, but they were quite confused to hear that the Cherokee label was the correct label and that no other option would be possible.

While most Delaware may own a Cherokee CDIB card, they are also quick to highlight the inaccuracies in the blood quantum fraction listed on the card. For example, one Delaware man offered that the CDIB card was in fact irrelevant to his Delaware identity, stating, "On my card it says I am one-quarter Cherokee, but my brother's is one-half Cherokee, but we have the same parents! They really don't know what they're doing down there." Discourses such as this are common and point out the constructed and artificial meanings associated with the blood quantum number. The critique of blood quantum here serves a dual purpose, as it is employed as an argument against the legitimacy of the Cherokee Nation as the administrator of the CDIB card as well as the relevance that blood quantum holds as a marker of Delaware identity. Since access to federal services in the Cherokee Nation is not dependent on the amount of Indian blood quantum listed on the CDIB, Delaware people remain ambivalent yet critical about their blood quantum inconsistencies.

Another popular way that the Delaware undermine the Cherokee label is by obtaining CDIB cards in both the Cherokee Nation and from other tribes in which they are eligible. This option is available only to those who can document descent from an ancestor listed on another tribal roll beyond the Cherokee Nation Dawes Roll, but there are a number of Delaware people who have CDIB cards and tribal membership cards from multiple tribes. While having multiple cards is illegal, it is one way that the Delaware resist a federal identification process that is not consistent with local group affiliations. Consider the following explanation given by a Delaware woman who spoke with me about her multiple tribal memberships and described why she applied for two CDIB cards. Her mother was full-blood Delaware and Shawnee and her father was full-blood Osage. Her CDIB card from the Cherokee Nation listed her as one-half Cherokee (even though she has no Cherokee ancestry), and her CDIB card from the Osage listed her as one-half Osage. When asked why she chose this form of identification she responded, "I can't change who I am, so I'm enrolled in all of my tribes and I'll keep it that way until they catch me."

This woman's explanation illustrates how some Delaware signify their multiple tribal identities beyond those limits imposed by the federal process. Maintaining CDIB cards from different tribes keeps an individual eligible for tribally specific programs and payments. Multiple CDIB cards also serve as a material reminder of one's tribal heritage to pass on to future generations and for one's own sense of self-identity. Having such an enrollment strategy is also more akin to the identification process as it existed prior to the self-determination era when administered directly by the federal government.[4] Those who choose this strategy do so as a form of self-empowerment and express through the practice that neither the federal government nor a tribal government should have the right to undermine one's multiple tribal identities. The result is that such individuals add to the Cherokee Nation's service population while simultaneously subverting the legality of the federal identification process through a covert act of resistance.

Ironically, the Delaware belief in the essential quality of kin group membership that drives some to enroll in more than one tribe can also work in concert with the motivations for some to enroll for a Cherokee CDIB card. A number of people can trace both Cherokee and Delaware descent, and being a member of both tribes is a point of pride for some individuals. Even Delaware people with no Cherokee genealogy believe that those with Cherokee ancestry should have the right to have a Cherokee CDIB card because such individuals of mixed Cherokee and Delaware descent also belong to a Cherokee family. Such a position is consistent with local notions of Delaware identity that describe family membership as a given quality of one's self and thus as an important marker of group membership. As one man explained, "I have a sister who is also Cherokee, she's my half sister; she was raised Delaware and I wouldn't ask her to feel any less towards the Cherokee side either. . . . I understand the politics behind all of this, but it's a God-given right to be who you are." Indicated here is that the ability to proclaim a dual heritage is important to sense of self that may transcend the present CDIB enrollment protocol. This man's explanation emphasizes the importance of Indian identity as one that is a birthright given to a person by virtue of descent. While his sister was raised Delaware and has a Delaware cultural background, she still retains the right to be Cherokee as well as Delaware by virtue of her Cherokee parentage.

Though the Delaware have doubts about, and generally critique, the Cherokee-administered CDIB process, my research with the Delaware found that most retain their Cherokee CDIB cards for a number of reasons, but the overwhelming justification offered was for access to the federal Indian services administered by the Cherokee Nation under self-determination. For instance, one Delaware woman stated that the CDIB card is only so "the government can have a list of names," and she has a card only so she can "use services and have the proof that the government wants." This response was typical and suggests an understanding that equates obtaining a CDIB card with a transaction in which genealogies are exchanged and false identities are tolerated for the promise of limited economic security.

Of the services cited for compelling Cherokee CDIB card ownership, reliable access to otherwise expensive health care service was the most common. In particular, having access to the health services provided through the Claremore Indian Hospital plays a pivotal role in convincing Delaware people to participate in the federal identification process. As one Delaware man explained, "I was wanting to go to the Indian hospital, I think I got it [CDIB card] from the hospital, through Tahlequah. One day a month they send their enrollment people. All I wanted was a card so I could get in the hospital." This man's response indicates that the Delaware see obtaining a CDIB card as a step they have to take in order to have access to critical federal health services provided at Indian hospital in Claremore. For most, the CDIB card is primarily considered to be an economic tool used to access health care. In actual practice then, the Delaware protect their genealogy, social structure, and cultural practices from imposed labels by understanding their participation as purely motivated by the need to have reliable access to health care.

Because of the central role played by health services in Delaware motivations for CDIB enrollment, an investigation of such services and their locations is necessary. The distribution and timing of health service centers in the vicinity of Delaware Country reveal the relatively recent introduction of Cherokee-sponsored services as well as the relationship between health care and local Delaware-Cherokee politics. Before 1989 the health service administered by the Osage Nation in Pawhuska was the closest facility, and the Osage also required the Delaware to have a CDIB card for service. The next closest facility was the Indian Health Service Hospital in Claremore, which also required the Delaware to have a CDIB card. Cherokee health care facilities were first introduced in Delaware Country with the building of a temporary health clinic in Nowata in 1989. Ironically, Nowata was the same city in which the Delaware Business Committee had originally hoped to establish health services prior to their loss of acknowledgment in 1979. A mobile unit from the Nowata facility served Bartlesville, Collinsville, Vinita, and South Coffeeville one day per week. The Nowata-based Cherokee health care clinic was relocated and expanded in 1997. Ironically, this expansion took place less than one year after the Department

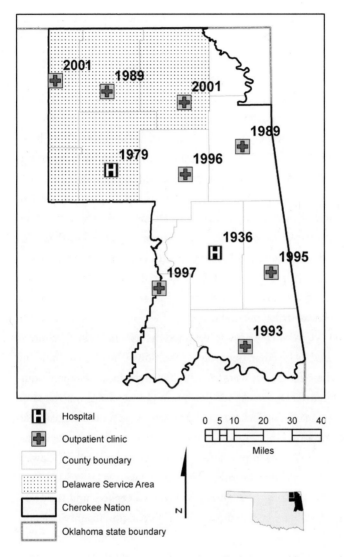

2001
1989
2001
1989
1979
1996
1936
1995
1997
1993

H	Hospital
+	Outpatient clinic
	County boundary
	Delaware Service Area
	Cherokee Nation
	Oklahoma state boundary

0 5 10   20   30   40
Miles

N

9. CHEROKEE NATION HEALTH SERVICES: The locations and year established for the health care services administered by the Cherokee Nation and the Indian Health Service within the Cherokee Nation Tribal Jurisdictional Service Area. The W. W. Hastings Indian Hospital in Tahlequah and the Claremore Indian Hospital at Claremore are run by the Indian Health Service. Map by Rebecca Dobbs.

of Interior restored the Delaware Tribe. All other Cherokee-sponsored health services that had previously been established were then concentrated in the mostly Cherokee-populated Ozark Plateau region of far eastern Oklahoma (Cherokee Nation of Oklahoma 2007a).

Construction of Cherokee-sponsored health care services expanded throughout Delaware Country in the years following restored recognition. A new clinic was built in Bartlesville in 2001. The Cherokee Health Clinic in Bartlesville was unique, though, because it was built with Cherokee Nation funds rather than federal funds, and thus the clinic initially promised to offer services to only Cherokee tribal members. This requirement obliged Delaware people to maintain and use their Cherokee CDIB cards in order to obtain health service at the clinic. The Cherokee-only health clinic was thus seen as a challenge to the Delaware Tribe's sovereignty during the years of restored recognition in the very city that served as the location for the Delaware tribal headquarters.

Indeed, most Delaware interpreted the new Bartlesville clinic as motivated by less than benevolent intentions. The plans to build the new Cherokee facility were made public in the local newspaper during Memorial Day weekend. This last weekend of May was the same weekend that many Delaware families converged for the annual Delaware Powwow. The timeliness of the Cherokee advertisement gave the new clinic a maximum amount of publicity among the Delaware electorate camped at the powwow. As one Delaware leader explained, "With the lawsuit going on between the Cherokees and the Delawares, the Cherokees are moving in to Washington County to let the Delawares know that they're there and they are going to service the people." Indeed, in 2002 the U.S. District Court in Tulsa had ruled in favor of the Delaware Tribe's restored recognition, and the case was subsequently appealed to the Tenth District Court of Appeals at the time that the Bartlesville clinic was announced. The Delaware thus critically understood the motivations for the recent introduction of Cherokee-sponsored health services. Although the Delaware were in need and made use of Cherokee health services in Bartlesville, the Delaware did not regard the Cherokee Nation's presence as the norm. The existence of Cherokee-sponsored services in Delaware Country was considered a reaction to the success of the Delaware Tribe during the years of restored recognition and the Cherokee Nation's appeal that was then failing in the Tulsa district court.

Thus politics between the Delaware Tribe and the Cherokee Nation also plays a pivotal role in Delaware understandings of Cherokee CDIB enrollment. Some Delaware people consider the CDIB card to be overtly political rather than something that provides economic security. Another way that the Delaware justify their Cherokee CDIB cards is by minimalizing the political significance of the card, thus making the card something that is disconnected from their sense of self. Conversations similar to the following are common:

CONSULTANT: Yeah, I've got a card somewhere, but I don't know where it is.

OBERMEYER: Do you know what tribe it says?

CONSULTANT: Cherokee I think, but I'm not Cherokee.

OBERMEYER: Why is that?

CONSULTANT: It's some political thing with the Cherokees. It's a bunch of bologna, but I don't get involved, I try to stay independent.

Such arguments identify the CDIB card as political, which is considered somewhat distasteful to Delaware people. Having a CDIB card but claiming a neutral stance in the Cherokee-Delaware struggle distances an individual from what he or she would consider the manipulation of Delaware identity into a tool for political gain. One cannot choose to be Delaware, one is simply born Delaware. On the same line of reasoning, one cannot choose to be Cherokee unless born to a Cherokee family. Thus, misidentifying the Delaware as

Cherokee by Blood is considered a political act in some Delaware minds because it certainly doesn't reflect any actual reality. Claiming that the CDIB card is a political process keeps one's local identity separate from the more volatile or artificial realms of intertribal politics and the conflict between the competing Delaware and Cherokee tribal governments.

I was also told by many Delaware people that the Cherokee Nation used to enroll applicants as members of the Cherokee Nation when they applied for the CDIB card. As one Delaware man explained, "Back then they was enrolling you when they gave you a CDIB card, they enrolled you in the Cherokee Nation too." The protocol for simultaneous enrollment as Cherokee by Blood and as a Cherokee tribal member apparently occurred on a massive scale. The Cherokee Nation reportedly sent enrollment representatives to important service centers such as the Claremore Indian Hospital to enroll Delaware as Cherokee tribal members. As one Delaware woman relates, "I registered at Claremore, at the Indian hospital. In my work, I mean, they set up the table down there and everybody was registered. I don't know what for or why I had to even get it. I think it was to be able to doctor down there maybe. Because when I hired in, I didn't have a CDIB, but when they came around registering us, well, then I jumped in there and registered." As this woman's experience indicates, everybody was registering, but very little information was given as to why it was so important. Registration for acknowledged Indian status was considered routine, but not the awareness that such actions would ultimately include them as Cherokee citizens. The Cherokee Nation, on the other hand, benefited from the accepted and normalized practice of enrolling with the federal government, which worked to rapidly increase the distribution of Cherokee-issued CDIB cards among the Delaware in the early years of self-determination.

A large portion of the Delaware Tribe also applied for their Cherokee CDIB card in order to receive the Delaware per capita payments discussed in chapter 5 that would be administered only to those holding an Indian status. As one man related to me, "The reason I received my first card was when I turned eighteen and I received Delaware funds; I had to have a card at that point to get it." The Cherokee Nation was thus able to gain a number of younger Delaware enrollees under the auspices of the per capita payments. To be included in the per capita payment, eligible Delaware tribal members had to apply for a Cherokee-issued CDIB card, which automatically enrolled the applicant as a Cherokee Nation tribal member at the time. Ironically, the Delaware had to obtain a Cherokee CDIB card that listed the applicants as Cherokee by Blood in order to be awarded a land payment that was to be distributed to only Delaware descendants.

A history of using the CDIB for economic security and objectifying its meanings through political debates has instilled variously held convictions about the benefits of having a card that in some cases goes beyond material concerns. The CDIB card is also considered by some Delaware as a form of insurance that could potentially be relied upon during hard times. As one man's experience suggests, not only is the CDIB card considered something with which to access services, but it also lends peace of mind. As the man explained, "And as a matter of fact, that's the reason I got my daughter a card. Like I said, I never really had to carry a card as a child or as a teenager even, but when my daughter was born, for her to receive services from Claremore we all of a sudden had to have a card. So that is why I got hers; it is a good idea to have one anyway, but as a must that's the reason why I did that." In this man's recollection, he is explaining that although the card is ultimately about being able to access otherwise expensive services such as health care, it also has a tangential function as another form of identification similar to a driver's license or social security card. He feels that it would be considered almost irresponsible for people not to own a CDIB card or to obtain one for their children. The CDIB card's role as a tool for economic security has thus made owning a card a good idea, even for those who remember the time when there was no need to have a Cherokee CDIB card to access federal services.

Although the majority of Delaware people hold a Cherokee CDIB card, there are a significant number of Delaware people who are choosing other ways to resist what they consider to be irreconcilable problems with the Cherokee CDIB card. A growing body of Delaware people have chosen not to own a Cherokee CDIB card and have either obtained a CDIB card from another tribal government or simply decided not to apply for a CDIB card at all. Such individuals will often register under a different tribe when possible, either because they do not want to be registered as Cherokee or prefer to remain distant from the current Delaware-Cherokee struggle. Although enrolled in other tribes such as the Osage Nation, Peoria Tribe, Cheyenne-Arapaho Tribe, Comanche Nation, and Muscogee (Creek) Nation, non-Cherokee CDIB holders continue to participate in Delaware society and still have access to most federal Indian services in the region. Since the Cherokee Nation generally provides contract services to all Indians regardless of tribe, a CDIB card from any tribe allows the Delaware of mixed tribal heritage to receive services without having to be labeled Cherokee. In one case in particular, a full-blood Delaware woman registered all of her children and her grandchildren with her husband's tribe so that the entire family could receive services administered through the Cherokee Nation while not having to register as Cherokee.

Other Delaware who do not have an Indian heritage beyond those listed on the Cherokee Dawes Roll have relinquished their CDIB card ownership in the Cherokee Nation. Those seeking to end their Cherokee enrollment had to fill out a formal application to have their Cherokee CDIB card revoked. After leaving the Cherokee Nation, most retained or applied for a Delaware tribal membership card.

This mode of identification was becoming increasingly popular as the new Delaware Tribal membership cards were being accepted by the Claremore Indian Hospital during the Delaware Tribe's restored federal recognition. As one woman relayed to me, "We have our own numbers now, we're not running off the Cherokee numbers. . . . I have a piece of paper stating that I am Delaware, and it has a code on that piece of paper, and they go in and change the Cherokee code to the Delaware code, and that's put into the system. We have this little piece of paper that says please change; we are a member of the Delaware Tribe." The woman cited here is expressing the growing sense of pride among Delaware people during the years of restored recognition as more and more Delaware began using their Delaware cards rather than Cherokee CDIB cards. During the years of restored recognition, the Delaware were no longer reliant on the Cherokee CDIB card to get health service. Using the Delaware card was a way for Delaware people to indicate their independence from the Cherokee Nation in ways considered meaningful by the BIA. For a few years the Delaware truly had the option to be either Cherokee or Delaware, and a growing number chose Delaware at the Claremore Indian Hospital.

I also talked with some Delaware people who simply never applied for a Cherokee CDIB card and had only applied for the Delaware tribal membership card. Such individuals were never marked as Cherokee nor held a legal Indian status, but they actively participated as a Delaware tribal member. The man quoted below is a descendent of the prominent turn-of-the-twentieth-century Delaware lawyer Richard Adams, who worked on the Delaware Tribe's cases before the Supreme Court, as discussed in chapter 2.[5] As this Adams descendent explained to me,

I never had a certificate of blood quantum. . . . I don't know what would be the benefit, I am personally opposed to the enrollment and I think if for no other reason than to honor my deceased relatives who fought long and hard, most of the time a failing battle, for independent recognition from the Cherokee Nation. I have no desire to be a member of the Cherokee Tribe or to have a piece of paper in my wallet that says I am a member of the Cherokee Tribe. And I have no animosity toward the Cherokee; it's not that, it's just that I am not Cherokee, I'm Delaware.

Even when refusing to enroll, the man quoted above portrays the Cherokee CDIB card as insignificant compared to the long history of political struggle between the Cherokee Nation and the Delaware Tribe that is of most importance. He describes the card as simply a piece of paper that will provide him with no real benefits nor accurately signify his very proud memories of his Delaware ancestors. Enrollment for this Adams descendant is clearly tied only to his cultural heritage and current alignment with the Big House–inspired position on Cherokee membership. It is clear from his narrative that no Cherokee-sponsored benefits of today would motivate him to dishonor the past struggles of his Delaware relatives. The refusal to submit a personal identity to the Cherokee CDIB process suggests a consciousness that supersedes the limits imposed by Cherokee Nation. This is an overt voice of resistance not only to the federal Indian identification process but to the Cherokee Nation's authority as well.

In the quoted statements throughout this section, the Cherokee CDIB card and the blood quantum–based identity it provides has been shown to be irrelevant when it comes to the real issues of Delaware history in the Cherokee Nation and local notions of group identity. Those opposed to the Cherokee CDIB card emphasized the final point made in the last quoted narrative, which resonates with the point made by the head man dancer at the beginning of this section. Most Delaware agree on one basic and undeniable position: that they are Delaware, not Cherokee, no matter what the cards issued by the Cherokee Nation or the federal government say. The CDIB card may have become a useful resource for Delaware people, but not one that has instilled a connection with the Cherokee Nation or an acceptance of a blood quantum–based identity. Rather, the Delaware hold a commitment to their unique heritage while challenging the Cherokee Nation's handling of the CDIB card. However, the Cherokee Nation controls the CDIB enrollment process and thus does not allow such resounding Delaware voices of resistance to be heard or become known.

Thus is the diversity of Delaware engagements with the Cherokee-administered CDIB card. Generally critical of blood quantum and citizenship in the Cherokee Nation, most Delaware apply for and use Cherokee CDIB cards for the limited economic security that the card provides. A smaller number have a Cherokee CDIB card in order to mark their shared Delaware and Cherokee heritage. Others have decided to completely reject Cherokee identification and have done so by enrolling with other federally recognized tribes when possible or by revoking their Cherokee membership. A few, like the descendant of attorney Richard Adams quoted above, have even chosen never to apply for a Cherokee CDIB card as a measure of rejecting the Cherokee Nation's claims to power over Delaware people. It is within this diverse field of competing opinions toward Cherokee enrollment that the debate over Delaware enrollment in the Cherokee Nation continues to take place. The Delaware are critically aware of the utility and effectiveness of the federal identification process. The Delaware feel that their Cherokee-issued CDIB cards are a birthright for some, an economic necessity for others, and a nuisance that most try to resist, reject, or ignore.

CONCLUSION

I have occasionally been told by Delaware people that their CDIB card does not mean anything when it was clear that they understood that Cherokee CDIB ownership did, in fact, mean something. By stating that the CDIB card did not mean anything, Delaware informants were telling me that their locally held Delaware identity was very different from the ways in which such group expressions were codified by the federal government and the Cherokee Nation. They were also telling me that the card did not mean that they wished to be a part of the Cherokee Nation, nor did it mean that they were members of a Cherokee family. Indeed, it is the case that Delaware sense of identity bears little resemblance or meaning with the information presented on the Cherokee CDIB card, and no one wants anything other than complete independence from the Cherokee Nation. On another level, the Delaware also realize in ways that often go unsaid that the federal Indian identification process is one that can be potentially damaging to Delaware sovereignty and independence from the Cherokee Nation as well as potentially empowering for Delaware acknowledgment. It is not unclear to some Delaware that the Cherokee Nation controls the CDIB process and through such control can maintain a degree of jurisdictional authority over the Delaware Tribe and its members.

The self-determination policy may have provided tribal governments with the ability to take back greater control over the administration of federal Indian programs. Administrative control over federal institutions has indeed allowed self-determination tribes to correct and redesign the very institutions that were intended to disenfranchise and assimilate Indian people at the outset of the twentieth century. The transition from federal to tribal control over the federal Indian identification process has played a central role in providing tribal governments with greater sovereignty in establishing their own rules for citizenship. Empowered federally recognized tribes throughout North America today now maintain their own unique qualifications and can control their own enrollment process for tribal membership that more closely approximates local notions of tribal identity while expressing such identities in terms understandable to the federal government. Unfortunately, tribes are not allowed complete flexibility with federal institutions and must work within the federal regulations. Thus, single enrollment is often required to ensure that a tribe does not have an overlapping service population with another federally recognized tribe.

The new federal policy has, however, worked against the efforts of tribes such as the Delaware who are even further limited in the ability to claim authority over their own separate tribal membership. Rather, the need for marginal economic security often requires the Delaware to enroll as Cherokee by Blood and contribute to the powerbase of their rival tribal government. The Cherokee Nation's control of the federal Indian identification process thus makes it appear as though non-Cherokee Indian descendants of the Cherokee Nation Dawes Roll actually consent to enrollment as Cherokee by Blood.

Realizing the empowerment that came with single enrollment in the self-determination era and hoping to benefit from its implementation, Delaware tribal leaders began pushing for the Delaware Tribe to do away with dual enrollment in the Cherokee Nation during the years of restored recognition. However, the Delaware leadership met with considerable opposition from the Cherokee Nation and surprisingly from the Delaware constituency as well. In the following chapter I present the polarized positions taken by the Delaware on the single enrollment proposal and explain why this seemingly straightforward issue is so complex. There is a divide between those in the Delaware Tribe who do not think that Cherokee enrollment compromises Delaware federal recognition, while others see dual enrollment as an obstacle to complete Delaware independence that must be replaced with a Delaware-issued CDIB card. Such polarized Delaware views on single enrollment were often not made individually but were perspectives cleaved by the long-standing kin-based divisions between Christian and Big House platforms that could be traced back to removal. The Cherokee Nation also had a vested interest in sustaining Delaware CDIB enrollment and thus used their influence within the Delaware Tribe to work against the single enrollment initiative. Chapter 7 thus picks up the debate over single enrollment as it existed within the Delaware Tribe during the years of restored recognition to illustrate the difficulties presented to the Delaware Tribe when attempting to solidify their independence from the Cherokee Nation in the self-determination era.

7 Single Enrollment

Let Them Be Cherokees!
ANONYMOUS DELAWARE MAN, 2002

All the men in attendance at the first annual Tecumseh Celebration were asked to sit at a metal picnic table underneath the shelter outside of the Delaware Housing Authority office in Chelsea. One Delaware woman asked half-jokingly, "even the white men?" The lady running the event responded, "Yes, all the men be seated at the table; the girls have decided that they want to serve the men in the traditional way." So all of the men including myself took a seat at the picnic table. The girls served a small portion of water to everyone, then a Delaware man, invigorated with news of his first grandchild, prayed over the water, and we all drank. The food was served, consisting of potatoes, grape dumplings, vegetables, and two types of meat. As we began to eat, the conversation turned to different discussions about the greatness of Tecumseh and how his spirit had inspired both the Shawnee and Delaware people. During the meal I remained relatively quiet, content with enjoying the food and conversation.

After the meal people began to mingle, and I took the opportunity to visit with the new grandfather about his CDIB card. He explained to me that the card meant very little to him and that he only owned one in order to receive health services. He said, "Really, it's just a white man's card." Our discussion soon caught the attention of others who were listening close by, and a small group began gathering around us. One of the Delaware men who had joined our conversation began taking his card out of his wallet so I asked what was listed under the heading "Tribal Affiliation" on his card. The Delaware man responded, "Adopted Delaware," and his response suddenly enraged the grandfather, who had just told me how meaningless the CDIB card was. The grandfather corrected the man and those in earshot, stating that the card did not say "Adopted Delaware" and that the cards actually listed the Delaware as "Cherokee A.D." He continued, "A.D. stands for ADMITTED DELAWARE, not ADOPTED. We were admitted into the Cherokee Nation as equals, as a sovereign government. We are not children. They can't adopt us! We were ADMITTED!" Those of us who had heard the grandfather's words fell silent and pondered the subtle difference between admitted and adopted. It was indeed a subtlety with huge significance. "Admitted Delaware" meant equality with the Cherokee Nation, while "Adopted Delaware" indexed subordination.

Although brief, the exchange described above expresses the complexities that surround Delaware sentiments about the Cherokee Nation's control over Delaware enrollment. At base there exists a critical awareness of the CDIB card and its function as a form of federal identification. Delaware people recognize that having a CDIB card provides access to certain federal Indian services, but they challenge the significance that the card has on their own personal identity, as explained in the previous chapter. As the grandfather at the Tecumseh celebration articulated, the CDIB card is clearly seen as the federal government's way of certifying one's eligibility to receive certain federal services based on one's status as Indian, and the most important service from the Delaware view is health care.

Layered on top of this general critique of the federal Indian Identification process is a debate among Delaware tribal members about whether the Cherokee Nation should have the right to administer the CDIB enrollment for Delaware people. The arguments voiced in such contexts raise issues concerning the extent to which Delaware tribal members should remain enrolled in the Cherokee Nation and what implications, if any, could result from Cherokee enrollment. One side consists of individuals who do not see a contradiction with being dually enrolled or holding membership in both the Cherokee Nation and the Delaware Tribe. Such dual enrollment proponents are either of mixed Cherokee and Delaware descent or hesitant to give up Cherokee membership because doing so may compromise their access to needed federal services, especially those health-related services. On the other side there are a number of people within the Delaware Tribe who are not comfortable with a position subordinate to the Cherokee Nation and who believe that the Delaware Tribe should institute single enrollment, or membership in either the Delaware Tribe or the Cherokee Nation. Advocates supporting this "go it alone," position, as it is sometimes called, hold that separating Delaware membership from Cherokee membership is the only way to achieve lasting and complete self-governance for the Delaware Tribe given the requirements of current federal policy.

While opinions on enrollment policy differ within the Delaware Tribe, consistent among promoters of both positions is an overwhelming support for Delaware federal recognition and a surprisingly high rate of Cherokee CDIB card ownership. It appears contradictory to find that on the one hand there are dual enrollment advocates who are staunch leaders in the push for Delaware federal recognition, while on the other hand the proponents of single enrollment often hold a Cherokee CDIB card. In this chapter I explain why such realities of Delaware life are not inconsistent and refute the notion that the Delaware passively accept membership in the Cherokee Nation. Though most Delaware apply for and utilize the Cherokee CDIB card for access to federal services, some align themselves with the position once held by the Big House leaders and think that single enrollment is the best strategy, while others sympathize with the Christian-inspired platform and feel that dual enrollment is the safest route for achieving a lasting federal recognition status without also jeopardizing their status as acknowledged Indians in the process.

Further revealed in this chapter is how the Cherokee Nation's membership policy funnels the Delaware's choices for enrollment to make it appear as though some Delaware want to remain citizens in the Cherokee Nation despite existing but divided sentiments. The first section discusses the topic of the multiple tribal membership cards available to those eligible for the Cherokee CDIB card. There were three federally recognized tribes within the Cherokee Nation during the course of my fieldwork, and each continues to issue its own tribal membership card that is separate from, but sometimes connected with, the Cherokee CDIB card. Outlined here are the multiple options available to the Delaware and other non-Cherokee tribes in the Cherokee Nation for card ownership when the requirements for tribal membership cards are considered. The following section then presents the Delaware Tribe's effort to validate their own tribal membership card as a substitute for the Cherokee CDIB card and the Cherokee Nation's reaction to the legitimized Delaware card during the years of restored recognition. The final section then closes with an analysis of the proposed single enrollment policy that was eventually defeated during a referendum vote in 2001. Though the amendment failed to pass by a small margin, the events surrounding the balloting provide a clear illustration of the continued divisions within the Delaware Tribe and also reveal the Cherokee Nation's ability to limit Delaware efforts for complete tribal independence.

Delaware enrollment for the Cherokee CDIB card is facilitated through a complex system of CDIB and tribal membership card requirements, each of which provide different access to federal and tribally sponsored services. Since the Cherokee Nation administers the federal program services and can provide superior tribal services for the region, the Cherokee Nation is able to obtain consent for Cherokee enrollment among Cherokee Nation Dawes Roll descendants. Despite the Cherokee Nation's jurisdictional control, there are options available for Cherokee Nation Dawes Roll descendants when pursuing tribal and federal enrollment. Outlined in this section are the multiple options available to the non-Cherokee tribes in the Cherokee Nation for CDIB and tribal card enrollment. My discussion clarifies how Delaware options for enrollment are channeled toward enrollment in the Cherokee Nation because of the superior federal and tribal services the Cherokee offer. Thus, most Delaware possess a Cherokee CDIB card or a Cherokee tribal membership card not as a sign of consent to Cherokee authority but as a way to access the Cherokee-administered federal services that one or both cards provide.

There exists a potentially confusing array of tribal cards that Cherokee Nation Dawes Roll descendants can possess. The CDIB card, as described in the previous chapter, is only administered by the Cherokee Nation. The Cherokee Nation also issues a separate tribal membership card or blue card from the same Cherokee Nation Registration Department in Tahlequah. Although the CDIB and the Cherokee tribal membership card are issued from the same office, there are two different but linked application procedures that provide differing privileges for membership. Both cards certify lineal descent from a person on the Cherokee Nation Dawes Roll. The Cherokee CDIB card, however, is the federal Indian identification card that lists blood quantum and provides access to federally sponsored Indian programs and services. The Cherokee Nation tribal membership card is the Cherokee Nation citizenship verification card. The Cherokee Nation requires a person to hold both a CDIB card and a Cherokee Nation tribal membership card in order to vote or hold office in the Cherokee Nation (Cherokee Nation of Oklahoma 2007b).

While the Delaware Tribe was federally recognized there were three federally recognized tribes whose members were descendant from the Cherokee Nation Dawes Roll and thus eligible for the CDIB card and the Cherokee Nation tribal membership card. Such potential Cherokee Nation tribal members were also eligible for their own non-Cherokee Nation tribal membership cards as well. The Delaware Tribe issues their tribal membership card from the Delaware Enrollment Office in Bartlesville, Oklahoma. All lineal descendants of the 1904 Delaware Per Capita Roll are eligible for Delaware tribal membership. The Shawnee Tribe received federal recognition in 2000 and issues their own tribal membership cards from the Shawnee Tribe's Headquarters in Miami, Oklahoma.[1] Lineal descendants of those listed on any of the historic Shawnee rolls are eligible for Shawnee tribal membership. However, neither the Delaware nor the Shawnee tribal membership cards list a person's blood quantum because blood degree is not a requirement for tribal membership in either tribe. Both Delaware and Shawnee tribal membership cards certify a person as eligible to vote and hold office in his or her respective tribe and to have access to programs and services provided by the tribe. A CDIB card is not required for membership in the Delaware Tribe or the Shawnee Tribe. The Shawnee Tribe requires single enrollment, and thus Shawnee tribal members cannot also be members of another tribe. The Delaware Tribe does not require single enrollment, and therefore Delaware tribal members can also be members of another tribe that does not require single enrollment (enrollment director, Delaware Tribe, personal communication, July 12, 2007; enrollment director, Shawnee Tribe, personal communication, April 21, 2007). Thus, the Delaware can be tribal members of the Cherokee Nation and the Delaware Tribe while also holding a Cherokee CDIB. The Shawnee, on the other hand, can have a Cherokee CDIB but can only be a card-carrying tribal member of the Cherokee Nation or the Shawnee Tribe, not both.

The United Keetoowah Band of Cherokee (UKB) is the third federally recognized tribe whose members are descendants of the Cherokee Nation Dawes Roll and is the only tribe of the three that is historically and culturally linked to the Cherokee Nation. The UKB are federally recognized as distinct from the Cherokee Nation and are also headquartered in Tahlequah. The UKB require a CDIB card showing at least one-quarter degree of Cherokee blood for tribal membership. Potential UKB members must obtain their CDIB card from the Cherokee Nation Registration Department. Once the blood degree requirement is met with the CDIB card, UKB membership is then based on lineal descent from a person listed on the 1949 Kee-toowah Base Roll. The Keetoowah thus require a Cherokee CDIB card for all UKB tribal members; however, only a UKB tribal membership card provides voting rights and the ability to hold office. The UKB also requires single enrollment and does not allow those who have relinquished their UKB membership to ever be reinstated (Enroll-ment Office, United Keetoowah Band, personal communication, April 21, 2007). UKB members thus have a situation different from both the Delaware Tribe and the Shawnee Tribe. The UKB members must have Cherokee CDIB and a UKB tribal membership card and not also be enrolled with another tribe.

The complexity of card ownership among Dawes Roll descen-dants is remarkable, and table 3 graphically illustrates the situation. Some interesting ironies are revealed when the tribal membership requirements of all four tribes are compared. First, each tribe uses a different base roll for tribal membership, and only the Cherokee

Federally recognized tribes in 2004	Tribe's base roll	Issue CDIB card?	Require CDIB card for tribal membership?	Require single enrollment?
Cherokee Nation of Oklahoma	1906 Cherokee Nation Dawes Roll	Yes	Yes	Yes, but not Delaware and Shawnee
Delaware Tribe of Indians	1904 Delaware Per Capita Roll	No	No	No
Shawnee Tribe	Historic Shawnee Rolls	No	No	Yes
United Keetoowah Band	1949 Base Roll	No	Yes	Yes

3. TRIBAL ENROLLMENT IN THE CHEROKEE NATION: The four federally recognized tribes in 2004 whose members are descendants of Indian enrollees on the Cherokee Nation Dawes Roll and the requirements for tribal membership in each tribe. The four tribes use different base rolls, and only the Cherokee Nation can issue the CDIB card. Each of the four tribes also has different requirements for CDIB ownership and single enrollment.

Nation holds the contract with the BIA to issue CDIB cards. Cherokee control of the CDIB cards means that the members of the Shawnee Tribe and the Delaware Tribe can choose to obtain their CDIB cards from the Cherokee Nation while the UKB and the Cherokee Nation require CDIB enrollment for tribal members. Another interesting comparison is that only the Delaware Tribe allows dual enrollment whereas the Shawnee Tribe and the UKB require single enrollment. The Cherokee Nation also requires single enrollment except for the Delaware and the Shawnee, who are uniquely allowed to be dually enrolled in the Delaware Tribe or the Shawnee Tribe and the Cherokee Nation. However, since the Shawnee Tribe requires single enrollment as does the Keetoowah Band, the Cherokee exception on single enrollment really only applies to the Delaware, who remain the only

OPTION	Cherokee CDIB card	Cherokee tribal card	Delaware tribal card	Tribal membership	Blood quantum ID	Access to federal services
1	Yes	Yes	Yes	Cherokee Nation and Delaware Tribe	Cherokee	Yes
2	Yes	Yes	No	Cherokee Nation	Cherokee	Yes
3	Yes	No	Yes	Delaware Tribe	Cherokee	Yes
4	Yes	No	No	None	Cherokee	Yes
5	No	No	Yes	Delaware Tribe	None	No*
6	No	Yes	Yes	Impossible	Impossible	No
7	No	Yes	No	Impossible	Impossible	No
8	No	No	No	None	Non-Indian	No

4. DELAWARE ENROLLMENT OPTIONS: The eight hypothetical options available to the Delaware for tribal enrollment. Because of tribal membership requirements, options 6 and 7 are not allowed, and option 8 would leave one without a tribal membership or an Indian blood quantum. Options 1 and 3 are the most commonly found among the Delaware, although option 5 was growing in popularity during the years of restored recognition. Options 2 and 4 remain possibilities, but both were rarely chosen by the Delaware.
*Note: For a brief time during the years of restored recognition (2000–2004), the Delaware could access federal Indian program services at select service centers using only a Delaware card.

tribe of the three whose members can be dually enrolled with the Cherokee Nation.

The Delaware Tribe was relatively rare among federally recognized tribal governments because it did not require single enrollment during the years of restored recognition. Also unusual among acknowledged tribes is the Cherokee Nation's allowance for dual enrollment with the Delaware Tribe and the Shawnee Tribe. As a result some Delaware continued to be tribal members of the Delaware Tribe and the Cherokee Nation during the years of restored recognition, yet those rather large numbers of Delaware with Delaware, Shawnee, or Cherokee descent could still only get their CDIB card through the Cherokee Nation Registration Department. With three cards available to the majority of Delaware tribal members, there were mathematically eight possible options for Delaware card ownership, and such possibilities are presented in the left-hand side of table 4. On the right-hand side of the table are the tribal membership, blood quantum, and access to federal Indian services that would result from each option.

Table 4 shows that if the enrollment regulations of the federal government and the Cherokee Nation are considered, then the actual possibilities for Delaware enrollment are narrowed to only four. Options 5–8 are either impossible because of the Cherokee Nation's tribal membership requirements or would label a person as not possessing Indian blood or descent. Leaving aside option 5, or the single enrollment option, the requirement that Cherokee tribal members must have a Cherokee CDIB has made it impossible for the Delaware to be a Cherokee tribal member without also having a Cherokee CDIB card, thus making option 6 an impossibility. Even though the Delaware paid for the right to Cherokee citizenship in the agreement of 1867, the modern Cherokee protocol will not allow the Delaware to have a Delaware tribal membership card and a Cherokee tribal membership card without also having a Cherokee CDIB card. Similarly, option 7 is not possible either because one cannot have only a Cherokee tribal membership card without also having a Cherokee CDIB card, even if one chooses not to have a Delaware tribal membership card. The CDIB requirement for Cherokee tribal membership may appear logical, but in practice it actually narrows the Delaware choices because they cannot be a Cherokee tribal member without also having a Cherokee CDIB card. Option 8 is the final, no-action alternative in which a person chooses not to enroll for any tribal membership or a CDIB card. Doing so leaves a person without a legal federal Indian status and without tribal membership rights.

Of the four possible options left available, two options will not provide a person with voting rights in the Delaware Tribe. Option 2 is not popular, and few if any Delaware have opted for a Cherokee CDIB card and Cherokee tribal membership card without also applying for a Delaware tribal membership card. Having only a Cherokee CDIB and a Cherokee tribal membership card would effectively mark one as Cherokee and thus make the individual's Delaware identity invisible to outsiders, the federal government, and the Delaware Tribe. Option 4 is similar to option 2, as rarely would a person apply for a Cherokee CDIB card only and not also have a Cherokee tribal membership card and a Delaware tribal membership card if he or she wished to participate politically as a Delaware or a Cherokee tribal member. Option 4, however, is more often practiced that option 2 because it does provide access to federal Indian services and requires the least amount of application work.

Two of the first four options that provide an Indian blood quantum identity are the choices most often practiced by the Delaware. However, a formal survey would need to be undertaken to determine which of the two is the most popular. It is known that a portion of Delaware tribal members have a Cherokee-issued CDIB card and a tribal membership card from both the Cherokee Nation and the Delaware Tribe. Holding all three cards provides a person with a valid Indian blood quantum as well as full membership rights in both the Cherokee Nation and the Delaware Tribe. Option 1, or the dual enrollment option, is the only viable option for those Delaware who want the security of an Indian blood quantum while also ensuring a political voice in the Delaware Tribe and the Cherokee Nation, which claims them as citizens. While holding a Cherokee CDIB does not require one to also apply for Cherokee tribal membership, there are Cherokee policies in place that encourage people to do so. Cherokee tribal preference, for instance, is given for jobs with the Cherokee Nation and the distribution of federal services administered by the Cherokee Nation including educational scholarships. Thus, Delaware in need of employment, financial aid, and fundamental services are in many ways obliged to apply for a Cherokee CDIB card as well as a Cherokee tribal membership card in order to facilitate better access to Cherokee-sponsored services. Dual enrollment is the choice then that some Delaware select, but it is a strategy taken out of economic necessity rather than compliance to Cherokee authority.

Option 3, or the Cherokee CDIB and Delaware enrollment option, is a second alternative found among the Delaware. A significant portion of Delaware own a Cherokee CDIB card and a Delaware tribal membership card while not holding a Cherokee Nation membership card. There probably are Delaware people who apply for a Cherokee CDIB card and believe that this act enrolls them as Cherokee tribal members, as was once the standard protocol. Thus, such Cherokee CDIB card holders do not separately apply for the Cherokee tribal membership but do apply for a Delaware tribal membership card. Others who clearly understand the new Cherokee enrollment rules have simply chosen to obtain a Cherokee CDIB card for access to federal Indian services while choosing not to apply for a Cherokee tribal membership card as an expression of resistance to the Cherokee Nation. With escalated tensions between the Delaware Tribe and the Cherokee Nation, some have chosen to forego Cherokee tribal membership either out of disgust or in order to avoid the potentially contaminating effects that might come with such an association. Cherokee CDIB and Delaware enrollment is found most often among those Delaware who simply express their opposition to the Cherokee Nation in the Delaware way. One respected elder, for instance, explained that she had a Cherokee CDIB card and Delaware tribal membership card but would not involve herself in the Cherokee Nation and pursue Cherokee citizenship and voting rights. The elder simply refused to be a part of the Cherokee Nation and could never bring herself to enroll in a tribe for which she felt no particular connection and held so much dissatisfaction. Although choosing CDIB and Delaware enrollment is consistent with some Delaware sentiments, not enrolling also allows the Cherokee Nation to count a larger service population while also silencing the electoral voice of those Delaware who choose to speak their resistance in the culturally appropriate way of avoidance.

A third strategy, or option 5, was also found to some extent and was growing in popularity during the years of restored recognition. Single enrollment is the option in which one only enrolls for a Delaware tribal membership card and not a Cherokee CDIB or Cherokee tribal membership card. The option to identify only as a Delaware tribal member is the most obvious way for Delaware people to signify separation from the Cherokee Nation in the modern era. Since the Delaware Tribe does not require a Cherokee CDIB card or blood degree for membership in the Delaware Tribe, some have chosen to enroll only with the Delaware Tribe. Until the Delaware Tribe was restored federal recognition, and with termination today, choosing single enrollment would leave one without an Indian blood quantum identity and thus without access to federal Indian services.

Therefore, single enrollment was not popular until after 2001, when Delaware tribal leaders were able to convince the BIA and local administrative centers in Delaware Country and beyond to start accepting Delaware tribal membership cards as valid. Even once accomplished, however, many people were still reluctant to give up the security provided by the blood quantum listed on the Cherokee CDIB card and the incentives that came with Cherokee tribal membership. Most Delaware followed either dual enrollment or Cherokee CDIB and Delaware enrollment before federal recognition because the social services offered through the Cherokee Nation were well established and provided the economic motivation for Cherokee enrollment and CDIB card ownership. The restored Delaware Tribe recognized the very real economic motivations that drove most to enroll with the Cherokee Nation as well as the importance of the now standardized federal enrollment process for establishing a separate and sizeable service population in the self-determination era. The Delaware Tribe thus began efforts after recognition was restored to make option 5, or single enrollment, an economically feasible option for its membership.

CONSIDERING SINGLE ENROLLMENT

Though the vast majority of Delaware people support the Delaware Tribe's efforts for self-government, feelings are divided on the importance of enforcing the single enrollment option. Delaware positions regarding federal identification exist in essentially two diametrically opposed camps. In general, dual enrollment in the Cherokee Nation is not regarded by the Delaware as membership in the Cherokee Nation but an enrollment performed out of necessity to sustain either a blood quantum–based Indian identity or the access to Cherokee-administered services that such an enrollment provides. Some Delaware (who may or may not have Cherokee ancestry) support dual enrollment with the Cherokee Nation for the limited economic security provided while others favor single enrollment for Delaware tribal members. Both positions are promoted with the intention of maintaining federal recognition for the Delaware Tribe separate from the Cherokee Nation. I turn now to a discussion of the dual and single enrollment policies to illustrate how both are considered viable strategies for Delaware self-governance and are not veiled support for inclusion in the Cherokee Nation.

The two policies on enrollment can be traced to the divide between Big House and Christian attitudes toward Cherokee membership that occurred with removal. Many proponents of dual enrollment have a Cherokee CDIB card and vote in Cherokee and Delaware tribal elections and referenda. Dual enrollment advocates are accustomed to the Cherokee Nation's label, *Cherokee* (A.D.), used to identify Delaware people and often interpret *A.D.* to refer to "Adopted Delaware." Vocal leaders of those who wish to sustain dual enrollment base their position on the 1867 Cherokee Delaware agreement. The terms of the agreement provided that the Delaware Tribe pay the Cherokee Nation for the right to citizenship. The Delaware Tribe did indeed provide the agreed payment, and thus Delaware people hold the right to Cherokee citizenship. Delaware rights in the Cherokee Nation were later confirmed by the U.S. Supreme Court ruling in 1894 that the Delaware people would share in any per capita payments granted to the Cherokee Nation (Weslager 1972:447–449).

Although the Supreme Court upheld the Delaware's rights as citizens in the Cherokee Nation, the proponents of dual enrollment are quick to point out that there were no provisions in the 1867 Cherokee Delaware Agreement or the 1894 court case that provided for the Delaware Tribe to dissolve. The court decision allowed Delaware people, regardless of their tribal heritage, the right to be voting members of both the Cherokee Nation and the Delaware Tribe. The dually enrolled Delaware argue that it is their paid-for right, based on the agreement with the Cherokee Nation and the 1866 treaty with the federal government, to participate economically, politically, and culturally as both Delaware and Cherokee tribal members. As one Delaware man explained to me, "When you look back in history, why should we give up our rights with the Cherokees when our ancestors bought and paid for it?" This man's position is grounded in historical and legal precedent, but it is a stance that has become problematic with the single enrollment requirements of the self-determination era. Tribes seeking federal recognition must now be able to show that their membership is composed principally of persons who are not members of any other tribe (M. Miller 2004:45). Acknowledged tribes must show that they do not have an overlapping membership with another acknowledged tribe in order to take over the administration of programs and services. Remaining dually enrolled in the Cherokee Nation, or any other tribe for that matter, would thus potentially limit the Delaware Tribe's ability to achieve a secure federal recognition status as well as self-determination contracts given the new direction in federal policy.

Because some Delaware people vote and participate in Cherokee politics, campaigning Cherokee candidates often cater to the dually enrolled Delaware during an election and then distance themselves from the Delaware once elected. This strategy has worked to the benefit of Cherokee politicians, but it has also reinforced an increasing sense of political isolation and economic neglect among dually enrolled Delaware tribal members and has caused many to support those calling for single enrollment. This sense of betrayal felt by some Delaware was pointed out to me by one woman who recalled a town meeting hosted by the former Cherokee chief, Wilma Mankiller. The Delaware woman explained that she stood up and asked Chief Mankiller:

> "Why do I have to go to Claremore to go to the Indian Health Service? Why do I have to go to Pawhuska? Why isn't there a center in Bartlesville? Why isn't there child care in Bartlesville?" And this was back in the 90s so a lot of changes have been made, but I said, "You know, you treat us like a stepchild and you say you want us to be with you, but I can't get a scholarship from you, I can't get a response from the scholarship committee." She didn't really have an answer . . . and I said, "I guess you can pat my hand and say it's OK, but you haven't answered my question," and I sat down.

Most telling in this passage is the frustration voiced toward Cherokee political leaders who never live up to their promises. The Cherokee Nation may want the Delaware to be with them during an election year, but the Delaware are treated like unwanted children after the votes have been tallied. The woman's outrage also illustrates the consistency with which the Delaware approach the Cherokee Nation. The Cherokee Nation is not considered the Delaware Tribe's governing body, but the organization that controls access to federal services like health care and scholarships that are important to Delaware economic security.

A good number of Delaware tribal members, like the woman quoted above, were rallying around a movement for single enrollment while the Delaware Tribe was federally recognized. The possibility of single enrollment was gaining momentum as more Delaware were becoming outraged by the Cherokee Nation's neglect for Delaware Country and court appeals seeking Delaware termination. The single enrollment policy was put forward as a way to remain politically independent while allowing the Delaware Tribe to provide the necessary federal services that the Cherokee Nation was reluctant to supply at the time. Certain Delaware leaders refocused the long-standing position against membership in the Cherokee Nation that was associated with the former Big House leadership and proposed single enrollment as a way to meet the federal acknowledgment requirements cited above as well as the contract stipulations for administering federal services under the Self-Determination Act.

Single enrollment supporters did not see that prohibiting dual enrollment would threaten the integrity of the Delaware Tribe. One Delaware man made it clear to me that formally doing away with dual enrollment would be an opportunity to finally certify Delaware independence while allowing Delaware people an actual choice in tribal membership. He explained that "if they want to be Cherokees, then let them be Cherokees!" Single enrollment advocates also saw their position as one that was consistent with most tribes in Oklahoma. Tribal constitutions throughout the state including the Shawnee Tribe and the UKB do not allow enrollment in more than one tribe. Everyone understands that single enrollment is often inconsistent with the actual genealogical realities of most Indian people. Single enrollment, however, is required by the BIA and is pushed by its proponents as a new form of tribal identity that has an established precedent among Oklahoma Tribes and would have allowed the Delaware Tribe to separate their tribal membership from the Cherokee Nation for the purpose of administering federal contract services as well as conforming to the ideals of the Big House-associated platform.

Though it seems as if a clear line existed between single and dual enrollment policies, it was often difficult to clearly identify the boundaries between proponents of each side. The complication arose because there were individuals who were dually enrolled but vocal advocates of the single enrollment movement, whereas there were others who were not enrolled in the Cherokee Nation but supported those who were. Persons pushing for single enrollment also felt that they should not restrict others in their midst from their own freedoms of identification, or they would have been just as self-serving as the Cherokee Nation. Those advocating for dual enrollment understood that their position limited the Delaware Tribe's ability to take over the administration of federal services, while access to such services was the primary reason that most remained dually enrolled. Such fluidity and complexity in behavior and belief made it difficult for Delaware leaders to mobilize support for the single enrollment policy. The dilemma that faced the pro-single enrollment Delaware Tribal Council during the restored recognition years was how to provide the needed services while not jeopardizing the limited economic security and federal Indian identity of its membership, which was then provided in a limited capacity by the Cherokee Nation.

THE SINGLE ENROLLMENT REFERENDUM

The Department of the Interior initially suggested the policy of single enrollment to the Delaware Business Committee as early as 1974 (Carrigan and Chambers 1994:41). Single enrollment was suggested during this time as a way to identify Delaware people for the dual purpose of distributing per capita payments from successful land claims and establishing a separate tribal membership in preparation for the emerging self-determination era. In order to institute single enrollment, the Delaware Business Committee would first have to modify their existing tribal constitution adopted in 1958. Proposed drafts of the revised Delaware Constitution included a provision for single enrollment per the BIA's suggestion, but ironically such language was later rejected by the BIA because the enrollment clause did not include a reference to the Cherokee Nation as described in chapter 5. Rather than formally recognizing Delaware membership in the Cherokee Nation, the Delaware Tribal Council dropped the enrollment clause entirely.[2] The final draft constitution that proved acceptable to the Delaware did not include any enrollment stipulations and was ratified by the Delaware in 1982. Thus, today the Delaware Tribe places no limits on the enrollment of its members in non-Delaware tribes. As far as the 1982 Delaware Constitution is concerned, Delaware tribal members can be a member of any other tribe with whom they are eligible.

If the BIA would have accepted the Delaware Tribe's decision not to define their membership in relation to the Cherokee Nation in the 1982 constitution, then those choosing to remain in the Delaware Tribe would not have had to rely on the Cherokee Nation for their CDIB cards, and the Delaware Tribe would have been eligible to take over the administration of programs and services under the self-determination policy. Since the Delaware Tribe was not federally recognized until 1996 as a consequence of the BIA's refusal to accept the 1982 Constitution, the Cherokee Nation was the only tribal government eligible to apply for and administer federal services to the Delaware throughout the past few decades. As a result, the Cherokee Nation currently controls most of the federal services offered within the Cherokee Nation's jurisdictional boundaries and the vast majority of Delaware people have to enroll with the Cherokee Nation in order to have access to such services.

While federally recognized, the Delaware Tribe began efforts to secure control over the administration of needed federal services, yet they experienced some difficulties because most Delaware tribal members were also dually enrolled with the Cherokee Nation. The restored Delaware Tribe's requests to begin offering federal contract services were consistently rejected by the BIA on the basis that the Delaware tribal members were already dually enrolled with and provided services through the Cherokee Nation. Instituting single enrollment as originally suggested in 1982 was again proposed by tribal leaders during the restored recognition years as the only way for the Delaware Tribe to meet the BIA requirements, plus this would allow the Delaware Tribe to administer federal services to the local constituency.

The restored Delaware Tribe faced the awkward reality that complete Delaware sovereignty would actually work against the interests of the Cherokee Nation as well as the immediate interests of some Delaware tribal members. Establishing a separate tribal membership or service population as required under the Self-Determination Act regulations would decrease the Cherokee Nation's tribal membership by over ten thousand. Also, since the boundaries between Delaware Country and Cherokee Country were locally understood, there was a concern among the Cherokee that an independent Delaware Tribe might pursue its own land base within the Cherokee Nation. Because of the threat that Delaware self-rule posed, the Cherokee Nation was openly opposed to Delaware single enrollment and continuously appealed Delaware recognition in the federal courts between 1996 and 2004. Delaware tribal members would also feel the effect of complete Delaware autonomy because single enrollment would mean that each Delaware would have to renounce Cherokee enrollment in order to remain a Delaware tribal member. Revoking membership in the Cherokee Nation could potentially jeopardize the Delaware's access to the most reliable federal Indian services in Delaware Country at the time. Because the Delaware had been a nonrecognized tribe for the preceding seventeen years before recognition was restored, the Delaware Tribe had been denied the ability to contract for services or apply for most federal funding sources. Thus it was initially difficult for the restored Delaware Tribe to compete with the established Cherokee infrastructure and influence in the region. Delaware tribal members understood the tribe's difficult position, yet many felt they had no other alternative but to rely on their Cherokee membership for access to the existing, and in many ways superior, Cherokee-administered services despite their sympathetic political sentiments.

Cognizant of the difficult situation in which the Delaware Tribe was placed, elected Delaware leaders did try to work diplomatically with the Cherokee Nation in order to achieve a compromise that would allow Delaware self-government even before restored recognition. As reported in the previous section, prospective Cherokee candidates would actively campaign in Delaware Country and raise support among the Delaware electorate by promising to work with the Delaware Tribe toward their goal of remaining separate from the Cherokee Nation. The most recent Cherokee Nation chief followed in this tradition. Prior to being sworn into office in August 1999, Cherokee chief Chad Smith met with Delaware chief Dee Ketchum to discuss the Cherokee Nation's appeal against the Delaware Tribe's federal recognition. Previous Cherokee chief Joe Byrd had originally brought the lawsuit against the Delaware Tribe, and Chief Smith campaigned for Delaware votes by promising to rescind the appeal.

During the 1999 meeting Chief Smith again promised the Delaware chief that once sworn in he would repeal the lawsuit, and he suggested establishing a committee comprising three members from each tribe and a seventh chosen by the committee for the purpose of hammering out the details of Delaware recognition. Pleased with this show of support, Chief Ketchum proudly announced the meeting at the 1999 Delaware General Council, and a full-page story of the meeting ran on the front page of the *Delaware Indian News*. As a way to honor the Cherokee Nation, the newspaper editor even wrapped the text around the Cherokee Tribal Seal located in the center of the article (*Delaware Indian News* 1999:1).

In the meantime, discussions ensued over the lawsuit, and negotiations between the Delaware and Cherokee broke down over the issue of how the lawsuit was to be dismissed. The Delaware Tribe had hoped that the appeal would be dismissed *with prejudice*, thus ensuring that the appeal could never be refiled. The Cherokee Nation, on the other hand, wanted to ensure their future interests were protected and intended to dismiss the case *without prejudice* so that the appeal could be filed again if subsequent negotiations between the two tribes broke down. As Chief Smith explained to me,

> We voluntarily dismissed the pending action, and then I think it was whoever the chief was then and his lawyer said, "Well, you agreed to dismiss this *with prejudice*." I said, "Of course not. It would be silly to dismiss an issue that you could never revisit." So the idea was we were going to dismiss it *without prejudice*. If negotiations broke down, we could always go back to court. And so, the litigation process took off again, and it ended up in the Supreme Court, and the resolution was what the resolution was. . . . No lawyer in his right mind would dismiss a case pending negotiations and never have the option to refile it. (Emphasis added)

A little over a year later, Chief Smith informed Chief Ketchum that the Cherokee Nation would not dismiss the case *with prejudice* as the Delaware Tribe had hoped, and the appeal against Delaware recognition continued. Disappointed, Chief Ketchum returned to the 2000 Delaware General Council and informed the tribe of the Cherokee's decision but urged his fellow members to stand shoulder to shoulder (*Delaware Indian News* 2001:1). The January 2001 issue of the *Delaware Indian News* reported the Cherokee Nation's decision to continue the appeal on the front page, but this time without the Cherokee Tribal Seal and only half a page of text. When reached for comment on Chief Smith's decision, Chief Ketchum (*Delaware Indian News* 2001:2) wrote,

> I am extremely disappointed because I took him at his word. Chief Smith suggests he doesn't know what his tribal council wants him to do. But he could drop this lawsuit on his own just as Chief Byrd filed it on his own. With this decision, Chief Smith has made it clear he is trying to terminate the Delaware Tribe. We have tried to work things out, but Chief Smith has waged war on the Delaware People by saying we are not Delaware, we are Cherokee. We must stand up and be counted as the grandfather tribe that we are. My prayer is that my grandchildren will know that the Delaware Nation is still here and functioning. They will have heard their language spoken and their songs sung.

Although the Delaware chief had high hopes with the election of the new Cherokee chief, Chief Smith was constitutionally sworn to protect the interests of the Cherokee Nation, which included not allowing the Delaware Tribe unchecked independence within the jurisdictional boundaries of the Cherokee Nation. Once it was clear to Chief Ketchum that diplomatic efforts would not be productive in achieving complete separation, the only route available was to seek self-determination contracts for the Delaware Tribe on their own terms. The difficulty that such a strategy presented was that to "stand up and be counted," as Chief Ketchum urged, was heard by some Delaware people as a strategy that might compromise their CDIB enrollment in the process.

The Delaware Tribe thus began an aggressive effort to pursue complete separation from the Cherokee Nation. The clearest solution was to validate the Delaware Tribal membership card as one that provided the same legal federal Indian identity as the Cherokee CDIB card. Achieving BIA approval of the Delaware Tribal membership card would be facilitated if the Delaware card had the same information as the CDIB card. During the course of my work with the Delaware Tribe, I witnessed the transformation of the Delaware tribal membership cards as Delaware leaders labored to create a Delaware-only jurisdiction. Work began when the tribal lawyer and a Delaware tribal member began doing research on Delaware genealogy and added blood quantum amounts to the 1904 Delaware Per Capita Roll. The Delaware Tribal Enrollment Office then calculated and included blood quantum for the new tribal membership card. The new cards were white rather than blue, they had the tribal member's picture, and the most recent ones included blood quantum. The new Delaware tribal membership cards were almost identical in appearance to the Cherokee CDIB card. The only real difference was that the new Delaware card had a picture of the tribal member, and the Cherokee CDIB card does not. The picture was to more clearly identify the cardholder for voting and registration purposes. Although the older blue Delaware cards were still valid, the Delaware Tribe actively advertised the availability of the new white card in every issue of the tribal newspaper during the later years of restored recognition.

The popularity of the new card exploded when the Claremore Indian Hospital began accepting the Delaware card in place of the Cherokee CDIB card. As a result single enrollment did become more prevalent for a brief period from about 2001 to 2004 despite some Delaware reluctance and Cherokee opposition. It was also during this time that the BIA in Muskogee also agreed to start accepting the Delaware tribal membership cards in lieu of the Cherokee CDIB cards. The Delaware Tribe was also given a reservation number to identify their tribal constituency and a five-county service area that existed within Cherokee Nation's fourteen-county service area for certain BIA contract services. Although the Cherokee Nation continued to control the CDIB card process, the new Delaware tribal card was setting the stage for the Delaware to completely separate their population from that claimed by the Cherokee Nation. In the process the Delaware Tribe was required to adopt federal forms of Indian identity such as blood quantum and reservation numbers into their existing tribal governmental processes. But like other self-determination governments, the Delaware Tribe was incorporating federal terminology in order to achieve greater tribal sovereignty. Unlike most other self-determination governments though, the Delaware Tribe had to achieve such sovereignty by separating and identifying their constituency and jurisdiction that had long been claimed by the Cherokee Nation.

In 2001 the Delaware Tribal Council thus resurrected the longstanding idea of single enrollment as a means to finally separate their membership from the Cherokee Nation and to be eligible for contract services. A seemingly straightforward modification was needed in the Delaware enrollment policy. As an acknowledged tribe under the self-determination policy, the Delaware could define their own rules for tribal membership. Instituting single enrollment would thus require a referendum vote to amend the 1982 Delaware Constitution. The Tribal Council proposed to add a clause that would explicitly prohibit dual enrollment and unanimously agreed to put the amendment to a vote. The Delaware Constitution requires a two-thirds majority from the voting membership to pass an amendment so the Tribal Council began immediately promoting the single enrollment clause. The Delaware Tribal Council allocated funds for a mass mailing campaign designed to publicize the vote as well as to educate their resident and nonresident constituency concerning the need for single enrollment. Town meetings were held to answer questions and to inform people on the importance that the amendment had for the tribe's ability to compete for federal contracts. These meetings were held with the intent to show the thoughtful consideration that went into the proposed amendment and the importance of single enrollment for the political integrity of the tribe. Delaware leaders spoke at length in tribal meetings and in the tribal newspaper, explaining why it was necessary for the Delaware Tribe to institute single enrollment.

The referendum was also introduced in a way that tried to balance the sentiments between those who were intolerant of Cherokee membership with those who were more open to Cherokee membership. The amendment to the constitution was publicized as an innovative way for those on both sides of the enrollment debate to agree to disagree. Council members realized that there were a number of tribal members who would like to remain dually enrolled while others in the tribe were already practicing and supportive of single enrollment. Tribal leaders presented the amendment as a way to settle the debate over enrollment that had existed within the Delaware Tribe since removal. Passing a single enrollment clause was an issue of administrative compliance, but it was promoted locally as the Delaware way to resolve mounting tension in the tribe by allowing opposing groups to take separate paths.

The Tribal Council thus had to gain support for the amendment in the way considered appropriate by the local family leaders. Consider the language in Chief Ketchum's (2001:2) message urging tribal members to approve a single enrollment requirement: "We must follow the BIA's requirement. However, this is an individual matter of conscience for each Delaware to decide. We are not telling you to enroll or dis-enroll. We are not the enrollment police. The reason we are coming back to you so quickly for a re-vote on the constitution is that the revised Delaware Constitution is a high priority for the tribe to have in place so we can apply and receive servicing funds. This constitution also gives more power to the General Council and less power to the Tribal Council. We will follow your directives." Chief Ketchum's argument for the need to change the enrollment policy was offered in order to encourage people to vote for single enrollment so that the tribe would be able to meet the BIA requirements and offer the same contract services provided by other tribal governments in Oklahoma. However, the chief's call to action was tempered with qualifications that emphasized the power of the voting membership over the Tribal Council and the need to explain why the amendment must be done so "quickly." His message was published in the *Delaware Indian News* and thus was sent to both local and nonlocal members. Even though the need for single enrollment was clear, the elected leaders knew that they had to gain the support of the local leadership in order to obtain the required votes for the constitutional amendment. Thus, even those policy changes that were required by the BIA had to be instituted in a way that was consistent with the local decision-making process in order to be considered valid by the Delaware people. Although the chief and the Tribal Council were the recognized elected representatives, the true authority rested in the voting membership of the General Council, which pivoted on the decisions of the local family leadership.

The amendment vote took place in November 2001 and was held during the annual General Council meeting. Private balloting lasted from nine o'clock in the morning until five o'clock in the afternoon, and absentee voting was allowed. After the votes were tallied, tribal opinion was split down the middle with 163 votes cast in favor of the amendment and 160 opposed. Since a two-thirds majority was required to amend the constitution, the resolution did not pass. Many Tribal Council members were disheartened as they came to terms with what the vote meant for the Delaware Tribe's potential self-determination contracts. Chief Ketchum later reported on the vote and the subsequent BIA actions in the quarterly tribal newspaper.

He explained that as a result of the failed amendment the Delaware Tribe would not be eligible for the administration of contract services already offered by the Cherokee Nation due to an overlapping membership (Ketchum 2002:2).

Though crushing to the Tribal Council and the Delaware Tribe's bid for single enrollment, the results of the vote were less revealing than the actual political maneuvers that led to the vote's outcome. The split vote may at first appear to have been a split within the tribe over support for federal recognition, with roughly half of the local community wanting to remain members of the Cherokee Nation. However, such an interpretation would be entirely inaccurate and superficial. The reality was that not a single person wanted to remain with the Cherokee Nation, nor did anyone want to do away with the Delaware Tribe's federal recognition. The pursuant discussion shows that the failed amendment actually revealed the kin-based divisions between opposed Big House and Christian platforms that exist within the tribe today and that express different ideas about how federal recognition should be gained and at what cost self-government should be sought. Those who voted against the referendum were not voting against federal recognition, but against the potential to lose access to federal services if single enrollment was used to sustain such a status and against the very real possibility that the Cherokee appeal could result in termination of the Delaware Tribe.

Most surprising was that despite the Tribal Council's efforts, some voters were not convinced that the amendment was proposed in a thoughtful way. Several people explained to me that they felt as though the amendment was a decision that was being forced on the community and that such rash actions are usually considered to be potentially harmful. It turns out that rather than institute what some felt to be a rushed policy, a good number of Delaware who initially supported single enrollment or were not dually enrolled were persuaded to choose caution and to vote against the amendment. Consider the following explanation provided by one Delaware woman who was not dually enrolled with the Cherokee Nation for why she did not vote for the amendment: "It hasn't been that long before we got all this anyway. Now it's just a battle trying to get everything and they are trying to . . . they are trying to move too fast and push the people too fast. You know, they're turning around, and they are wanting too much overnight, you know. . . . The Cherokees, took a while for them to get started but the Delawares, the way the Tribal Council is doing, they're trying [to] push everything too fast and they're trying to push it on the people too fast." The temper of reservation explained in this statement was a pervasive sentiment held by some Delaware that resonated with the leadership expectations explained in chapter 5.

Another important factor in the amendment's failure was the perceived socioeconomic differences between the proponents of single enrollment and the rest of the Delaware constituency. The most vocal proponents of single enrollment were the elected leaders who represented kinship constituencies from the local urban centers (Bartlesville and Dewey) of Washington County. Those lineages from beyond the urban spaces of Washington County associated the region with apprehension because of the concentration of wealth in the local cities. As one man explained to me, "Washington County is power and greed; they think they are the upper crust of the Delaware Tribe. If you're not from Washington County, you're not a true Delaware. . . . Anything outside of Washington County, in my opinion, is taken for granted, not recognized, not a part of, not important." In many ways this man's testimony is understandable when we consider the modern composition of the local economy in the context of the regionally associated Delaware lineages. Bartlesville is the county seat for Washington County and also the core region for the regional economy. Washington County is currently almost five times larger in population than neighboring

Nowata County, and this contrast is even more apparent considering that Nowata County is over one hundred square miles larger in area. Also, from 1959 to 1989 Washington County recorded the highest per capita income in the state of Oklahoma, surpassing the metropolitan areas of Tulsa and Oklahoma City, while Nowata, Craig, and Rogers counties have remained almost consistently below the state income average for the same thirty-year period (U.S. Census Bureau 2007).[3] The concentration of wealth in Washington County is centered in the city of Bartlesville and is most likely the result of the revenues generated by the Phillips Petroleum Corporation, which has been headquartered in Bartlesville since its organization in the early twentieth century.[4] Washington County is thus materially juxtaposed as the economic center, with Nowata, Craig, and Rogers counties as the rural hinterland of Delaware Country.

The man's statement also hints at a sensibility within the Delaware Tribe that further contributed to the amendment's failure. The city of Bartlesville is the location of the tribal headquarters, the Delaware Community Center, and the majority of the tribal offices. Much like the way that some Americans who live outside of Washington DC feel disconnected from national politics, the Delaware living outside of Bartlesville often felt left out of the major tribal decision-making processes. With the Bartlesville-based leadership leading the call for single enrollment, some family constituencies beyond southern Washington County were skeptical of the movement and were concerned about who would benefit if the amendment passed.

The final and most important contributor to the amendment's failure was the Cherokee Nation. Recognizing the potential threat to their jurisdictional authority that a single enrollment policy would pose, Cherokee political representatives embarked on a strategy to undermine the amendment. The Cherokee Nation worked to destabilize the single enrollment effort by threatening to remove Delaware access to federal Indian services if the amendment passed. Cherokee leaders recognized the geographic and socioeconomic differences in the Delaware Tribe and relied on such spatially divided sentiments. Cherokee representatives began focusing their threats on Delaware leaders who represented lineages from beyond Washington County to target those who felt somewhat removed from the Bartlesville-oriented, single enrollment movement. Such non-Bartlesville leaders were also more likely to represent a higher percentage of constituents who would be more reluctant to risk the loss of Cherokee-sponsored services.

Delaware persons on both sides of the enrollment debate informed me that the Cherokee Nation spread information through campaign fliers in the mail and by word of mouth against the single enroll-ment amendment. The Cherokee warned the Delaware that if the amendment passed, the Cherokee Nation would restrict those who relinquished Cherokee membership from ever re-applying. The Cherokee threat was of considerable concern for the vast majority of dually enrolled Delaware people. Since the Cherokee Nation was then appealing the Delaware's federal recognition, it was uncertain if the Delaware Tribe would remain a recognized government fol-lowing the court case. The dually enrolled constituency feared that if the Cherokee Nation won their appeal against the Delaware's federal recognition, then Delaware eligibility for federal services would be lost. As one man explained, "If we resign as Cherokees, and we lose our case, then we're not Delawares, then what are we?!" The con-cern that this man voiced is consistent with the prevailing Delaware sentiment. Many feared that if they gave up their rights to Cherokee membership, then they would run the dual risk of losing federal acknowledgment and access to critical services that such a status provided if the Cherokee appeal was successful.

When faced with the Cherokee warnings, some elected leaders who initially supported single enrollment were not prepared to risk the possibility of squandering their kin-based constituency's access to federal services already provided by the Cherokee Nation. These concerned Delaware leaders thus mobilized their own local and absentee constituencies just days before the election in order to ensure that the amendment failed. For those who were concerned about the financial impact that single enrollment might have for them and their families in the long run, the Cherokee message served as a viable threat and kept many on the side of maintaining dual enrollment despite their desire to maintain Delaware federal recognition.

The Tribal Council thus faced considerable opposition to its proposed single enrollment policy during the years of restored recognition even through a good portion of Delaware tribal members actually practiced single enrollment. While some questioned the immediate need for officially implementing single enrollment, others were concerned that such a policy change might ultimately compromise the access to federal services disproportionately required by the non-Bartlesville constituency. The result was that a significant portion of the active voters in the Delaware Tribe were not convinced that single enrollment was either economically feasible or carefully considered. The Tribal Council was thus unable to implement single enrollment as required by the BIA despite their calls to action. As shown, though, the vote against single enrollment was not a vote against Delaware self-governance. The amendment's failure was clearly a product of the Cherokee Nation's ability to influence the votes of the economically dependent and historically divided Delaware constituency through its administrative control of the enrollment process, which provided the most secure and reliable access to federal Indian services in the region.

The Delaware Tribe was thus not able to move forward without difficult challenges from the Cherokee Nation as well as internal dissent. The Cherokee Nation held considerable influence with those tribal members who either depended on or benefited from health-related services contracted through the Cherokee Nation.

The Cherokee Nation could thus effect the Delaware Tribal government through their influence on the Delaware who were members of both tribes, were sympathetic to the Christian platform on Cherokee membership, or were dependent on Cherokee-sponsored services. Ultimately, the Cherokee Nation's appeal was successful, leaving the Delaware with no other option but to return to or maintain Cherokee enrollment. Without federal recognition, most Delaware today, despite their political positions, have resorted to dual enrollment and have a Delaware tribal membership card and one or both of the Cherokee Nation–issued cards. Nonetheless, it is important to emphasize that many Delaware followed the Big House position on Cherokee membership and renounced their Cherokee enrollment when single enrollment was made available. The viability of the Delaware tribal membership card did replace the Delaware's reliance on the Cherokee-issued CDIB card for a brief period during the years of restored recognition, thus reflecting the critical way in which the Delaware utilize their potential for Cherokee enrollment.

CONCLUSION

Despite their best efforts the Delaware Tribal Council was never able to establish single enrollment, and today the Delaware continue to have the potential to be dually enrolled as citizens of the Delaware Tribe and the Cherokee Nation. Instituting single enrollment would have certainly been a tremendous victory for the Delaware Tribe at the time. Establishing a tribal body without overlapping membership would have been a great step toward completely separating the Delaware Tribe from the economic influence of the Cherokee Nation. On the other hand it may have also been a blessing that single enrollment did not pass, considering the Cherokee Nation's successful appeal against the Delaware's federal recognition. Because of the dual enrollment allowance, the Delaware people today sustain an acknowledged Indian status though the Delaware Tribe is no longer federally recognized. However, the Delaware must register with the Cherokee Nation and hold a Cherokee CDIB card in order to hold such a mis-acknowledged status.

Regardless of the amendment's outcome, it was clear that both sides equally supported the Delaware Tribe's federal recognition. While Delaware people continue to be generally critical about blood quantum and the Cherokee CDIB card, most have retained their CDIB cards for economic and now political viability. The debate over single enrollment has subsided for the moment as the elected Delaware leaders now struggle to simply regain acknowledgment. Though many Delaware hold a Cherokee CDIB card and some have a Cherokee tribal membership card, their voluntary enrollments should not be read as support for the Cherokee Nation. In most cases Delaware enrollment in the Cherokee Nation is the result of the practical economic realities of federal Indian policy within which the Delaware live today. Those who remain dually enrolled are aware that having a Cherokee CDIB card may in fact hinder their ultimate goal of Delaware self-governance, but card ownership has become a necessary fact of life for those dealing with the economic adversity and health needs that can be a factor in the Indian communities and urban areas of Delaware Country.

Considered to be blood descendants of another federally recognized tribe, the Delaware were required to either enroll with the Cherokee Nation or to choose what some considered to be a risky strategy of complete separation and create their own tribally specific service population. As explained in this chapter, making the move toward complete independence was not without reaction from the Cherokee Nation, which sought to influence Delaware detractors and encourage people to remain enrolled in the Cherokee Nation through the lure of better health care services. Ultimately, complete independence can only be achieved in the self-determination era if single enrollment is realized, and some Delaware simply may not be able to make such a choice.

The Delaware Tribe's failure to dissolve dual enrollment may be interpreted by some as an indication that the Delaware wished to remain part of the Cherokee Nation. I hope that I have demonstrated here that such an interpretation is entirely inaccurate. The Delaware remain divided on the issue of single enrollment today, not because some want to be Cherokee but because enrollment, according to modern policy, holds two principal but overlapping meanings: tribal membership and service population. Such multi-vocality is understood by Delaware people in the context of a long historical debate that has existed within the Delaware Tribe over the issue of their potential Cherokee membership and what such membership should actually mean. Some Delaware who are sympathetic with the Big House platform reject Cherokee membership because it is regarded as tribal membership in another tribe, which would compromise their Delaware identity and separateness from the Cherokee Nation. Others see Cherokee membership as simply inclusion in the only possible Indian service population available to them, and thus they accept Cherokee membership for the access to the programs and services it provides. Inclusion in a service population is separate from tribal membership, and thus such individuals who are open to Cherokee enrollment do not see that such an action would undermine their Delaware identity or the independence of the Delaware Tribe. Because of these historically situated and divided sentiments about Cherokee membership, those who voted against single enrollment may be more appropriately interpreted as voting against what some aligned with the Christian platform would consider the unrealistic conflation of tribal membership and service population that is imposed on every tribal government in order to hold an acknowledged status and contract for programs and services under the self-determination policy.

It is in such contexts then that one must consider that although a number of Delaware people actively utilize services through the Cherokee Nation, none of them want to be Cherokee, nor do they want to give up being Delaware. Everyone knows and is proud of their shared Delaware heritage, and some are equally proud of their Cherokee ancestry. The reality was that some lineage leaders in the community who wanted to solidify their separateness from the Cherokee Nation in the modern era sided with the Tribal Council's Big House–inspired referendum and voted to institute single enrollment and meet the BIA requirements. Other Delaware sympathetic to the Christian platform, however, did not recognize the immediacy of the BIA's policy, nor did they see the need to conflate Delaware tribal membership with the creation of a Delaware service population in the process. Influenced heavily by the Cherokee Nation, enough individuals saw single enrollment as a risky financial strategy instead of a nuanced way to promote and sustain Delaware tribal independence. While the competing platforms on membership in the Cherokee Nation can be traced to removal, the reality was that dual enrollment continued because a significant portion of Delaware voters sided with the Christian-inspired perspective that wanted to continue the possibility for membership in the Cherokee Nation but only because dual enrollment was the only reliable way for the Delaware to gain access to those vital programs and services only available through inclusion in the Cherokee Nation's service population. Unfortunately, dual enrollment is also a policy that compromises the Delaware Tribe's long-standing effort to remain separate from the Cherokee Nation, given the combined meanings of tribal membership and service population in modern understandings of tribal enrollment. Indeed, the choice to not institute single enrollment today will likely require Delaware tribal members to continue as members of the Cherokee Nation's service population in order to simply survive as Delaware Indians in the self-determination era. However, Delaware enrollment in the Cherokee Nation, both today and in the past, is a compromise that some Delaware are compelled to make in order to maintain an acknowledged Indian status while remaining dedicated to the goal of preserving the Delaware Tribe as an independent tribal government resident in the Cherokee Nation.

⑧ Conclusion

They will have heard their language
spoken and their songs sung.
CHIEF DEE KETCHUM, 2001

In my office as I worked on the final editing of this book, my cell phone rang on the desk beside me. I was sometimes startled at the sound of my cell phone because calls had not been coming very often. The cell was not my own, but one of the few pieces of tribal equipment that I still possessed. The tribal cell phone is the number for the Delaware Tribe's NAGPRA Program, and phone calls once brought inquiries from federal agencies or private companies about the potential for impacting Delaware cultural and religious sites as was required under federal law. After the loss of recognition, however, the frequency of such calls decreased at the same time that the news coming from the other end increasingly was not good and often revolved around the issue of lost recognition. The message from this midmorning call was similar. It was a representative from Harvard's Peabody Museum calling to notify the Delaware Tribe that the museum's Delaware collection, about which they initially consulted the tribe in 1999, was now ready to be repatriated. The items would be available for return after a notice had been posted for thirty days in the federal register.

The initial good news then turned sour as the Peabody representative proceeded to explain that since the Delaware Tribe was not federally recognized, according to federal law the Peabody Museum could not list the items as culturally affiliated with the Delaware Tribe. In the federal register the notice would read, "officials of the Peabody Museum of Archaeology and Ethnology also have determined that, pursuant to 25 U.S.C 3001 [2], there is a relationship of shared group identity that can be reasonably traced between the Native American human remains and associated funerary objects and the Cherokee Nation, Oklahoma, on behalf of the Delaware Tribe of Indians" (U.S. Department of Interior 2007:41525). The Peabody representative explained that she had already been in contact with the NAGPRA representative for the Cherokee Nation and that the Cherokee had deferred the issue and right to repatriate to the Delaware Tribe. However, if the Delaware Tribe wanted to move forward on repatriating the human remains, the Delaware Tribe would have to act as representatives of the Cherokee Nation as it was the Cherokee, not the Delaware, who held standing as an acknowledged tribe under federal law.

Such a repatriation issue presented a quandary for the Delaware Tribe and me that reflected the difficult position within which tribes like the Delaware are placed everyday. Should the Delaware move forward on this important repatriation in order to return and rebury excavated Delaware graves as was the goal of the NAGPRA program? Or would doing so be read by the Department of the Interior, Congress, and the federal judiciary as an indication that the Delaware have indeed accepted their merger with the Cherokee Nation? What emerges from such questions is the complexity of the federal relationship with the Delaware Tribe, which has often not been well understood but which has now been explained with this research. To repatriate without federal recognition, the Delaware have no other option but to do so through the Cherokee Nation. Presented with no other recourse, the Delaware and I can choose to do nothing and let the items continue to sit on the shelves at the museum, or we can take action and rebury the items under the auspices of the Cherokee Nation as would be in line with the mission of the Delaware Tribe's unacknowledged, but known-to-exist, NAGPRA program.

Like the difficult repatriation issue, this work presents the similar dilemma facing Delaware families, but often on a much more personal and emergent scale. Delaware families who are caring for a sick elderly parent, an injured breadwinning spouse, or an aspiring youngster must make the same choice, and the decisions made are understandably easy. The Delaware overwhelmingly choose to care for their elders, heal their spouses, and look after their children's education, but the only option available to do so requires that the prescriptions, hospital care, and scholarship assistance is sought through the Cherokee Nation. As this work shows, when the Delaware rightfully look after and follow through on important and even life-threatening issues that take place everyday, such actions should not detract from the parallel existence of a distinct Delaware community and long-lasting independent political organization that certainly meets the federal acknowledgment criteria.

With the recent loss of federal acknowledgment, the Cherokee Nation now stands in a pivotal and powerful position with regard to the Delaware Tribe's restoration as well as the Delaware's continued access to what are often necessary programs and services. Indeed, it is the Cherokee Nation on whom many Delaware now must rely for the medical and social support that is sometimes needed, given the unknown but inevitable circumstances that will eventually come to pass for some Delaware families. The need to remain a part of the Cherokee Nation's service population has thus brought many Delaware to return as members of the Cherokee Nation, and the Cherokee Nation thus holds the desirable position of remaining as the tribal government for Delaware people and retaining the right to administer services and programs to its Delaware constituency.

With such an outcome, it is not difficult to see why the Cherokee Nation has been so concerned about the Delaware Tribe's federal acknowledgment. The reality is that in the recent past the Cherokee Nation has been openly opposed to Delaware acknowledgment, yet such challenges have been carried out only in order to protect the substantial Cherokee interests and sovereignty in their treaty-guaranteed territory. Moving against Delaware recognition is understandable from the Cherokee viewpoint, and Cherokee actions should not be demonized since other tribes, including the Delaware, would do the same if their integrity and territorial jurisdiction were similarly threatened. As Cherokee chief Chad Smith explained to me,

I'm constitutionally sworn to defend the Cherokee Nation; and it's not, Cherokee Nation is not counties. It is an area that is defined by metes and bounds description in 1838 and memorialized in a fee patent beginning in 1846. That's the Cherokee Nation, and within the Cherokee Nation we believe that there cannot be another tribe that exercises a government-to-government relationship with the United States. . . . Those principles stay the same regardless of what form the Delawares choose. That was our objection with the courts, that would be our objection to Congress; that would be our objection with the Executive Branch with acknowledgment. . . . If you've got another tribe here saying, "Well we're the governance of this particular part of the Cherokee Nation." Well, that is something that we would object to. I took an oath of office to defend our constitution and our government. . . . And, if the shoe was on the other foot, the Delawares would be exactly the same. If they had a particular treaty territory, they would not want some other tribe to come in and assert some authority there.

The Cherokee Nation's guiding principle remains the conviction to maintain supreme jurisdictional authority within the historic boundaries of the Cherokee Nation, while being very aware of the continued existence and distinctiveness of the Delaware Tribe and the Shawnee Tribe. With such realities in mind, the Cherokee Nation offered two separate agreements to the Shawnee Tribe and the Delaware Tribe that would allow for the conditional acknowledgment of both. The Shawnee Tribe was the first to accept the agreement and did receive conditional acknowledgment during Chief Smith's administration. The Delaware did not initially accept the Cherokee proposal but did revisit the agreement following the 2004 judicial termination. The Delaware and the Cherokee have since worked out an agreement that would allow the Delaware Tribe separate recognition yet maintain Cherokee authority within the Cherokee Nation. The first section of this chapter reviews a draft of the 2007 Cherokee-Delaware Agreement and provides an analysis of its major provisions. What emerges is that the agreement is not so different from the 1867 Cherokee-Delaware Agreement and may ultimately prove just as difficult to carry out in the context of future federal policy given the similarities.

In light of the substantial power held by the Cherokee Nation and the motivation to remain opposed to Delaware acknowledgment, one may wonder why Chief Smith has been so open to working with the Shawnee and Delaware on providing opportunities for recognition that do not infringe on Cherokee authority. Chief Smith justifies his efforts with the following statement to me:

> The reality of it is, is that it was just good public policy. The tribe could negotiate something else that would save us some money, save the Delawares some money, and try to use those moneys for something that has some tangible return and value . . . we'd relieve some friction between the Cherokee Nation and the Delawares. I mean everyone wants to get along and get onto more productive issues. . . . We've made the commitment; I've made the personal commitment to support them in federal recognition as long as

it doesn't infringe upon the rights of the Cherokee Nation and our territories.

The Cherokee Nation then holds an understandable interest in the acknowledgment decisions for the Delaware and the Shawnee. Indeed, the place to begin our critical attention is not on the position held by the Cherokee Nation, who will justifiably work to maintain their authority, but on the federal structure in place that has pitted the interests of the Delaware and the Cherokee in opposition. The Delaware case presents an uncommon type of tribal government and community for whom the current self-determination policies on enrollment remain problematic. The second section here revisits the special situation faced by the Delaware and explores one possibility for the acknowledgment of such groups. The San Juan Southern Paiute acknowledgment presents a singular but empowering model for the Delaware and other groups to consider given the current federal policy on tribal enrollment. However, as it stands, the Paiute model is an illuminating but difficult example to follow and will result in inevitable challenges from the Cherokee Nation and a potentially long waiting period. The Paiute example clarifies some of the nuances in the Federal Acknowledgment Process and the need to differentiate between tribal enrollment and service population with reference to certain tribes. It remains to be seen, however, whether such clarification will be useful for the Delaware.

2007 CHEROKEE-DELAWARE AGREEMENT

The underlying issues driving the 2007 Cherokee-Delaware Agreement are multiple, but the politics that led to the development of the agreement actually clarify the unequal situation within which tribes like the Delaware are placed. Evident in the terms of the 2007 Cherokee-Delaware Agreement is the powerful role that can be played by a federally recognized tribe in the processes surrounding federal recognition for certain groups. The Delaware Tribe is placed in a difficult situation by being obliged to negotiate with the Cherokee Nation. Tribal Council members were reportedly informed by U.S. congressmen following the 2004 judicial termination that the Delaware must seek terms with the Cherokee Nation if there was ever to be any hope for separate recognition. However, it was the Cherokee Nation that sought the termination of the Delaware Tribe, and it would seem contradictory for Congress to instruct the Delaware to deal with the very tribe that sought their initial termination. Regardless, the Delaware Tribe has been told that they must negotiate with the Cherokee Nation in order to restore a modified form of federal recognition. With very little financial resources and even less federal backing, the Delaware Tribe was thus obliged to sit down at the table with the Cherokee Nation and negotiate for Delaware recognition while it is clear to all that the Delaware are at an unmistakable disadvantage in the process. Under self-determination, the Cherokee Nation holds the federal relationship and thus controls the programs and services on which the Delaware rely and holds the lobbying power in Washington DC to block any potential legislation providing for Delaware recognition that does not meet with Cherokee approval. The reason that the Delaware must come to terms with the Cherokee Nation is not the fault of either the Delaware or the Cherokee but the current federal structure within which both groups must operate in order to maintain their acknowledged position. Indeed, it is the U.S. federal government, not the Cherokee Nation nor the Delaware people, that has provided the Delaware with no other option but to negotiate with the Cherokee Nation for acknowledgment.

One hundred and forty years following the signing of the 1867 Cherokee-Delaware Agreement, Delaware chief Jerry Douglas and Cherokee principal chief Chad Smith (2007) signed another Cherokee-Delaware agreement that would restore the federal recognition of the Delaware Tribe dated January 18, 2007. This agreement received overwhelming support from the Delaware voters, with over 80 percent of ballots cast in favor of moving forward on the agreement with the Cherokee Nation. The vast majority of support for the agreement and voter turnout came from absentee voters, with approximately one thousand absentee votes cast in the referendum compared with just under fifty walk-in votes. Interestingly, absentee voters vastly supported the agreement (85 percent in favor) while the few walk-in votes cast showed very little support for the agreement (25 percent in favor) among local Delaware. The striking contrast in support likely reflects Chief Douglas's electoral support, which remains predominately among absentee voters. As revealed in the 2006 election, Chief Douglas and his platform were popular among absentee voters while the local resident community largely did not support his approach. Once in office, Douglas worked diligently with Chief Smith on the final agreement in order fulfill his decidedly Christian-inspired campaign platform of regaining recognition as efficiently as possible and through diplomatic concessions to the Cherokee Nation if necessary. The strong absentee support presents a compelling voice in the Delaware Tribe that is impossible to ignore, although it may not be a voice that is satisfactory to some in the local resident community.

As explained in chapter 4, although the BIA had earlier certified that the Delaware Tribe was eligible to reorganize under the Oklahoma Indian Welfare Act, the business committee declined to do so. With such reorganization still potentially available, the Delaware Tribe was instructed to simply restore federal recognition by modifying its existing constitution into one that was consistent with the OIWA. The Cherokee Nation agreed to not appeal the Delaware Tribe's reorganization as long as the revised constitution remained constrained by the 2007 Cherokee-Delaware Agreement. With no other immediate options available, the Delaware Tribe voted to adopt a revised OIWA constitution on May 27, 2009. The Delaware Tribe was restored to the list of federally recognized tribes on August 11, 2009.[1]

The major provisions of the 2007 Cherokee-Delaware Agreement are thus worth reviewing in order to understand the relationship that now exists between the Delaware Tribe and the Cherokee Nation. The Delaware Tribe's acknowledgment as articulated in the agreement would remain an acknowledged status subject to Cherokee oversight for those tribal programs, services, and businesses carried out in Delaware Country as would be consistent with Cherokee principles. The restoration of Delaware recognition will thus not be completely separate as some, if not most, of the Delaware Tribe's local authority will be carried out under Cherokee authority per the agreement, which could potentially mold the Delaware Tribe into a local extension of the Cherokee Nation.

The 2007 Cherokee-Delaware Agreement includes four basic sections that outline the terms for the Delaware's federal recognition. The first and most lengthy section deals with the distribution of the remaining funds from various land claims that are still held in trust awaiting final determination. Access to and control over the Delaware Trust Fund that initially sparked the current Cherokee-Delaware struggle thus continues to play a role in contemporary negotiations. The bulk of the payout goes to the Delaware Tribe, although other Delaware-descended entities (Delaware Nation, Idaho Delaware, and Kansas Delaware) are included in the distribution. The Cherokee Nation will not be awarded any moneys or administration of the fund distribution, nor does the Cherokee Nation make any claim to such funds.

The second major section addresses the status of the federally recognized Delaware Tribe. Under the agreement the Delaware were restored to full federal recognition and included on the list of federally recognized tribes, and thus they are now eligible for those programs and services available to recognized Indian tribes. The members of the Delaware Tribe will also retain the right to be eligible for programs and services administered by the Cherokee Nation.

However, the Cherokee Nation will continue to hold all authority over the administration of Delaware programs and services provided within the Cherokee Nation. In order for the Delaware Tribe to administer such programs and services, the Cherokee Nation and the Delaware Tribe will have to enter into a written agreement concerning the operation of locally administered programs and services. Such agreements are to be written, and the Delaware Tribe will be allowed to offer programs and services, only if the Cherokee Nation is ineligible or declines to apply. The Delaware Tribe is eligible, however, to administer without Cherokee approval those programs and services that do not occur within the Cherokee Nation's jurisdictional boundary and thus outside of Delaware Country.

The third major issue addressed is the status of tribal and individual lands. The agreement recognizes the Delaware Tribe's right to establish trust lands that exist outside of the Cherokee Nation and within the former reservation boundaries and occupational areas of the Delaware Tribe. Considering the Delaware Tribe's different historic occupational areas, this condition makes available key locations for potential trust properties throughout the Midwest and Northeast. Within the Cherokee Nation where the Delaware live today, however, the conditions are much more limiting. The Cherokee Nation will retain exclusive jurisdiction over trust lands that exist within the Cherokee Nation. No land can be placed in trust by the restored Delaware Tribe without the written consent of the Cherokee Nation. Furthermore, the Cherokee Nation will have the right to tax and regulate the activities of the Delaware Tribe and tribal businesses on trust lands within the Cherokee Nation. The Delaware Tribe will, however, be able to operate tribal businesses without Cherokee regulation or taxes if the operations are located outside trust lands. The Delaware Tribe will also not be allowed to establish or conduct gaming enterprises in Delaware Country without the Cherokee Nation's written consent.

The final major issue addressed is the status of the Delaware government, membership, and assets of the Delaware Tribe. The Delaware Tribal Council as it exists today is recognized as the federally recognized governing body, and the tribal membership consists of the lineal descendants of the 1904 Delaware Per Capita Roll. There was apparently no need to recognize the Delaware Trust Board as it was organized for the sole purpose of overseeing the administration of programs funded by the interest from the Delaware Trust Fund. Presumably the Delaware Trust Board will exist alongside the Tribal Council as it has since 1991. The Delaware Tribe will also retain all assets received during the years of restored recognition. Thus, for all intents and purposes, the Delaware tribal government as it exists today is still considered by all parties a viable, representative, and authoritative voice for the Delaware.

Not only will Delaware recognition be conditional under the 2007 Cherokee-Delaware Agreement, but the stipulations in the agreement look remarkably similar to the 1867 Cherokee-Delaware Agreement that has long been the catalyst for tense relations between the two tribes. Under the terms of the 2007 Cherokee-Delaware Agreement, the Delaware Tribe has achieved federal recognition for their existing governmental structure and membership while the membership will likely remain dually enrolled in order to maintain access to both Cherokee-and Delaware-sponsored programs and services. Delaware-sponsored programs and services administered in the Cherokee Nation will effectively work as a compliment to the existing Cherokee services, as the Cherokee Nation will not likely approve those Delaware proposals that would appear to duplicate or compete with existing Cherokee-sponsored programs and services. As Chief Smith describes,

> You know there is very talented people in this program, there is very talented Delawares around. . . . If we can get those folks

to help us work on the expansion of services, you know. We've been very successful expanding our health care system. We built a facility in Muscogee, we built a new one in Nowata. So we have some size and some assets small tribes would not necessarily have. Joint venture programs and the ability to bond and fund those ... So if we could develop a better working relationship between the community and the health professionals, we could expand that health care system there. We can work with them on ideas of local concern.

Thus, Delaware recognition will effectively enhance the already superior federal Indian programs and services administered and sponsored by the Cherokee Nation. Such an improvement will work to the benefit of Indian people living in the Cherokee Nation Jurisdictional Service Area but will also place the Delaware Tribe in a clearly subordinate position in the process.

Just as in the 1867 Cherokee-Delaware Agreement, the 2007 Cherokee-Delaware Agreement promises to preserve the organization and distinct cultural identity of the Delaware Tribe while also requiring that the Delaware exist under Cherokee authority as a consequence of occupying a portion of the Cherokee Nation. In order to remain in control over the region now occupied by the Delaware, the Cherokee Nation will maintain supreme jurisdiction over any trust lands in the Cherokee Nation, while the Delaware Tribe will be able to establish trust properties and tribal businesses within the Cherokee Nation given Cherokee consent. Just as in the 1867 Cherokee-Delaware Agreement, the Delaware purchased and held the right to occupy Cherokee lands but apparently not the right to alienate such lands from the Cherokee Nation as was promised in the 1866 Delaware Treaty. Thus, it appears that the status of the Delaware Tribe in the Cherokee Nation according to the 2007 Cherokee-Delaware Agreement may not be much different from the position once stipulated in the 1867 Cherokee-Delaware Agreement. Although there was reportedly no intention to mimic the 1867 agreement, the 2007 agreement is best understood as a revision of a generations-old agreement, reworked to fit the requirements of contemporary self-determination policy as well as the local authority of the Cherokee Nation.

It is on this issue that Chief Smith disagrees with my interpretation that the 2007 Cherokee-Delaware Agreement is a mirror image of the 1867 Cherokee-Delaware Agreement. Chief Smith points out that the 1867 Cherokee-Delaware Agreement provided for the Delaware to become members of the Cherokee Nation whereas the 2007 Cherokee-Delaware Agreement gives the Delaware Tribe the right to choose whether or not to institute single enrollment. As Chief Smith described, "The way I read the 1867 treaty was that the Delawares were expatriated from their tribal government and became citizens of the Cherokee Nation. The agreement, to me, does quite the opposite. It recognizes the Delawares as a tribal government and implicitly gives them the decision of how they want to form or reform their tribal government; either as dual members with the Cherokee Nation or separate members." Chief Smith's argument is certainly valid and is based on the Cherokee Nation's similar agreement and relationship with the Shawnee Tribe. Following acknowledgment, the Shawnee Tribe did institute single enrollment, and thus the Shawnee must now choose between membership in the Cherokee Nation or Shawnee Tribe, but not both, as described in the previous chapter. Chief Smith is correct that the Delaware Tribe will also have the choice to institute single enrollment as did the Shawnee. However, what this book has demonstrated is that the seemingly logical choice to institute single enrollment is influenced by many factors that can complicate this apparently straightforward decision. The Delaware have a long and divided history over the issue of Cherokee citizenship that began with removal, and today the debates must now also take into consideration that federal policies and practices tend to equate inclusion in the Cherokee service population with tribal membership in the Cherokee Nation. The decision to institute single enrollment is not as simple as declaring the Delaware Tribe's independence from the Cherokee Nation. The Delaware Tribe has long declared such independence while also holding citizenship for economic and political reasons in the Cherokee Nation. Establishing single enrollment today may be viewed by some as a risky financial strategy or an unnecessary loss of a once-paid-for right. Others will be willing to institute single enrollment in order to finally follow through with the historic Big House protests that demanded the right to remain separate from the Cherokee Nation. None of these decisions will be easy, nor are they likely to have universal support.

While the 2007 Cherokee-Delaware Agreement has provided the hoped-for acknowledgment, it remains to be seen if the 2007 Cherokee-Delaware Agreement will actually end the long-standing dispute over the Delaware Tribe's position in the Cherokee Nation that initially began with removal. Although the 2007 agreement may be the best solution to allow for Delaware acknowledgment at the moment, the agreement will not likely end the historic debate within the Delaware Tribe over the issue of their potential membership in the Cherokee Nation. Rather, the 2007 Cherokee-Delaware Agreement will likely add a new dimension to an age-old dispute.

DELAWARE TRIBE AND THE FEDERAL ACKNOWLEDGMENT PROCESS?

The Delaware are not alone in the struggle to maintain their sovereignty against the challenges from another acknowledged tribal entity. A brief review of one such tribe that faced a situation similar to the Delaware Tribe but that achieved acknowledgment through the Federal Acknowledgment Process helps conclude this study and contrasts the intertribal agreement route forced on the Delaware by

Congress. The San Juan Paiute stand as a comparative example of a tribe whose experience was remarkably similar to the Delaware. The Paiute were able to achieve acknowledgment through the Federal Acknowledgment Process rather than through an intertribal agreement, and thus the Paiute experience can suggest another possible route for certain tribes to follow in order to achieve federal recognition. However, as recognition stands today, achieving acknowledgment will still place petitioning tribes like the Delaware against the formidable power of host acknowledged tribes, and formal federal recognition for constituent tribes may take away political and economic resources from acknowledged groups.

The San Juan Southern Paiute Tribe presents another case that may shed light on what appears to be the end of the tunnel for groups like the Delaware. Although the Paiute were once claimed by the Navajo as members of the Navajo Nation, the Paiute successfully petitioned and achieved separate federal recognition through the FAP in 1989. In doing so the Paiute were faced with challenges from the Navajo Nation while under FAP review, and the Navajo Nation immediately appealed the Department of Interior's decision in federal court following recognition. The Navajo challenges and appeals were ultimately defeated, and the San Juan Paiute are today a federally recognized tribe headquartered near Tuba City, Arizona. Like the Delaware, the San Juan Paiute had maintained a distinct and identifiable Indian community and a separate political organization, and were facing some indifference and discrimination from the Navajo Nation, which claimed the Paiute as members at the outset of the self-determination era. Although some Paiute held Navajo census numbers whereas others were intermarried with Navajo spouses, the Paiute petition was able to demonstrate that such enrollees and spouses "had not acquired or used [Navajo census numbers] with the intent and understanding of becoming members of the Navajo Tribe. Census numbers were found to have been issued routinely by the Bureau and or tribal census clerks as a part of a Bureau process" (U.S. Department of Interior 1989:51504). Thus the Paiute were able to demonstrate that their membership was not principally composed of those enrolled in any other acknowledged Indian Tribe, although some Paiute held forms of identification that formerly included them as part of the Navajo Nation's service population. Recognition has brought significant empowerment for the Paiute, enabling them to contract for programs and services and work out a treaty with the Navajo Nation to establish a separate Paiute reservation within the boundaries of the Navajo Nation (Pamela Bunte, personal communication, July 31, 2007).

The Paiute were able to show, as I have sought to demonstrate is the case for the Delaware, that they may have once been enumerated on rolls and census now used by other host tribes, but such enrollment occurred because they were either obliged to do so for access to federal resources or because they were presented with no other option to sustain an acknowledged Indian status. Thus, it would appear that if the Delaware Tribe and other similar groups were able to follow the Paiute model, that they too could achieve separate acknowledgment. The burden for the Delaware would be to demonstrate that the Delaware Tribe does not consist principally of persons enrolled in another acknowledged Indian tribe for purposes other than the access to federal services that such enrollment provides. Whether the Delaware can accomplish such a task remains to be seen; however, it is encouraging to know that an option does exist for certain tribes like the Delaware seeking separate acknowledgment.

What is most evident from a comparison of the Delaware case with that of the Paiute is that the Delaware, like most tribes in their situation, remain as distinct, vital, and persistent Indian communities living within the boundaries of another — often a more powerful federally recognized tribe whose position is elevated by the self-determination relationship. As this work reveals, the Delaware and the Cherokee were brought together as a consequence of the removal policy, and the Delaware have remained a distinct community with an independent political organization throughout. A unique Delaware landscape was established with removal that continues to inform contemporary life and political action in the present. Delaware group identity is very much evident despite the disempowerment that came with Oklahoma statehood and the assimilation goals of twentieth-century federal policy. Shocked with the loss of federal recognition in the self-determination era, Delaware leaders reorganized their governmental structure in order to preserve Delaware independence from the Cherokee Nation while establishing an organization that would provide access to the significant Delaware Trust Fund. The contemporary leadership stands today as representatives of the diverse Delaware Tribe whose predecessors maintained a distinct community, political organization, and continued relationship with the federal government.

Despite the vitality of the Delaware community and political organization, the Delaware case and the 2007 Cherokee-Delaware Agreement reveal the vested interests and powerful roles played by host recognized tribal governments in the modern era. Such power is buttressed by the self-determination policy that provides significant political and economic resources to those tribes that can meet the standards proposed by the BIA and supported by federally recognized tribes. My research with the Delaware has found that the single enrollment requirement in the FAP and in self-determination contracts clearly provides acknowledged tribes with significant economic and political advantages. The Cherokee Nation's contract with the federal government to administer the CDIB card allows the Cherokee Nation to create a matrix by which the Delaware must apply for Cherokee by Blood status in order to receive programs and services, which sometimes contain a Cherokee preference. The Cherokee Nation can thus influence Delaware enrollment in the Cherokee Nation for access to

Cherokee-administered services while rendering the Delaware's bid for separate acknowledgment difficult because the Delaware Tribe cannot meet the single enrollment criteria. The central importance of tribal enrollment in allowing and limiting the acknowledgment efforts for tribes like the Delaware is thus clarified with this work.

Through the CDIB and tribal enrollment process, federally recognized tribes can manufacture what appears to be consent to inclusion within a host tribe when such acquiescence is actually done out of the need to access what are sometimes necessary federally funded Indian programs and services. As is shown with this book, the Delaware were choosing to enroll as Delaware when doing so conferred or was promising to confer the same access to federal Indian services that was provided through Cherokee enrollment. Support for single Delaware enrollment declined, however, when such an enrollment strategy appeared to threaten the Delaware's access to Cherokee-controlled programs and services. Thus, tribal enrollment in the self-determination era has come to mean more than the meaning of tribal membership as is defined by the Federal Acknowledgment Process. Under self-determination contracts and compacts, tribal membership is often equated with an acknowledged tribe's service population, whereas the FAP definition is much more complex. The FAP defines tribal membership as "an individual who meets the membership requirement of the tribe as set forth in its governing document and has consistently maintained tribal relations with the tribe or is listed on the tribal rolls of that tribe as a member" (Procedures 1994). While the Delaware and Shawnee are specifically listed as members of the Cherokee Nation in the Cherokee Constitution, it is demonstrated here that the Delaware have not consistently maintained tribal relations with the Cherokee Nation despite their inclusion by the Cherokee Nation. Also, it is questionable whether the Cherokee Nation Dawes Roll is a tribal roll or more in line with a reservation-wide roll. Indeed, the Cherokee Nation Dawes Roll lists members of different Indian tribes as well as non-Indians who were once residents in the Cherokee Nation and are no longer eligible for tribal membership.

A comparative look at the Delaware and Paiute cases indicates that recognition for such groups today would inevitably work against the interests of acknowledged tribes. Paiute recognition resulted in a loss of land for the Navajo Nation as the Navajo have now turned over 5,400 acres to the Paiute. Termination of the Delaware Tribe was sought precisely so that the Cherokee would not lose jurisdiction over certain territories as had the Navajo. Once Cherokee authority was no longer threatened, then amicable negotiations resumed with the intent of achieving Delaware recognition, but not at the expense of Cherokee sovereignty. The reason that recognized tribes oppose the acknowledgment of constituent tribes is not due to any special dislike that exists between tribes but because of the challenge that such groups present to tribal sovereignty as it is defined and carried out under federal policy in the self-determination era. Thus, the true path to take for correcting the situation is not through recourse to more intertribal agreements. It is not the fault of the tribes who are pitted as antagonists in what can sometimes be an unworkable situation. The real recourse is to take a critical look at the self-determination policy and, in particular, who is allowed control over the flow of federal resources, which perpetuates such intertribal disputes. The Paiute case, however, does provide some hope for a truly separate acknowledgment for certain deserving tribes and indicates that the Federal Acknowledgment Process is sophisticated enough to make important and empowering distinctions concerning tribal enrollment as it exists in the modern era.

Despite the enlightening example that the Paiute provide, it is also important to point out one last comparison that exists between the Delaware and the Paiute that is working against Delaware efforts at the moment. The motivation for the Delaware to achieve federal recognition is to better meet the local needs of their community that are either being neglected or ignored by their host tribal government. The Paiute were faced with discrimination from local Navajo leaders, and the Paiute leadership felt as if their needs were not being given weight by the Navajo-controlled tribal structure (Bunte and Franklin 1987:279–283). Fortunately, the Paiute were able to utilize the Federal Acknowledgement Process and achieve recognition in order to ensure that Paiute interests and needs were met. Unfortunately though, because of the tremendous workload and exacting research carried out by the Office of Federal Acknowledgment, the process of undergoing recognition through the Federal Acknowledgement Process can take a decade or more (M. Miller 2004:64). Sometimes tribes like the Delaware and their constituencies do not have the luxury to wait for a potential positive finding as did the Paiute.

Self-determination is thus a word that carries multiple meanings for the Delaware. In its broadest definition the term refers to the Delaware ideal that they hold the freedom to choose their own political status, fate, or course of action without compulsion. With reference to contemporary federal Indian policy, however, *self-determination* takes on an even stricter meaning. Self-determination policy recognizes the freedom of an acknowledged Indian tribe to take over federally administered programs and services, yet this is a right that is reserved for only those acknowledged Indian tribes that do not also have an overlapping membership with other acknowledged tribes. The practice of self-determination for acknowledged Indian tribes today, or the taking over of programs and services, is thus limited by the enrollment requirement in the self-determination policy. As this chapter describes, some tribes may hold federal acknowledgment, such as the Delaware from 1996 to 2004, but are claimed as constituent parts of, or exist as members of, existing tribes that hold federal acknowledgment and that have already claimed their right to self-determination through federal policy. It is therefore acknowledged here that self-determination for Indian tribes under federal policy is not easily available for tribes like the Delaware as a consequence of the single enrollment requirement. However, as is also shown with this book, the ideal of self-determination may indeed be practiced in the everyday lives of Delaware people who still have not accepted their tribal membership in the Cherokee Nation or accepted that a single enrollment requirement should so limit their claims of self-determination. The Delaware Tribe is thus presented as a given group of people who have yet to accept their inclusion in the Cherokee Nation and continue to search for ways to formally codify their freedom to choose their own political status, fate, or course of action without being compelled by federal policy to compromise on the issue of Cherokee membership.

Thus, such historic tribes as the Delaware will follow the directives of their group and pursue another agreement or other recourse to meet the pressing and sometimes critical care required by their constituents. However, the point made with this study is that the Delaware Tribe's choice to negotiate with the Cherokee Nation is not freely chosen but is a decision considered necessary in light of the way in which programs and services are administered under the self-determination policy and because the Delaware lack any other expedient option through the FAP. Delaware families are in need of federal assistance, and the Delaware Tribe requires federal recognition in order to provide such assistance, as only the Delaware would know best how to care for their own families and loved ones. The most efficient and less oppositional way to follow through at the moment, however, is to seek terms with the Cherokee Nation.

While acknowledgment for the Delaware may require concessions to the Cherokee Nation, the Delaware and their tribal government will inevitably continue as a distinct community and political organization, as will be clear to subsequent observers. The members and elected leaders will hold to the pursuit of tribal sovereignty and independence while moving forward in a way that will not compromise the Delaware's deeply held beliefs about who they are and a sincere conviction of their separate existence apart from the Cherokee Nation despite their divided sentiments toward the Cherokee Nation. The 2007 Cherokee-Delaware Agreement may be considered by some to be potentially fatal to the unconditional acknowledgment efforts of the Delaware Tribe that will likely resurface in the future. But from the view of the elected leadership of the Delaware Tribe today, it would be more responsible to look after the immediate needs of family and friends than to potentially jeopardize such important obligations with a long-drawn-out waiting period that would likely result if acknowledgment was pursued through the FAP. Indeed, as a result of self-determination policy and congressional urging, it appears that the Delaware Tribe may well remain in a Cherokee Nation in order to rightfully look after the very needs of the community, families, and loved ones that they were elected to represent.

Notes

1. INTRODUCTION

1. Robert J. Franklin's (1984) dissertation discusses the role of federal policy in San Juan Southern Paiute society.

2. Examples of other confederated acknowledged tribes would include the Confederated Tribes of the Umatilla Reservation and the Assiniboine and Sioux Tribes of the Ft. Peck Reservation, as well as many others.

3. For the historical development of the concept of federal acknowledgment, see also William W. Quinn Jr. (1990).

4. Such important research on petitioning tribes in eastern North America includes, but is not limited to, Jack Campisi's (1991) ethnography of the Mashpee struggle, David Wilkins's (1993) work with the Lumbee, Anne McCulloch and David Wilkins's (1995) discussion of the Catawba and the Lumbee difficulties with federal recognition, and Anthony Paredes's (1992) ethnography of the Poarch Creek's efforts for federal recognition. William Starna's (1996) work presents the case of the Wampanoag, Samuel Cook (2002) describes the Monacan's persistence without federal recognition and William W. Quinn Jr. (1993) provides an analysis of the special case presented by southeastern Indians in general. Representative of work among unacknowledged peoples of the West Coast is Les Field's (1999) survey of unacknowledged groups in California, and Frank Porter (1990) discusses federal recognition among the several smaller tribes of western Washington. There are also the numerous reports and notes submitted by researchers working for petitioning tribes and the federal government that document and detail the history and culture of petitioning tribes throughout the United States (Campisi 2004:768). Such work remains regionally focused on tribes from the East and West Coasts, and the Delaware case study will balance the literature with an example from a tribe from the Southern Plains.

5. James W. Brown and Rita J. Kohn (2007) have since edited and published many of the Delaware interviews from the Doris Duke Collection and the Oklahoma Historical Society.

6. Jackson and Levine (2002) and Jackson (2003b) provide a thorough outline of the development of Pan-Indianism in anthropology and critique the usefulness of such a model.

2. REMOVAL AND THE CHEROKEE-DELAWARE AGREEMENT

1. The authorities to which I am referring are the 2004 United States Court of Appeals for the Tenth Circuit, which stated, "Based on the foregoing, the DOI's conclusion the Delawares preserved their tribal identity under the 1866 Cherokee Treaty and 1867 Agreement is clearly contrary to Supreme Court precedent" (Cherokee Nation v. Norton, 241F Supp. 2d 1368 [2004]:4).

2. For a general overview on the archaeology of this region I refer the reader to the major works of Herbert Kraft (1974, 1977, 1984, 1986).

3. For more information on the history of Dutch colonialism in New Netherland see van Laer (1924), Brasser (1974), Weslager (1972, 1986), and Kraft (1996).

4. Although officially loyal to the English through the Iroquois, the Delaware never relinquished the right to make their own political decisions (Weslager 1972:196–218; Goddard 1978:223). During the French and Indian War, for example, Delaware leaders pledged loyalty to both the French and the English simultaneously (Weslager 1972:221–260). In the American Revolution, the majority of Delaware leaders initially aided the Americans but later switched to the British as more and more Delaware were forced westward during the course of the war (Weslager 1972:294–315).

5. That indigenous political systems of Woodland peoples have shifted over time is well documented. For the impact of the fur trade on the indigenous political systems of the Northeast see Cayton and Teute (1998), Jennings (1975), and White (1991). The historical literature also describes the impact that forced relocations and the so-called king-making policies of the British had on the Delaware clan structure and the centralization of Delaware governance (Thurman 1973; Wallace 1947, 1956, 1970; Schutt 2007). The reader is directed to Goddard (1978:225) for an overview of Delaware clan-based political organization. While the antiquity of the

Delaware clan system of governance is unknown, such a governing system is associated with village leadership, which indicates that it probably existed prior to the arrival of Europeans. Jay Miller (1989:2–3) indicates that the Delaware aboriginal political system was founded on a symbolic connection between a chief who was the paramount leader of the clan that was associated with its own town. The ascendancy of clan identity as the primary system of governance over town affiliation in the eighteenth century was probably due to the refugee experience during that era. Despite such significant pressures on the Delaware to centralize authority, appointed Delaware chiefs frequently faced opposition groups within the tribe who gave voice to their dissent by recognizing their own leadership and alliances with enemy forces (Weslager 1972:296).

6. The historical migrations of the divergent Delaware groups are generalized here. For a more rigorous review of the multiple Delaware migrations, see Goddard (1978) and Weslager (1972, 1978).

7. There were individuals who likely veiled their indigenous descent throughout the American Revolution in order to remain in their homelands.

8. Research on the short period of Delaware occupation in southwest Missouri has been nonexistent, yet this is an important time period for understanding the cultural changes that took place in Delaware society as they adapted to and became familiar with the peoples and ecology of the Prairie Plains region. See Gina S. Powell and Neal H. Lopinot's (2003) multiyear archaeological work on the Delaware occupation in Missouri as well as Melissa Ann Eaton's (n.d.) unpublished dissertation for the most comprehensive work on the Delaware in Missouri.

9. Following the nativistic movement in 1806, led by Chief Anderson and described in detail by Jay Miller (1994), the Delaware banned Christian missionaries from access to the tribe. Later, when Issac McCoy traveled to the Delaware settlements on the White River, some chiefs promised him that he could return after the tribe was relocated west of the Mississippi. McCoy kept in contact with the Delaware during their sojourn in southwest Missouri, and when the Delaware finally relocated to their reserve in what would later be northeast Kansas, he was the official

surveyor of the Delaware reserve. In 1836 Rev. Ira Blanchard established a Baptist mission school near Edwardsville. After the mission was destroyed by a flood, Rev. John Pratt rebuilt it on higher ground, and prominent Delaware leaders such as Charles Journeycake and John and James Conner were active in this church. Pratt later stepped down from the mission after being appointed the Delaware agent in 1864 (Weslager 1972:370, 384–385). The Methodists were the first to establish a mission on the Delaware Reserve. In 1832 the Methodists built a church and school five miles north of the old Delaware Crossing, and soon the Christian Church community was established. Captain Ketchum, the first Christian Delaware chief, was converted in this church and is laid to rest at the Christian Church cemetery (Weslager 1972:388). The Moravians of United Brethren were the last to build, constructing their mission in 1837 on the north bank of the Kansas River near the town of Munsee. Not surprisingly, the congregation was mostly Munsee and included a few Stockbridge families as well (Weslager 1972:384). These Baptist- and Methodist-based Delaware communities held together in the removal to Indian Territory while many of the Moravian Christian Delaware remained in Kansas or moved to the Stockbridge Munsee Reservation in Wisconsin.

10. In Kansas, Captain Ketchum was the first Christian Delaware principal chief, but he was also of the Turtle clan and was appointed as principal chief through matrilineal ascendancy even though he was a converted Methodist. Ketchum served from 1849 to 1858 and was succeeded by his maternal nephew and fellow Christian, John Conner, also of the Turtle clan (Weslager 1972:387–390).

11. For the most recent historical treatment of Delaware removal to Oklahoma, see Haake (2001, 2002a, 2002b, 2007).

12. Though by no means exhaustive, the reader should consult the recently published *Handbook of North American Indians: Southeast*, vol. 14, for a recent synthesis of anthropological work on the ethnology and ethnohistory of southeastern peoples. On the Green Corn Ceremony, I found the selections in Witthoft (1949), Hudson (1976:365–375), and Jackson (2003a:235–240) to be the most comprehensive.

13. The Delaware Tribe was the first tribe to sign a treaty with the Amer-

ican government, doing so on September 17, 1778 (Weslager 1972:304).

14. On July 14, 1951, the Delaware General Council passed a resolution to formally adopt five named persons, granting them full political and property rights, who were not listed on the 1867 roll but who later joined the tribe in Indian Territory and directly purchased their citizenship rights from the Cherokee Nation (Carrigan and Chambers, 1994:36–37).

15. The Osage, Kaw, Pawnee, Otoe, and Missouria are all Central Plains tribes that were relocated to reservations on land ceded by the Cherokee Nation. The only tribe with a reservation on the land formerly known as the Cherokee Outlet is the Tonkawa Tribe, who originally occupied the southern plains of Texas.

3. DELAWARE COUNTRY

1. Shawnee Country is also within the Cherokee Nation, but the Shawnee Tribe has held federal acknowledgment since 2000. Like the Delaware Tribe, the Shawnee Tribe was relocated from a reservation in Kansas to take up residence in the Cherokee Nation in the years following the end of the American Civil War. While some Shawnee families settled in the Delaware communities, the distinctively Shawnee settlements predominated at three locations: Hogan Creek (Fairland), White Oak, and Bird Creek (Sperry) (Shawnee Tribe 2007). The Shawnee built their still active ceremonial grounds at White Oak along Pryor Creek and also established the now moribund Spybuck grounds along Bird Creek (see Howard 1981 for detailed discussion of Shawnee settlement). Along with the Shawnee, there was an equally significant Cherokee population in Delaware Country, yet I have learned of no evidence for a Cherokee ceremonial ground in the region. I have been told that a Cherokee Church did exist at one time in the predominately Cherokee settlement of Matoaka south of Bartlesville. However, the culturally conservative Cherokee settlements were and continue to be located within the Ozark Plateau region south and east of the Grand River (Bays 1998:76; Sturm 2002:12, 146–150; Warhaftig 1968: 511).

2. While settled in what would later become eastern Ohio, the Delaware Council (then called Lupwaaeenoawuk, or wise men) was faced with the

decision of whether or not to allow Christian Delaware onto the council. This matter became increasingly important due to the success of the Moravians and their conversion of many Delaware during the eighteenth century. After much discussion, the council agreed that converts could be allowed on the council (Weslager 1972:288).

3. It is also interesting to note the parallel between the federal agents in Kansas and the Moravian missionaries in Ohio. Obviously, the Delaware agent was a strong voice in the Delaware Council just as Weslager (1972:289) reports that Moravian ministers such as John Heckewelder and David Zeisberger were also counted in the councils held in the eighteenth century. Ever since the American Revolution, the United States has negotiated with the Delaware Council through these intermediaries, and in this alliance Christian Delaware are often associated historically with the pro-American sentiment.

4. While in Kansas, the Delaware signed five treaties with the United States prior to the Treaty of 1866 (Carrigan and Chambers 1994:A92).

5. The delegation did include Captain Sarcoxie's son, who is reported to have been the last person to bring in another form of the Big House Ceremony in Kansas (Grumet 2001:73). He later became a Baptist preacher in Indian Territory. John Conner had only recently moved to Kansas in 1860. Prior to this, he lived on the Texas frontier as a leader and landowner among the western Delaware. Black Beaver was among the delegation as well; his presence was probably due to the fact that the western Delaware, along with other tribes loyal to the Union, fled from Oklahoma Territory to different agencies in Kansas during the Civil War (Hale 1987:74–80).

6. Bays (1998:178) adds that since the oil companies recruited families from Pennsylvania and Ohio to work in the oil fields, a much more northern Appalachian folk culture developed in the towns of this region as opposed to the cultural orientation more similar to that of the southeastern United States that predominates in the Ozark Plateau region of the Cherokee Nation.

7. The Delaware Big House was gaining a considerable amount of attention at the turn of the century. First, it was central to the work of Richard Adams (1904, 1997), a Delaware lawyer who hoped to use its description

as a way to win the pending court cases with the Cherokee Nation. In 1903 U.S. senators attended the ceremony, and with the impending allotment of Indian Territory, Charlie Elkhair asked the Senate to set aside land for the Delaware Big House (Carrigan and Chambers 1994:24). Ten acres were carved out of Walter Wilson's allotment and set aside for the Big House, which is identified as the Delaware church on the allotment maps. In the early twentieth century the ceremony also caught the attention of ethnographers working with tribes in Oklahoma. Their work soon sparked a considerable tradition in anthropology devoted to reconstructing and preserving the accounts of the observance (Michelson 1912; Harrington 1913; Speck 1931, 1937; J. Miller 1980b, Grumet 2001).

8. For more information on the Plains-derived powwow see Powers (1990), on the powwow in western and central Oklahoma in particular see Lassiter (1998) and Ellis (2003). Jackson (2003b) describes the unique manifestation of the powwow in eastern woodland contexts such as exists with the Delaware.

4. GOVERNMENT TO GOVERNMENT

1. The regional centers that developed after statehood were often given Delaware names, which may come as little surprise since many of the towns in Delaware Country were often founded by Delaware and intermarried non-Indian entrepreneurs (Teague 1967; Cranor 1985). Charles Journeycake's non-Indian sons-in-law founded Bartlesville, Dewey, and Nowata. Journeycake's daughter, Nannie Journeycake Pratt, married Jacob Bartles, a non-Indian trader and entrepreneur who had lived with and fought alongside the Delaware while in Kansas. The couple moved to the Silverlake area in 1873, where Bartles established a trading post on the Caney River. In 1874 Bartles moved his store from Silverlake to Turkey Creek, where Bartlesville developed. His success encouraged other intermarried white entrepreneurs including George Keeler, William Johnstone, and Nelson Carr. In 1899, after losing a bid for a railroad depot, Bartles moved his store four miles up the Caney River and re-established his business in one of his wheat fields. Soon the town of Dewey developed, and the railroad opened a depot in the community (Teague 1967:116). Bartles's wife, Nannie, started holding the

first church services and later founded the First Baptist Church in Dewey. Today the church is locally known as the Journeycake Church. Nowata actually started as a centrally located railroad depot that quickly attracted local businessmen. J. E. Campbell, also a non-Indian man who had married another of Charles Journeycake's daughters, opened the first store in Nowata, and Jacob Bartles soon followed his brother-in-law's lead (Cranor 1985). Nowata, Alluwe, Lenapah, Ketchum, and Delaware are town names derived from the Delaware language and presence in the region. For more complete descriptions of the history of each town see Teague (1967).

2. The Oklahoma Historical Society has an account from Albert Exendine, a Delaware cattle rancher, who recounts how he was forced to cede an entire ranch to the federal government during the shift to statehood (Exendine n.d., 1972).

3. See also Leslie Hewes's (1942, 1944, 1977) work that contrasts the relatively unproductive and underdeveloped region of the Oklahoma Ozark Plateau with the surrounding prairie plains regions.

4. George Bullette was from Alluwe, and after his wife died he moved closer to his sister, Minnie Fouts, who had adopted his daughter. Bullette's allotment was located next to Minnie Fouts and other siblings in the Post Oak community. Joseph Bartles lived in the town of Dewey, and his allotment was located just outside the city limits. John Young, a Baptist, established a small settlement at Caney Fork in the vicinity of the Big House community (Teague 1967; Cranor 1991, 1985).

5. Frank Speck's political support of the Delaware traditional leaders is consistent with his support of other indigenous peoples (see Rountree 1990:219–242). Speck was very much involved in the communities with which he worked as he felt that involvement in local politics was an important dimension of anthropological research (Gleach 2002:504). Charlie Webber first introduced Frank Speck to local community leaders, and in 1929 they began corresponding directly with Speck about Delaware culture. It is from this correspondence that Speck obtained most of his ethnographic data for his major works on Delaware culture and religion (Speck 1931, 1937). See Obermeyer (2007) for more on Speck's collaborative work with the Big House community and leadership.

6. See Pamela Wallace (2002) for another discussion of the impact of the Indian Claims Commission Act.

7. Delaware demographic history is not unusual among eastern Oklahoma tribes. In Warhaftig's (1968) study of the Cherokee, for instance, he identified what he classed as the Tribal Cherokee and the Legal Cherokee. The tribal population was defined as the aggregate of individuals who functioned as participants in the distinctly Cherokee ceremonial institutions associated with the Cherokee settlements. Legal Cherokees, on the other hand, were those who had political rights within the Cherokee Nation but who were variously removed from this more socially and culturally conservative Cherokee group. Roark-Calnek (1977:18–40) observed the development of this distinction during the course of her fieldwork with the Eastern Delaware in the early 1970s.

5. SELF-DETERMINATION

1. Family Night is not publicized but is locally known. Families gather to prepare their camps, eat, and visit, as they do each year. After supper, as night begins to fall, some men will build a fire in the traditional way, using flint and steel. After the fire is lit, everyone settles in around the large arena either on the benches or in lawn chairs for a night of social dancing. Included in the event are stomp dancing from local leaders and from visiting tribes and other social dances such as the Cherokee, Women, Bean, Duck, and Stirrup dances. See Rementer and Donnell (1995) for more information on the Delaware social dances.

2. Although men figured prominently in the described event, women play an integral role as well. Many Delaware women serve the community either informally or as elected officials.

3. I have paraphrased this story for the sake of brevity, but the original telling was recorded by Truman Michelson when working with the northern Washington County Delaware in the early twentieth century. A written transcription of Michelson's recording can be found in Bierhorst (1995:47–56).

4. See also Weslager (1978:251), who provides a breakdown of the Delaware Tribe's membership and lists the number of Delaware living in each state in 1977.

5. Prior chiefs did not earn a salary. Economic flexibility was previously an assumed requirement for tribal leaders, who had reportedly spent large sums of their own money to either get tribal programs going or to keep them in operation after federally appropriated funds were spent. With federal recognition restored, the office of chief became a full-time job and a salaried position for the first time. Only the most recent chiefs — Dee Ketchum, Joe Brooks, and Jerry Douglas — have earned a salary.

6. CHEROKEE BY BLOOD

1. A copy of the original roll listing the Delaware Indians who elected to move to Indian Territory in 1867 can also be found in the Mary Smith Witcher collection at the Oklahoma Historical Society and in the Bartlesville Public Library in Bartlesville, Oklahoma.

2. Being Native Cherokee as stipulated in the 1867 agreement meant to the Delaware that they were Native, or Indians, who had the same rights as other Cherokee citizens, but it did not, by extension, mean the absurd assumption that the Delaware were now somehow descended from Cherokee people or members of a Cherokee family, as the labels *Cherokee* and *Cherokee (A.D.)* would imply. Unfortunately for the Delaware, it is just such an illogical conclusion that the federal government considers legal today.

3. The critique of blood-based definitions of identity was first articulated by feminist scholars interested in the cultural reproduction of colonial power in Latin America. See Stoler (1989, 1995), Stolcke (1991), Alonso (1994, 1995), and Smith (1997) for further discussion. Scholars critical of the blood quantum–based definition of Indian identity in North America describe blood quantum as a method of genocide. Such critics argue that as intermarriage with non-Indians proceeds through time as it has in the past, each successive generation will theoretically become less Indian. A legal identity based on the rule of hypodescent would thus serve as a convenient way to steadily relieve the federal government of its treaty responsibilities all the while defining Indian identities out of existence (Churchill 1993; Jaimes 1992).

4. Dual enrollment beyond the Cherokee Nation is slightly risky; any-

one who is caught doing so is forced to relinquish their membership in all but one tribe. Fortunately for those who choose this strategy, enforcement is largely left to each individual tribal government. Thus, my example used in the text refers to a real person, but the tribal affiliations have been altered in order to preserve my consultant's anonymity.

5. I refer the reader to Adams (1904, 1997) for those interested in his work.

7. SINGLE ENROLLMENT

1. The Shawnee began efforts in the 1980s to separate from the Cherokee Nation, and to do so they agreed not to seek jurisdiction within the Cherokee Nation's jurisdictional boundaries. In return the Cherokee Nation supported the Shawnee Tribe's federal recognition. In 2000 Congress enacted Public Law 106–568, the Shawnee Tribe Status Act, which restored Shawnee federal recognition (Shawnee Tribe Status Act 2000). The Shawnee Tribe established their tribal headquarters in Miami, Oklahoma, located beyond the Cherokee Nation Jurisdictional Area. A field office near White Oak, Oklahoma, and another in Sperry, Oklahoma, were later abandoned because both existed within the Cherokee Nation's jurisdiction. The Cherokee Nation also purchased and put into trust the land on which the Shawnee White Oak ceremonial grounds sits, and currently holds the land for the Shawnee community. Visit the Shawnee Tribe's Web site (www.shawnee-tribe.org) for contact information and contemporary tribal events, programs, and administrative locations.

2. Ironically, the BIA interprets the exclusion of single enrollment as including the possibility of dual enrollment in the Cherokee Nation since the Delaware Constitution does not specifically state otherwise.

3. The only exception is in 1989, when Rogers County did raise its per capita income and exceeded the state average, probably as a result of people moving northward from Tulsa County (U.S. Census Bureau 2007).

4. Phillips Petroleum Company combined their operations with Conoco in 2003 and moved their headquarters out of Bartlesville and relocated to Houston, Texas.

8. CONCLUSION

1. Most who voted in favor of the constitution were actually voting to restore the Delaware Tribe's federal recognition and either did not support the 2007 Cherokee-Delaware Agreement or viewed the agreement as a necessary but unwanted concession in order to achieve the ultimate goal of federal acknowledgment. While the final vote totals in the referendum appear to reflect a consensus among the Delaware electorate, many Delaware voters simply chose not to participate in the referendum and did not cast ballots to stop the proposed constitution. These voters did not support the revised constitution because they did not want the Delaware Tribe to be bound by the 2007 Cherokee-Delaware Agreement. However, those who chose not to participate did support the restoration of the Delaware Tribe's federal acknowledgment but not in a way that appeared to concede any form of membership in or authority to the Cherokee Nation. They did not want to vote against the new constitution because doing so would have appeared to indicate that they did not want the Delaware Tribe restored. However, they also did not support the revised constitution because it was constrained by the 2007 Cherokee-Delaware Agreement. Thus the nonparticipating electorate, most of whom were members of the local community with a more separatist view of the Cherokee Nation, simply voiced their dissent in the traditional way by not participating in the referendum vote.

References

Adams, Richard. 1904. *Ancient Religion of the Delaware Indians: Observations and Reflections*. Washington DC: Law Reporter.

———. 1997. *Legends of the Delaware Indians and Picture Writing*.
Deborah Nichols, ed. James Rementer, transcriptions. Syracuse
NY: Syracuse University Press.

Alonso, Ana Maria. 1994. "The Politics of Space, Time and Substance:
State Formation, Nationalism and Ethnicity." *Annual Review of
Anthropology* 23:379–406.

———. 1995. *Thread of Blood. Colonialism, Revolution, and Gender on
Mexico's Northern Frontier*. Tucson: University of Arizona Press.

Basso, Keith. 1996. *Wisdom Sits in Places: Landscape and Language
among the Western Apache*. Albuquerque: University of New
Mexico Press, 1996.

Bays, Brad. 1998. *Townsite Settlement and Dispossession in the Cherokee
Nation, 1866–1907*. New York: Garland.

Bierhorst, John, ed. 1995. *The White Deer and Other Stories Told by the
Lenape*. New York: William Morrow.

Biolsi, Thomas. 1992. *Organizing the Lakota: The Political Economy of
the New Deal on the Pine Ridge and Rosebud Reservations*. Tucson:
University of Arizona Press.

———. 1995. "The Birth of the Reservation: Making the Modern Individual among the Lakota." *American Ethnologist* 22(1):28–53.

Blu, Karen I. 1996. "Where Do You Stay At? Homeplace and Com-
munity among the Lumbee." In *Senses of Place*. Steven Feld and
Keith Basso, eds. Pp. 197–227. Santa Fe NM: School of American
Research Press.

Brasser, Ted. 1974. *Riding on the Frontier's Crest: Mahican Indian Culture
and Culture Change*. National Museum of Man Mercury Series,
Ethnology Division Paper 13. Ottawa: National Museum of
Canada.

Brown, James W., and Rita T. Kohn, eds. 2007. *Long Journey Home:*

Oral Histories of Contemporary Delaware Indians. Bloomington:
Indiana University Press.

Bunte, Pamela Ann, and Robert J. Franklin. 1987. *From the Sands to the
Mountain: Change and Persistence in a Southern Paiute Community.*
Lincoln: University of Nebraska Press.

Burns, Louis, 1994. "Lu tsa ka Le Ah ke ho, 'Can't Go Beyond': Allot-
ting the Osage Reservation, 1906–1909." *Chronicles of Oklahoma*
72(2):200–211.

Butler, La Follette. 1979. Letter to Mr. Henry Secondine, 24 May.
Bartlesville OK: Delaware Tribe of Indians Collection.

Calloway, Colin G. 2004. *First Peoples: A Documentary Survey of American Indian History.* 2nd edition. Boston: Bedford/St. Martin's.

Campisi, Jack. 1991. *The Mashpee Indians: Tribe on Trial.* Syracuse NY:
Syracuse University Press.

———. 2004. "Resurgence and Recognition." In *Handbook of North
American Indians,* vol. 14: *Southeast.* William C. Sturtevant and
Raymond D. Fogelson, eds. Pp. 760–768. Washington DC: Smith-
sonian Institution.

Carrigan, Gina, and Clayton Chambers. 1994. *A Lesson in Administra-
tive Termination: An Analysis of the Legal Status of the Delaware
Tribe of Indians.* 2nd edition. Bartlesville OK: Delaware Tribe of
Indians.

Carter, Kent. 1997. "Snakes and Scribes: The Dawes Commission and
the Enrollment of the Creeks." *Chronicles of Oklahoma* 75(4):384–
413.

Cayton, Andrew, and Fredrika Teute, eds. 1998. *Contact Points: American Frontiers from the Mohawk Valley to the Mississippi, 1750–1830.*
Chapel Hill: University of North Carolina Press.

Cherokee Nation v. Norton. 2004. 241F Supp. 2d 1368.

Cherokee Nation of Oklahoma. 2007a. Clinics and Hospitals. Electronic document, http://www.cherokee.org/home.aspx?section=
health&service=HealthClinics, accessed August 4, 2007.

———. 2007b. Tribal registration: Frequently Asked Question (FAQ).
Electronic document, http://www.cherokee.org/home. aspx

?section=services&service=Registration&ID=TKeffDhl7iU=, accessed August 4, 2007.

Churchill, Ward. 1993. *Struggle for the Land*. Monroe ME: Common Courage Press.

Conner, John. 1866. Letter to Wm. P. Ross, 9 Dec. Kansas Collection, vol. 10:46–48. Lawrence KS: University of Kansas Libraries.

Cook, Samuel. 2002. "The Monacan Indian Nation: Asserting Tribal Sovereignty in the Absence of Federal Recognition." *Wicazo Sa Review* 17(2):91–116.

Cramer, Renee Ann. 2005. *Cash, Color and Colonialism: The Politics of Tribal Acknowledgment*. Norman: University of Oklahoma Press.

Cranor, Ruby. 1985. *Caney Valley Ghost Towns and Settlements*. Self-published manuscript. Bartlesville OK: Bartlesville Public Library.

———. 1991. *Kik Tha We Nund: The Delaware Chief William Anderson and His Descendants*. Self-published manuscript. Bartlesville OK: Bartlesville Public Library.

Dean, Nora Thompson. 1978. "Delaware Indian Reminiscences." *Bulletin of the Archaeological Society of New Jersey* 35:1–17.

Debo, Angie. 1940. *And Still the Waters Run: The Betrayal of the Five Civilized Tribes*. Norman: University of Oklahoma Press.

Delaware Indian News. 1999. Cherokees to End Battle against Delaware Tribe. *Delaware Indian News* 22(4), October 1:1.

———. 2001. Cherokees Seek to Terminate the Delaware Tribe. *Delaware Indian News* 24(1), January 1:1.

Delaware Tribe of Indians. 1982. Constitution and Bylaws of the Delaware Tribe. Copy in the author's possession. Bartlesville OK: Delaware Tribe of Indians.

———. 1990. Trust Document of the Delaware Tribe of Indians. Approved 31 October. Copy in the author's possession. Bartlesville OK: Delaware Tribe of Indians.

———. 1991. Delaware Tribe of Indians Proposed Master Plan. 3 June. Copy in the author's possession. Bartlesville OK: Delaware Tribe of Indians.

Dickson-Gilmore, E. Jane. 1999. "Factionalist Competition and the Assumption of Imposition in the Kahnawake Mohawk Nation." *Ethnohistory* 46(3):429–450.

Douglas, Jerry, and Chad Smith. 2007. Letter and Draft Legislation providing for the Federal Recognition of the Delaware Tribe to Dan Boren. 18 January. Copy in the author's possession.

Eaton, Melissa Ann. N.d. "Against the Grain: Culture Change, Revitalization, and Identity at Delaware Village, Southwest Missouri, 1821–1831." Ph.D. dissertation, College of William and Mary.

Ellis, Clyde. 2003. *A Dancing People: Powwow Culture on the Southern Plains*. Lawrence: University of Kansas Press.

Esber, George S., Jr. 1992. "Shortcomings of the Self-Determination Policy." In *State and Reservation: New Perspectives in Federal Indian Policy*. George Castile and Robert L. Bee, eds. Pp. 212–223. Tucson: University of Arizona Press.

Exendine, Albert A. N.d. Interview with Exendine, Albert A. [cLL 331.A-B], Delaware Indian Oral History Collection, Oklahoma Historical Society, Oklahoma City.

———. 1972. Interview with Exendine, Albert A. 30 September. [cLL 488.1.A-B], Delaware Indian Oral History Collection, Oklahoma Historical Society, Oklahoma City.

Falleaf, Captain. 1868. Petition to Commissioner of Indian Affairs. 16 January. M234, roll 275. National Archives, Washington DC.

Falleaf, Fred. 1969. T-377–2 (Second of Three Interviews). Interviewed by J. W. Tyner. Delaware Indian Oral History vol. 31, Doris Duke Indian Oral History Collection, Western History Collections, University of Oklahoma, Norman.

Falleaf, George. 1932. Resolution. 26 January. Copy in the author's possession.

Farley, A. 1955. *The Delaware Indians in Kansas: 1829–1867*. Lawrence: Kansas Historical Society.

Farring, Bob. 1978. Memo for the Record. 24 February. Reprinted in *A Lesson in Administrative Termination: An Analysis of the Legal Status of the Delaware Tribe of Indians*. Gina Carrigan and Clayton

Chambers, eds. 2nd edition. Pp. A67–A69. Bartlesville OK: Delaware Tribe of Indians.

Feld, Steven, and Keith Basso, eds. 1996. *Senses of Place*. Santa Fe NM: School of American Research Press.

Field, Les. 1999. "Complications and Collaborations: Anthropologists and the 'Unacknowledged Tribes' of California." *Current Anthropology* 40(2):193–209.

Fogelson, Raymond D. 2004. "Cherokee in the East." In *Handbook of North American Indians*, vol. 14: *Southeast*. Raymond D. Fogelson and William Sturtevant, eds. Pp. 337–353. Washington DC: Smithsonian Institution.

Foreman, Grant. 1942. *A History of Oklahoma*. Norman: University of Oklahoma Press.

Foucault, Michel. 1983. "The Subject and Power." In *Michel Foucault: Beyond Structuralism and Hermeneutics*. Hubert L. Dreyfus and Paul Rabinow, eds. Pp. 208–226. Chicago: University of Chicago Press.

Fowler, Loretta. 2002. *Tribal Sovereignty and the Historical Imagination*. Lincoln: University of Nebraska Press.

Franklin, Robert J. 1984. "The Role of Structure, Agency and Communication in the Development of Federal Policy toward the San Juan Southern Paiute Tribe." Ph.D. dissertation, Department of Anthropology, Indiana University.

Gearing, Fred. 1962. *Priests and Warriors: Social Structures for Cherokee Politics in the 18th Century*. American Anthropologist, Memoir 93, vol. 64(5), part 2. [Menasha WI]: American Anthropological Association.

Gleach, Frederic W. 2002. "Anthropological Professionalization and the Virginia Indians at the Turn of the Century." *American Anthropologist* 104(2):499–507.

Goddard, Ives. 1978. "Delaware." In *Handbook of North American Indians*, vol. 15: *Northeast*. Bruce Trigger and William Sturtevant, eds. Pp. 213–239. Washington DC: Smithsonian Institution.

Grumet, Robert S., ed. 2001. *Voices from the Delaware Big House Ceremony*. Norman: University of Oklahoma Press.

Haake, Claudia. 2001. "Resistance Is (Not) Futile — Two Native American Histories of Change and Survival: Removal of Delawares
and Yaquis in the United States and Mexico." Ph.D. dissertation,
Department of History, Bielefeld University, Germany.

——. 2002a. "Delaware Identity in the Cherokee Nation." *Indigenous
Nations Studies Journal* 3(1):19–44.

——. 2002b. "Identity, Sovereignty, and Power: The Cherokee-
Delaware Agreement of 1867, Past and Present." *American Indian
Quarterly* 26(3):418–435.

——. 2007. *The State, Removal and Indigenous Peoples in the United
States and Mexico, 1620–2000*. London: Routledge.

Hagan, William. 2003. *Taking Indian Lands: The Cherokee (Jerome)
Commission, 1889–1893*. Norman: University of Oklahoma Press.

Hale, Duane. 1987. *Peacemakers on the Frontier: A History of the Delaware Tribe of Western Oklahoma*. Anadarko OK: Delaware Tribe of
Western Oklahoma Press.

Hamill, James F. 2003. "Show Me Your CDIB: Blood Quantum and
Indian Identity among Indian People of Oklahoma." *American
Behavioral Scientist* 47(3):267–282.

Harrington, Mark. 1913. "A Preliminary Sketch of Lenape Culture."
American Anthropologist 15:208–235.

Hewes, Leslie. 1942. "The Oklahoma Ozarks as the Land of the Cherokees." *Geographical Review* 32:269–281.

——. 1944. "Cherokee Occupancy in the Oklahoma Ozarks and
Prairie Plains. *Chronicles of Oklahoma* 22:324–337.

——. 1977. *Occupying the Cherokee Country of Oklahoma*. University
of Nebraska Studies, n.s. 57. Lincoln: Board of Regents of the
University of Nebraska Press.

Holm, Tom. 1979. "Indian Lobbyists: Cherokee Opposition to the
Allotment of Tribal Lands." *American Indian Quarterly* 5(2):115–
134.

Howard, James. 1955. "Pan-Indian Culture of Oklahoma." *Scientific
Monthly* 81(5):220–250.

——. 1970. "Bringing Back the Fire: The Revival of a Natchez-Cherokee Ceremonial Ground." *American Indian Crafts and Culture* 4(1):9–12.

———. 1980. "Discussion: Social Contexts of Late Nineteenth and Early Twentieth Century Delaware Religion." *Papers in Anthropology* 21(2):153–161.

———. 1981. *Shawnee! The Ceremonialism of a Native Indian Tribe and Its Cultural Background.* Athens: Ohio University Press.

Hudson, Charles M. 1976. *The Southeastern Indians.* Knoxville: University of Tennessee Press.

Hurt, Douglas Allan. 2000. "The Shaping of a Creek (Muscogee) Homeland in Indian Territory, 1828–1907." Ph.D. dissertation, Department of Geography, University of Oklahoma.

Jackson, Jason Baird. 2003a. *Yuchi Ceremonial Life: Performance, Meaning and Tradition in a Contemporary American Indian Community.* Lincoln: University of Nebraska Press.

———. 2003b. "The Opposite of Powwow: Ignoring and Incorporating the Intertribal War Dance in the Oklahoma Stomp Dance Community." *Plains Anthropologist* 48(187):237–253.

Jackson, Jason Baird, and Victoria Lindsay Levine. 2002. "Singing for Garfish: Music and Community Life in Eastern Oklahoma." *Ethnomusicology* 46(2):284–306.

Jaimes, M. Annette, ed. 1992. *State of Native America: Genocide, Colonization and Resistance.* Boston: South End Press.

Jennings, Francis. 1975. *The Invasion of America.* Chapel Hill: University of North Carolina Press.

Kappler, Charles J., ed. 1913. *Indian Affairs: Laws and Treaties*, vol. 3: *Laws.* Washington DC: Government Printing Office.

Ketchum, Dee. 2001. "A Message from Chief Dee Ketchum." *Delaware Indian News* 24(4), October 1:2.

———. 2002. "A Tribal Update from Chief Dee Ketchum: Dual Enrollment Reduces Tribal Funding." *Delaware Indian News* 25(1), January 1:2.

King, Duane, ed. 1979. *The Cherokee Indian Nation: A Troubled History.* Knoxville: University of Tennessee Press.

———. 2004. "Cherokee in the West: History since 1776." In *Handbook of North American Indians*, vol. 14: *Southeast*. Raymond D. Fogelson and William Sturtevant, eds. Pp. 354–372. Washington DC: Smithsonian Institution.

Kraft, Herbert, ed. 1974. *A Delaware Indian Symposium*. Anthropological Series, no. 4. Harrisburg: Pennsylvania History and Museum Commission.

———. 1977. *The Minisink Settlements: An Investigation into a Prehistoric and Early Historic Site in Sussex County, New Jersey*. South Orange NJ: Seton Hall University Museum.

———, ed. 1984. *The Lenape Indian: A Symposium*. Archaeological Research Center, no. 7. South Orange NJ: Seton Hall University Museum.

———. 1986. *The Lenape: Archaeology, History and Ethnography*. Newark: New Jersey Historical Society.

———. 1996. *The Dutch, the Indians and the Quest for Copper: Pahaquarry and the Old Mine Road*. South Orange NJ: Seton Hall University Museum.

Lassiter, Luke E. 1998. *The Power of Kiowa Song: A Collaborative Ethnography*. Tucson: University of Arizona Press.

Lewis, David. 1991. "Reservation Leadership and the Progressive-Traditional Dichotomy: William Walsh and the Northern Utes, 1865–1928." *Ethnohistory* 38(2):124–148.

McCulloch, Anne, and David Wilkins. 1995. "Constructing Nations within States: The Quest for Federal Recognition by the Catawba and Lumbee Tribes." *American Indian Quarterly* 19(3):361–390.

McLaughlin, Michael. 1996. "The Dawes Act, or Indian General Allotment Act of 1887: The Continuing Burden of Allotment: A Selective Annotated Bibliography." *American Indian Culture and Research Journal* 20(2):59–105.

Michelson, Truman. 1912. Ethnological and Linguistic Field Notes from the Munsee in Kansas and the Delaware in Oklahoma. Manuscript 2776, National Anthropological Archives, Washington DC. Smithsonian Institution.

Miller, Bruce Granville. 2003. *Invisible Indigenes: The Politics of Nonrecognition*. Lincoln: University of Nebraska Press.

Miller, Jay. 1975. "Kwulakan: The Delaware Side of the Their Movement West." *Pennsylvania Archaeologist* 45(4):45–46.

———. 1977. "A Struckon Model of Delaware Culture and the Positioning of Mediators." *American Ethnologist* 6:791–802.

———. 1980a. "The Matter of the (Thoughtful) Heart: Centrality, Focality or Overlap." *Journal of Anthropological Research* 36:338–342.

———. 1980b. "A Structuralist Analysis of the Delaware Big House Rite." *Papers in Anthropology* 21(2):107–134.

———. 1989. "Delaware Traditions from Kansas, NahKoman to Isaac McCoy." *Plains Anthropologist* 34:1–6.

———. 1994. "The 1806 Purge among the Indiana Delaware: Sorcery, Gender, Boundaries and Legitimacy." *Ethnohistory* 41(2):245–266.

———. 1997. "Old Religion among the Delawares: The Gamwing (Big House Rite)." *Ethnohistory* 44(1):113–134.

Miller, Mark Edwin. 2004. *Forgotten Tribes: Unrecognized Indians and the Federal Acknowledgment Process*. Lincoln: University of Nebraska Press.

Miner, Craig. 1976. *The Corporation and the Indian: Tribal Sovereignty and Industrial Development in Indian Territory, 1865–1907*. Columbia: University of Missouri Press.

Morgan, Lewis Henry. 1959. *The Indian Journals, 1859–1862*. Leslie White, ed. Ann Arbor: University of Michigan Press.

Nagel, Joane. 1995. "American Indian Ethnic Renewal: Politics and the Resurgence of Identity." *American Sociological Review* 60:947–965.

Newcomb, William. 1955. "A Note on Cherokee-Delaware Pan-Indianism." *American Anthropologist* 57(5):1041–1045.

———. 1956a. *The Culture and Acculturation of the Delaware Indians*. Anthropological Papers 10. Ann Arbor: University of Michigan, Museum of Anthropology.

———. 1956b. "The Peyote Cult of the Delaware Indians." *Texas Journal of Science* 8:202–211.

Obermeyer, Brice. 2003. "Delaware Identity in a Cherokee Nation: An Ethnography of Power." Ph.D. dissertation, Department of Anthropology, University of Oklahoma, Norman.

———. 2005. "Lessons from Salt Creek: Maintaining Tribal Identity among the Black Indians of the Five Civilized Tribes." In *Race, Roots and Relations: Native and African Americans*. Terry Straus, ed. Pp. 54–62. Chicago: Albatross Press.

———. 2007. "Salvaging the Delaware Big House Ceremony: The History and Legacy of Frank Speck's Collaboration with the Oklahoma Delaware." *Histories of Anthropology Annual*, vol. 3. Regna Darnell and Frederic W. Gleach, eds. Pp.184–198, Lincoln: University of Nebraska Press.

Paredes, Anthony. 1992. "Federal Recognition and the Poarch Creek Indians." In *Indians of the Southeastern United States in the Late Twentieth Century*. Anthony Paredes, ed. Tuscaloosa: University of Alabama Press.

Penn, William. 1857[1683]. *Watson's Annals of Philadelphia and Pennsylvania*. Vol. 2, *Indians*, pt. 1. Electronic document, http://www.usgwarchives.org/pa/philadelphia/watsontoc.htm, accessed 9 January 2009.

Petrullo, Vincenzo. 1934. *The Diabolical Root: A Study of Peyotism, the New Indian Religion, among the Delaware*. Philadelphia: University of Pennsylvania Press.

Porter, Frank. 1990. "In Search of Recognition: Federal Indian Policy and the Landless Tribes of Western Washington." *American Indian Quarterly* 14(2):113–132.

Powell, Gina S., and Neal H. Lopinot. 2003. "In Search of Delaware Town, an Early Nineteenth Century Delaware Settlement in Southwest Missouri." Unpublished paper in the author's possession.

Powers, William. 1990. *War Dance: Plains Indian Musical Performance*. Tucson: University of Arizona Press.

Pratt, John G. 1867. Letter to Thomas Murphy. 6 August. M234, Roll 275, National Archives, Washington DC.

Prewitt, Terry. 1981. *Tradition and Culture Change in the Oklahoma Delaware Big House Community, 1867–1924*. Contributions in Archaeology no. 9. Tulsa: University of Tulsa Laboratory of Archaeology.

———. 2001. "Introduction: The Big House Described." In *Voices from the Delaware Big House Ceremony*. Robert Grumet, ed. Pp. 3–22. Norman: University of Oklahoma Press.

Procedures for Establishing That an American Indian Group Exists as an Indian Tribe. 1994. 25 C.F.R. Part 83.1–13. Electronic document, http://www.und.edu/dept/indian/Treaties/existence%20tribe.pdf, accessed August 10, 2007.

Prucha, Francis Paul, ed. 1975. *Documents of United States Indian Policy*. Lincoln: University of Nebraska Press.

———. 1988. "United States Indian Policies, 1815–1860." In *Handbook of North American Indians*, vol. 4: *History of Indian-White Relations*. William C. Sturtevant and Wilcomb E. Washburn, eds. Pp. 40–50. Washington DC: Smithsonian Institution.

Quinn, William W., Jr. 1990. "Federal Acknowledgment of American Indian Tribes: The Historical Development of a Legal Concept." *American Journal of Legal History* 34(4):331–364.

———. 1993. "Southeastern Indians: The Quest for Federal Acknowledgment and a New Legal Status." *Ethnic Forum: Journal of Ethnic Studies and Ethnic Bibliography* 13(1):34–52.

Records of the Bureau of Indian Affairs. 1871. List of Delawares who elected to remove to Indian Territory. Record Group 75, 7RA74. Federal Archives and Records Center, Fort Worth TX.

———. 1880. Index and Census of the Cherokee Nation. Record Group 75, Schedules 1 6. P2072 (formerly 7RA07). Federal Archives and Records Center Fort Worth TX.

———. 1904. Records of the Commissioner to the Five Civilized Tribes: Rolls of the Delaware Tribe and Shawnee Tribe. Record Group 75, 7RA26, roll 1. Federal Archives and Records Center, Fort Worth TX.

———. 1907. Final Rolls of Citizens and Freedmen of the Five Civi-

lized Tribes in Indian Territory, Cherokee Nation (as approved
by the Secretary of the Interior on or before March 4, 1908 with
supplements dated September 25, 1914). Record Group 75, T529,
roll 2. Federal Archives and Records Center, Fort Worth TX.

Rementer, James, and Doug Donnell. 1995. "Social Dances of the
Lenape and Other North-Eastern Indian Tribes." In *Remain-
ing Ourselves: Music and Tribal Memories: Traditional Music in
Contemporary Communities.* Dayna Bowker Lee, ed. Pp. 37–41.
Oklahoma City: Arts Council of Oklahoma.

Results.gov. 2007. Ross Swimmer — Department of the Interior. Electronic document, http://www.whitehouse.gov/results/
leadership/bio_522.html, accessed August 5, 2007.

Roark-Calnek, Sue. 1977. "Indian Way in Oklahoma: Transactions
in Honor and Legitimacy." Ph.D. dissertation, Department of
Anthropology, Bryn Mawr College.

———. 1980. "Delaware Religion and Ethnic Identity: The Last Fifty
Years." *Papers in Anthropology* 21(2):135–152.

Rountree, Helen. 1990. *Pocahontas's People: The Powhatan Indians of
Virginia through Four Centuries.* Norman: University of Oklahoma
Press.

Sarcoxie, Chief Anderson. 1867. Petition to Commissioner of Indian
Affairs. 13 June, M234, roll 275. National Archives, Washington DC.

Schutt, Amy. 2007. *Peoples of the River Valleys: The Odyssey of the Delaware Indians.* Philadelphia: University of Pennsylvania Press.

Seneca, Martin E. 1979. "Message to Members of the Cherokee
Delaware Tribe." 7 June. Reprinted in *A Lesson in Administrative
Termination: An Analysis of the Legal Status of the Delaware Tribe
of Indians.* 2nd edition. Gina Carrigan and Clayton Chambers,
eds. Pp. A77–A80. Bartlesville OK: Delaware Tribe of Indians.

Shawnee Tribe. 2007. The Shawnee in History. Electronic document,
http://www.shawnee-tribe.com/history.htm, accessed August 24,
2007.

Shawnee Tribe Status Act, Public Law 106–568. (27 December 2000),
161 Stat. 1658.

Shimony, Annemarie Anrod. 1994. *Conservatism among the Iroquois at the Six Nations Reserve*. Syracuse NY: Syracuse University Press.

Smith, Carol. 1997. "The Symbolics of Blood: Mestizaje in the Americas." *Identities: Global Studies in Culture and Power* 3(4):495–522.

Snipp, Matthew C. 1989. *American Indians: The First of This Land*. New York: Russell Sage Foundation.

Speck, Frank. 1931. *A Study of the Delaware Big House Ceremony*. Publications of the Pennsylvania Historical Commission, no. 2. Harrisburg: Pennsylvania Historical Commission.

———. 1937. *Oklahoma Delaware Ceremonies, Feasts and Dances*. Memoirs of the American Philosophical Society, no. 7. Philadelphia: American Philosophical Society.

Starna, William. 1996. "'We'll All Be Together Again': The Federal Acknowledgment of the Wampanoag Tribe of Gay Head." *Northeast Anthropology* 51:3–12.

Stolcke, Verena. 1991. "Conquering Women." NACLA *Report on the Americas* 24(5):23–28.

Stoler, Ann. 1989. "Making Empire Respectable: The Politics of Race and Sexual Morality in Twentieth Century Colonial Cultures." *American Ethnologist* 16(4):634–660.

———. 1995. *Race and the Education of Desire: Foucault's History of Sexuality and Colonial Order of Things*. Durham NC: Duke University Press.

Strong, Pauline, and Barrik Van Winkle. 1996. "'Indian Blood': Reflections on the Reckoning and Refiguring of Native North American Identity." *Cultural Anthropology* 11(4):547–576.

Sturm, Circe. 2002. *Blood Politics: Race, Culture and Identity in the Cherokee Nation of Oklahoma*. Berkeley: University of California Press.

Swimmer, Ross O. 1977. Letter to Dr. Perry Johnson. 28 November. Reprinted in *A Lesson in Administrative Termination: An Analysis of the Legal Status of the Delaware Tribe of Indians*. Gina Carrigan and Clayton Chambers, eds. 2nd edition. Pp. A65–A66. Bartlesville OK: Delaware Tribe of Indians.

———. 1978. Letter to Mr. Forrest J. Gerard. 27 February. Reprinted in *A Lesson in Administrative Termination: An Analysis of the Legal Status of the Delaware Tribe of Indians*. Gina Carrigan and Clayton Chambers, eds. 2nd edition. Pp. A70 –A71. Bartlesville OK: Delaware Tribe of Indians.

Teague, Margaret. 1967. *History of Washington County and Surrounding Area*. Bartlesville OK: Bartlesville Historical Commission.

Thornton, Russell. 1987. *American Indian Holocaust and Survival: A Population History since 1492*. Norman: University of Oklahoma Press.

Thurman, Melburn. 1973. "The Delaware Indians: A Study in Ethnohistory." Ph.D. dissertation, University of California, Santa Barbara.

Tolley, Sara-Larus. 2006. *Quest for Tribal Acknowledgment: California's Honey Lake Maidus*. Norman: University of Oklahoma Press.

Township Maps of the Cherokee Nation. N.d. Bound maps in the possession of the Washington County Assessor's Office. Washington DC: U.S. Government Printing Office.

United States Census Bureau. 2007. Table C3, Per Capita Income by County: 1959, 1969, 1979, 1989. Electronic document, http://www.census.gov/hhes/www/income/histinc/county/county3.html, accessed August 4, 2007.

United States Department of Interior, National Park Service. "Notice of Intent to Repatriate Cultural Items: Peabody Museum of Archaeology and Ethnology, Harvard University, Cambridge MA." Washington DC: *Federal Register* 72 no. 145 (July 30, 2007):41524–41525.

United States Department of Interior, Office of Federal Acknowledgment. "Notice of Final Determination That the San Juan Southern Paiute Tribe Exists as an Indian Tribe." Washington DC: Federal Register 54 no. 240 (December 29, 1989):51502–51505.

Van Laer, A. J. F., ed. and trans. 1924. *Documents Relating to New Netherland, 1624–1626, in the Henry Huntington Library*. Henry Huntington Library and Art Gallery, San Marino CA.

Voegelin, Charles F. 1946. "Delaware, an Eastern Algonquian Lan-

guage." In *Linguistic Structures of Native America*. Cornelius
Osgood, ed. Viking Fund Publications in Anthropology no. 6. Pp.
130–157. New York: Viking.

Wallace, Anthony F. C. 1947. "Women, Land and Society: Three
Aspects of Aboriginal Delaware Life." *Pennsylvania Archaeologist*
17:1–35.

———. 1956. "Political Organization and Land Tenure among the
Northeastern Indians, 1600–1830." *Southwest Journal of Anthropology* 13:301–321.

———. 1970. *King of the Delawares: Teedyuscung, 1700–1763*. Freeport
NY: Books for the Libraries Press.

Wallace, Pamela. 2002. "Indian Claims Commission: Political Complexity and Contrasting Concepts of Identity." *Ethnohistory*
49(4):743–767.

Wallis, Michael. 1988. *Oil Man: The Story of Frank Phillips and the Birth
of Phillips Petroleum*. New York: Doubleday.

Warhaftig, Albert. 1968. "The Tribal Cherokee Population of Eastern
Oklahoma." *Current Anthropology* 9:510–518.

Washington, Joe. 1929. AGREEMENT. 15 June. Fred Washington Collection, copy in the author's possession.

Weslager, Clinton A. 1972. *The Delaware Indians: A History*. New
Brunswick NJ: Rutgers University Press.

———. 1978. *The Delaware Indian Westward Migration*. Wallingford PA:
Middle Atlantic Press.

———. 1986. *The Swedes and the Dutch at New Castle with Highlights
in the History of the Delaware Valley, 1638–1664*. Wilmington DE:
Middle Atlantic Press.

White, Richard. 1991. *The Middle Ground: Indians, Empires and Republics in the Great Lakes Region, 1650–1815*. Cambridge: Cambridge
University Press.

Wilkins, David. 1993. "Breaking into the Intergovernmental Matrix:
The Lumbee Tribe's Efforts to Secure Federal Acknowledgment."
Publius: The Journal of Federalism 23(4):123–142.

Witthoft, John. 1949. *Green Corn Ceremonialism in the Eastern Wood-*

lands. Occasional Paper from the Museum of Anthropology of the University of Michigan, no. 13. Ann Arbor: University of Michigan Press.

Young, Claiborne Addison. 1958. "A Walking Tour in Indian Territory, 1874." *Chronicles of Oklahoma* 36(2):176–177.

Zeisberger, David. 1910. *David Zeisberger's History of the North American Indians.* Archer Butler Hulbert, ed. William Nathaniel Schwarze, trans. Columbus: Ohio State Archaeological Society.

Index

Adams, Richard, 213

administrative centers, *110*

Administrative Procedures Act (APA), 61–62

Algonquian dialect speakers, 38

Alluwe OK, 73–74, 85, 92

American Revolution, 43, 280n4, 281n7

Anadarko OK, 44

Anderson, William, 47, 82

APA. *See* Administrative Procedures Act (APA)

Apache Indians, 74–75

Arapaho Indians, 13

Argall, Samuel, 38

Armstrong, Arthur, 131

Armstrong, Charles, 82

Armstrong, Henry, 131

Articles of Agreement between the Cherokee Nation and the Delawares. See Cherokee-Delaware Agreement (1867)

Assiniboine, 13

Bartles, Jacob, 120–21, 139, 285n1

Bartles, Joseph, 131, 286n4

Bartlesville Indian Women's Club, 1, 105

Bartlesville OK, 104, 121, 248–49, 285n1

Basso, Keith, 74–75

BIA. *See* Bureau of Indian Affairs (BIA)

"Big Fish and the Sun" story, 151–55, 287n3

Big House Ceremony (Gamwing), 41, 45, 69–72, 113, 134–36, 284n7; discontinuation of, 87, 94–96

Big House Committee, 135–37

Big House community, 93, 112–14; and cultural preservation, 132–35; and political organization, 132–36; and resistance to Cherokee tribal membership, 235; and single enrollment referendum, 254; and tribal government, 172–73

Biolsi, Thomas, 193

Black Beaver (Delaware leader), 82, 284n5

Blanchard, Ira, 281n9

blood quantum, 182–84, 201–3, 288n3; and CDIB cards, 214; and Delaware Per Capita Roll, 242; and enrollment options, 229; and land rights, 186–87; and single enrollment, 231; and tribal identity, 190–96

Blu, Karen I., 75

Branch of Acknowledgment and Recognition (BAR). *See* Office of Federal Acknowledgment (OFA)

Brooks, Joe, 173, 175

Bullette, George, 131, 286n4

Bunte, Pamela Ann, 12

Bureau of Indian Affairs (BIA): and APA, 62; and Cherokee Nation Dawes Roll, 191; and Delaware Business Committee, 145; and Delaware Constitution, 237, 289n2; and Delaware tribal membership cards, 242; and Delaware Trust Fund, 166–68; and federal recognition, 10, 16–17; and land allotments, 123; and land claims award, 162; and self-determination policy, 8–9; and tribal enrollment, 119; and tribal membership, 141–42

Byrd, Joe, 61, 239

California Creek community, 93

Cape Girardeau MO, 44

Carrigan, Gina, 28–29

CDIB. *See* Certificate Degree of Indian Blood (CDIB)

CDIB cards, 187, 212; and blood quantum, 201, 214; Delaware interpretations of, 219–20; and Indian identity, 194–97; and multiple tribal memberships,

203–5; and tribal affiliation, 220

Certificate Degree of Indian Blood (CDIB), 32, 180–81, 187–88. *See also* CDIB CARDS; Cherokee CDIB cards

Chambers, Clayton, 28–29

Cherokee, Eastern Band of, 52

Cherokee by adoption, 182–83, 185, 220

Cherokee by blood, 182–91, 195, 210, 217

Cherokee CDIB cards, 187, 189–91, *190*, 212; and access to federal services, 195, 205–8, 211–12, 215, 220–24, 252, 273; and blood quantum, 201, 214; Cherokee Nation's control of, 181–82, 192, 203, 215–16, 226, 272–73; Delaware interpretations of, 200–203, 208–14, 219–20; enrollment process for, 196–200; and Indian identity, 194–97; and land claims awards, 210–11; and multiple tribal memberships, 203–5; requirements for, 223–24; revoked by request, 212–13; and single enrollment, 229–30; and tribal affiliation, 220; and United Keetoowah Band of Cherokee Indians, 225

Cherokee citizenship, and blood quantum, 201

Cherokee-Dawes Agreement
(1902), 128
Cherokee-Delaware Agreement
(1867), 35–37, 57–66, 82–83,
117, 132, 267–68; and tribal
membership, 182, 233, 288n2
Cherokee-Delaware Agreement
(2007), 33, 233, 260–69, 277
Cherokee Executive Committee,
138
Cherokee Health Clinic, 208
Cherokee membership provision: and Delaware internal
divisions, 67–68; and Delaware resistance to, 77
Cherokee Nation, 56, 203; and
Christianity, 51; and cultural
accommodation, 37; cultural
affinities of, 49; history of,
3–4, 50–51; membership
policy, 222; and OIWA, 138;
and opposition to Delaware
recognition, 259, 262; origins
of, 48–50; political organization, 50; and removals, 3–4,
37, 46, 50, 51–52; and single enrollment referendum, 248–51;
social organization, 49–50, 52;
tribal government, 2, 51
Cherokee Nation Dawes Roll, 183,
186–88, 273; and BIA, 191; and
tribal membership, 224–25
Cherokee Nation health care
services, 206–8, 207, 266–67

Cherokee Nation Jurisdictional
Area, 102, 191, 207, 223, 237,
241, 265, 267, 289n1
Cherokee Nation of Oklahoma v.
Babbitt (1996), 61
Cherokee Nation of Oklahoma v.
Babbitt (1997), 61–62, 239–41
Cherokee Nation of Oklahoma v.
Norton (2002), 62
Cherokee Nation of Oklahoma v.
Norton (2004), 61–62, 117
Cherokee Nation tribal enroll-
ment, 226
Cherokee Nation Tribal Jurisdic-
tion Area, 1
Cherokee Nation v. Georgia (1831),
51
Cherokee Nation v. Journeycake
(1894), 60, 185
Cherokee Phoenix, 51, 52
Cherokee service area, 191. See
also federal contract services
Cherokee Treaty (1866), 54–55,
57, 83
Cherokee tribal membership
card, 223–24
Cheyenne Indians, 13
CHR. See Committee Health
Representatives program
(CHR)
Christian community, 69–72,
77–78, 84–85, 109, 111–14; and
Delaware Business Commit-
tee, 131–32; and political

Christian community (*cont.*)
organization, 130; and support
of dual enrollment, 222; and
tribal government, 80–81, 104,
172–73
Christianity: and Cherokee Nation, 51; and Delaware Tribe,
45, 47–48, 281n9. *See also*
Christian community
clan system, 42–43, 48, 280n5;
and political organization, 87;
and tribal government, 80–82,
282n10; and Tribal Seal, 113
Claremore Indian Hospital,
205–6, 213, 242
Committee Health Representatives program (CHR), 162–63
confederated tribes, 12, 279n2
Conner, James, 82, 130, 281n9
Conner, John, 54–55, 81–83,
85–86, 281n9, 282n10
Conner lineage, 79
consolidated tribes, 12–13, 18
CPC. *See* Cultural Preservation
Committee (CPC)
Cramer, Renee Ann, 19
Cranor, Ruby, 28
Creek Indians. *See* Muscogee
(Creek) Indians
cultural diversity, origins of,
79–80
cultural geography, 68–75, 101–3
cultural identity, 100, 103, 111,
201–2. *See also* tribal identity

cultural practices, revitalization
of, 173–74
cultural preservation, 68, 132–35,
171–75
Cultural Preservation Committee
(CPC), 172–73
cultural sites, *110*

Davis, Anna, 125–26
Dawes Act. *See* General Allot-
ment Act
Dawes Commission, 184–86
Dean, Nora Thompson, 134
Deer, Ada, 17
Delaware Treaty (1866), 53–55, 57
Delaware Business Committee,
58–59, 103, 118, 128–32, 135–42,
161–66, 176; and BIA, 145; and
land claims, 186; and religion,
149; and single enrollment,
236–37
Delaware Bylaws and Constitu-
tion (1962), 139
Delaware chiefs, responsibilities
of, 134. *See also* leadership
Delaware Child Care Program,
103
Delaware Community, 23–24
Delaware Constitution (1982),
237, 243–44, 289n2
Delaware Country, 1–3, 66–67,
109–10, 127–28, 140–41; cultural
geography of, 68–75, 101, 103
Delaware Days, 24, 108

Delaware Executive Council, 135–37

Delaware General Council, 24, 104, 167–68, 244

Delaware Grievance Committee, 149

Delaware homeland, 39

Delaware Housing Authority, 103

Delaware Indian News, 240–41, 244

Delaware Indian Per Capita Roll (1904), 140, 142–43, 166, 186, 265–66; and blood quantum, 242; and tribal membership, 224

Delaware Indians v. Cherokee (1904), 60

Delaware-Muncee Tribe, 53, 61

Delaware Powwow, 24, 72, 77, 143, 146–49, 174, 287n1; and cultural identity, 107–8

Delaware Service Area, 103–4, 111, 243

Delaware Treaty (1866), 53, 58, 81, 83

Delaware Tribal Business Committee v. Weeks (1977), 60–61

Delaware Tribal Council, 80–81, 129–30, 166–67, 169–70; and Cherokee-Delaware Agreement (2007), 265–66; and religion, 283n2, 284n3; and single enrollment, 243–46, 250–52

Delaware tribal membership cards, 212–13, 224, 242

Delaware Tribal Seal, *112*, 112–14

Delaware Tribe: author's work with, 25–27; chairmen and chiefs of, *171*; demography of, 142–44; headquarters of, 103–4; origins of, 3–4, 37–42; and relationship with Cherokee Nation, 234–35; and relationship with U.S. government, 117–19, 145, 161

Delaware Tribe Service Area, 1

Delaware Trust Board, 167–70, 172, 266

Delaware Trust Fund, 151, 165, 272; and BIA, 166–68; and Cherokee-Delaware Agreement (2007), 264

de la Warr, Lord (Sir Thomas West), 38

delegation to Washington, 81–82, 284n5

demographics: of Cherokee Nation, 287n7; of Delaware Tribe, 142–44, 287n7

Department of the Interior (DOI), 61; and *Cherokee Nation of Oklahoma v. Norton*, 117; and single enrollment, 236; and tribal government, 131

Dewey Fair Building, 105

Dewey OK, 105, 121, *122*, 131, 139, 285n1

DOI. *See* Department of the
Interior (DOI)
Donnell, Doug, 109
Douglas, Jerry, 175–76, 262–63
dual enrollment, 221, 226–30,
251–52; and access to federal
services, 232; and Cherokee-
Delaware Agreement (1867),
233; and Cherokee-Delaware
Agreement (2007), 266; and
religion, 222, 254; risks of,
288n4

Eagle Ridge dance ground, 109,
172
Eastern Band of Cherokee, 52
economic development, 121,
285n1
elections, 157–61
Elkhair, Charlie, 87, 134–36; and
"Big Fish and the Sun" story,
151
Elkhair, Ray, 106
enrollment. *See also* tribal membership
enrollment in Cherokee Nation, 202, 251–52; opposition
to, 213–14, 235; and religion,
232–33
enrollment options, 227, 227–32
enrollment policy, 11, 18–21, 194
Esber, George S., 9
ethnography, 11–12, 71, 76;
author's, 24–27, 29–30; of

Cherokee, 188; and Speck,
134–35, 286n5
European encroachment, 41–42,
50

factionalism, ethnology of, 76
Falleaf, Captain, 73, 83, 84
Falleaf, Fred, 73–76
Falleaf, George, 107, 135–36
Falleaf, John, 107, 135
Falleaf, Numerous, 107
Falleaf lineage, 79
Fallen Timbers, Battle of (1795),
45
family. *See* lineage
FAP. *See* Federal Acknowledgment Process (FAP)
Federal Acknowledgment Process (FAP), 8, 17–20, 165, 231,
261, 269–74
federal contract services, 20–22;
and CDIB cards, 195, 205–8,
211–12, 215, 220–24, 252, 273;
and Cherokee-Delaware
Agreement (2007), 264–65;
and Cherokee Nation, 262;
Cherokee Nation control of,
237–38; and dual enrollment,
232; and population size, 189;
and single enrollment, 231,
236, 238; and single enrollment referendum, 244
federal recognition, 2, 5, 10–11, 14,
17–19; conditional, 260, 262,

266; and cultural identity, 100; and Delaware Tribal Council, 169; efforts to restore, 176; and Indian identification process, 216; proposal for Delaware recognition (2007), 262–63; support for, 252; termination of, 26, 61–62, 117–18, 145, 165, 175–76, 274; ways to obtain, 16–17

Final Rolls of Citizens and Freedmen of the Five Civilized Tribes, Cherokee Nation (BIA, 1907). *See* Cherokee Nation Dawes Roll

First Nations (Canada), 43–44

Five Civilized Tribes, 184–85

Five Civilized Tribes Act (1906), 129

Flint, Sam, 133

Foucault, Michel, 192–93

Fowler, Loretta, 76

Franklin, Robert J., 12

freedmen, 4

French and Indian War, 280n4

Frenchman, Frank, 135

Ft. Belknap Indian Community, 13

gaming, 19, 263, 265

Gamwing. *See* Big House Ceremony (Gamwing)

General Allotment Act (Dawes Act, 1887), 119, 128, 183; and land allotments, 121, 123

General Council, 157

Gnadenhutten Massacre, 43

Grandfathers, 15

Great Britain, 41–42, 43, 280n4, 280n5

Green Corn Ceremony, 49

Gros Ventre Indians, 13

Hamill, James, 194

Health, Education and Welfare, Department of, 8

Hill, Rose, 107

Howard, James, 12

Hurt, Douglas Allen, 75

identity. *See* cultural identity; Indian identity; tribal identity

Indian Claims Commission, 138–41, 161

Indian Claims Commission Act (1946), 138

Indian Health Services, 164

Indian identification process, 181–82, 188, 215–17; critique of, 221; and cultural identity, 202; and exercise of power, 192–93; and federal recognition, 216; and land rights, 192–93; resistance to, 214

Indian identity: and blood quantum, 202; and CDIB cards, 194–97; and cultural participation, 201–2

Indian Removal Act (1830), 51

Indian Reservation Road (IRR)
program, 25–26
Indian Self-Determination and
Education Act (1975), 8, 20,
164, 187–88, 191. *See also* self-
determination policy
Interior, Department of. *See* DOI
intermarriage, 92, 93, 133
internal tribal divisions, 67–68,
72–77, 79–80, 84–87, 135–36,
217, 246; origins of, 79–80;
permeability of, 89–90
Intertribal Indian Club of
Bartlesville (IICOB), 105
IRR. *See* Indian Reservation
Road (IRR) program
Iroquoian dialects, 48–49
Iroquois Indians, 42

Jackson, Andrew, 51
Jackson, Colonel (Wolf Clan
leader), 87
Jackson, Jason Baird, 11–12, 114
Johnson, Fielding, 80
Journeycake, Charles, 74, 80–82,
85–86, 130–31, 281n9
Journeycake, Isaac, 82
Journeycake lineage, 79

Kansas Delaware Roll (1867),
182, 288n1
Kansas River, 47, 282n9
Keeler, W. W., 132, 138, 163–64
Keetoowah Indians. *See* United

Keetoowah Band of Cherokee
Indians
Ketchum, Captain, 281n9, 282n10
Ketchum, David, 1–2
Ketchum, Dee, 173, 239–41,
244–45
Ketchum, James, 82, 85, 130
Ketchum, Lewis, 172
kin-based divisions. *See* internal
tribal divisions; lineage
Kishelemukong (the creator), 41

Lakota (Sioux) Indians, 193
land allotments, 60, 90–92, 91,
101, 119–28, 122, 183–85, 286n2
land claims award, 141–42,
161–62, 172, 186; and CDIB
cards, 210–11; and Cherokee-
Delaware Agreement (2007),
264; and single enrollment,
237
land rights, 186–87; and Indian
identification process, 192–93
leadership, 149–57; Delaware
ideals of, 161, 177
Lenape (Delaware people), 40
Lenape (language), 71–72, 92,
94–98, 148, 174
lineage: and elections, 158–59;
and internal divisions, 73–79;
and settlement patterns,
72–73, 85; and single enrollment, 217, 247–49; and single

enrollment referendum, 246,
254; and tribal government,
172
lineage-based divisions. *See* internal tribal divisions
line communities, 70, 79, 87–90,
88, 100–101, 121
Longbone, Jack, 135
Longbone, Willie, 126, 135
Lumbee Indians, 75

Mahican Indians, 44
Maidu Indians, 19
Mankiller, Wilma, 234
McCoy, Isaac, 281n9
McCracken, Horace, 139
Miller, Andrew, 131
Miller, Bruce Granville, 6
Miller, Mark Edwin, 17
Missouri River Railroad Company, 81, 84
Moravians, 43, 281n9, 283n2
multiple enrollment, 203–5, 237
Munsee speakers, 37–42, 43–44
Muscogee (Creek) Indians, 4, 13,
75, 192

NAGPRA. *See* Native American
Graves Protection and Repatriation Act (NAGPRA),
Natchez Indians, 4, 12, 192
Native American Graves Protection and Repatriation Act
(NAGPRA), 25–26, 96, 256–58

nativistic movement, 281n9
Navajo Nation, 12, 14, 270, 274
New Hope Indian Methodist
Church, 105–6, 125
Nowata County, 248
Nowata OK, 121, 163, 285n1

OFA. *See* Office of Federal Acknowledgment
Office of Federal Acknowledgment (OFA), 17–19
Office of Indian Trust Transition,
164–65
oil industry, 125–26
OIWA. *See* Oklahoma Indian
Welfare Act (OIWA)
Oklahoma, settlement in, 54–55,
67–68
Oklahoma Indian Welfare Act
(OIWA) (1936), 137–39, 144,
266
Old Settlers (first Cherokee in
Oklahoma), 50
Operation Eagle, 105
Osage Indians, 1, 106, 126, 132–33,
206

Pace, Bill, 106
Peabody Museum, 256–57
Phillips, Frank, 125–26
Phillips Petroleum Company, 125,
132, 248, 289n4
political organization, 36–37,
42–43, 129–30, 132–37, 170

political views: and religion, 78, 83, 87; and settlement patterns, 72–73, 84–87
population, 140–43, *143*; and federal contract services, 189
powwows, 285n8. *See also* Delaware Powwow
Pratt, John, 80–82, 84, 281n9
Pratt, Nannie Journeycake, 120, 285n1
Prewitt, Terry, 93–94
problem solving, ideals of, 154. *See also* leadership

Redcorn, Katherine, 73
religion, 40–41; and Cherokee Nation, 49; and cultural identity, 100; and cultural preservation, 68; and Delaware Business Committee, 149; and dual enrollment, 254; and internal tribal divisions, 77; Moravians, 43; and political organization, 130–32, 137, 170–71; and political views, 78, 83; and proposal for Delaware recognition (2007), 263; revitalization movement, 45; and settlement patterns, 72, 84–87, 89–90, 92–93, 111; and single enrollment referendum, 254; and tribal government, 80–81, 172–73, 282n10, 283n2, 284n3; and tribal identity,

70–72, 100, 114–15; and Tribal Seal, 112–13; and views on Cherokee tribal membership, 235; and views on enrollment, 232–33. *See also* Big House Ceremony (Gamwing); Big House community; Christian community; Christianity
religious tensions, 68–70. *See also* internal tribal divisions; religion
removals, 75; of Cherokee, 3–4, 37, *46*, 50–52; of Delaware, 2–4, 36–37, 44–45, *46*, 53–54, 57–58, 84–85; and retention of identity, 280n1; of Shawnee, 57–58
reservation number, 242–43
reservations, 44, 86, 283n15
Roark-Calnek, Sue, 70, 78, 114, 133
Rose Hill Baptist Church, 107
Ross, William P., 54

San Juan Southern Paiute Indians, 12, 261, 269–71, 274–75
Sarcoxie, Anderson, 82–83, 84, 86, 179
Sarcoxie, John (Big John), 82–83, 86, 130, 131, 284n5
Sarcoxie, John, Jr. (Little John), 131
Sarcoxie lineage, 79, 82–83
Secondine, Fillmore, 131

Secondine, Henry, 172

Secondine, John, 131

self-determination policy, 5–11, 187, 191, 261, 272; and Delaware Tribe, 243, 275–76; and single enrollment, 233–34, 237; and tribal membership, 216. *See also* Indian Self-Determination and Education Act (1975)

self-government, 149, 239, 242, 252–53

Senate Committee on Indian Affairs, 263

Seneca Indians, 44

Sequoyah (Cherokee leader), 51

service areas, *102*

service populations, 22–23; of Cherokee Nation, 258; and FAP, 231; and multiple memberships, 204–5; and tribal membership, 253–54, 268, 273

settlement patterns, 286n4; and internal tribal divisions, 79–80, 84–87; and land allotments, 90–92; and lineage, 72–73, 85; non-Indian, 92–93, 284n6; and political views, 72–73, 84–87; and religion, 72, 84–87, 89–90, 92–93, 111

Shawnee Indians, 12, 225, 283n1; and Big House community, 133; within Cherokee Nation, 1, 4, 260–61, 273; and dual enrollment, 226–27; and federal recognition, 289n1; history of, 45; and Indian identity process, 192; and religion, 58, 106; removal of, 57; and single enrollment, 224–26, 235, 268; and Tecumseh Celebration, 219

Simon, James, 130

single enrollment, 217–18, 221–22, 224–27, 229–39, 243–44, 250–53; and Cherokee-Delaware Agreement (2007), 268–69; and FAP, 272; and lineage, 247–49

single enrollment referendum, 243–51, 254

Six Nations, 41–42

Six Nations Reserve (Canada), 43

Smith, Chad, 192, 239–41, 259–62, 266, 268

social dances, 146–48

social organization, 40, 45–46. *See also* lineage

socioeconomic differences, and support for single enrollment, 247–49

Speck, Frank, 134–35, 286n5

stomp dances, 106–9, 143, 287n1

Strong, Pauline, 193

Sturm, Circe, 188

subtribes, 14–15

Sullivan, John, 263

Swimmer, Ross, 163–65
Sykes, Thomas, 80

Tahlequah OK, 198
Tecumseh Celebration, 219
ten percent plan, 162, 165
Thompson, James H., 135–36
Tiblow, Henry, 82
Tolley, Sara-Luis, 19
Townsend, Bruce, 172
tradition, defined, 114
Trail of Tears, 37, 52. *See also* removals
treaties with U.S., 117, 284n4
Treaty of Greenville, 45
Treaty of New Echota, 51–52
Treaty Party, 51–52
tribal government, 2, 15, 18, 131, 266; 1962 reorganization, 139–40; 1982 restructuring, 166; Cherokee, 2, 51; and Cherokee-Delaware Agreement (2007), 265–66; and clan system, 80–82, 282n10; and federal recognition termination, 175–76; and internal divisions, 135–36; and lineage, 172; and religion, 80–81, 104, 172–73, 282n10, 283n2, 284n3; reservation-wide, 13
tribal identity, 109–10; and blood quantum, 190–96; and cultural landscape, 103, 111; and multiple memberships, 204–5; and religion, 71–72, 100, 114–15; retention of, 98–100; and single enrollment, 236
tribal membership, 119, 141–45, 178–81, 187–88, 222, 229, 256; and access to federal services, 20–22; and Cherokee-Delaware Agreement (1867), 182, 288n2; and Cherokee-Delaware Agreement (2007), 265–66; and Cherokee Nation Dawes Roll, 224–25; and Delaware Per Capita Roll (1904), 224; and FAP, 273–74; and individual identity, 205; and land allotments, 183–85; multiple memberships, 203–5, 221, 237; and non-resident tribal members, 143–44, 157–58; re-establishment of, 283n14; and religion, 235; requirements compared, 225–26; and self-determination policy, 216; and service populations, 253–54, 268, 273. *See also* dual enrollment; single enrollment
tribe, definition and use of term, 15–16
trust lands, 265, 267

unacknowledged tribes, 19–20
Unami speakers, 37–42
United Keetoowah Band of Cherokee Indians (UKB), 138–39, 225–26, 235
U.S. government, relationship

with Delaware Tribe, 117–19,
145, 161

Van Winkle, Barrik, 193
voting rights, 233; and tribal
membership, 225

Washington, Fred, 135
Washington, Joe, 135
Washington County, 247–48
Webber, James Charlie, 135–36,
286n5
Weslager, Clinton A., 27–28
White, Samuel, 135

Wild Onion Dinner, 1, 24, 105
Wilson, Reuben, 136
women, in Delaware community,
287n2
Worchester v. Georgia (1832), 51

Xingwikaon (last functioning Big
House), 41, 86, 109

Young, John, 82, 131, 286n4
Yuchi Indians, 12

Zeisberger, David, 43
Zunigha, Curtis, 173